Causes and Consequences of Feelings

This engaging, scholarly, and up-to-date book by one of the leading social psychologists in the world reviews the rapidly growing body of research on the antecedents and consequences of positive and negative affect. Starting with studies that identify the dimensions along which affective experience can be located, it considers whether good and bad feelings are opposite ends of a bipolar continuum or are independent dimensions. It then looks at the many conditions that can determine whether an experience is felt as pleasant or unpleasant and examines how feelings can influence thought, memory, and action. For example, the author shows how people's ideas about what had caused their feelings influence the judgments they make at that time, how their level of mental activity determines what effect their mood has on their susceptibility to persuasion, and how judgments and problem solving are sometimes helped and sometimes hurt by positive feelings. He also discusses the controversies regarding the impact of personal traumas on memory, the influence of emotion arousal on the accuracy of eyewitness testimony, and the effect of unusually hot weather on violent crimes.

Leonard Berkowitz is Vilas Research Professor Emeritus in the Department of Psychology, University of Wisconsin–Madison. He is the author of *Aggression: Its Causes, Consequences and Control.*

STUDIES IN EMOTION AND SOCIAL INTERACTION
Second Series

Series Editors

Keith Oatley
University of Toronto

Antony Manstead
University of Amsterdam

This series is jointly published by the Cambridge University Press and the Editions de la Maison des Sciences de l'Homme, as part of the joint publishing agreement established in 1977 between the Fondation de la Maison des Sciences de l'Homme and the Syndics of the Cambridge University Press.

Cette collection est publiée co-édition par Cambridge University Press et les Editions de la Maison des Sciences de l'Homme. Elle s'intègre dans le programme de co-édition établi en 1977 par la Fondation de la Maison des Sciences de l'Homme et les Syndics de Cambridge University Press.

Titles published in the Second Series:

The Psychology of Facial Expression
Edited by James A. Russell and José Miguel Fernández-Dols

Emotions, the Social Bond, and Human Reality: Part/Whole Analysis
Thomas J. Scheff

Intersubjective Communication and Emotion in Early Ontogeny
Stein Bråten

The Social Context of Nonverbal Behavior
Edited by Pierre Philippot, Robert S. Feldman, and Erik J. Coats

Communicating Emotion: Social, Moral, and Cultural Processes
Sally Planalp

Feeling and Thinking
Edited by Joseph P. Forgas

For a list of titles in the First Series of Studies in Emotion and Social Interaction, see the page following the index.

Causes and Consequences of Feelings

Leonard Berkowitz

CAMBRIDGE
UNIVERSITY PRESS

& Editions de la Maison des Sciences de l'Homme
Paris

PUBLISHED BY THE PRESS SYNDICATE OF THE UNIVERSITY OF CAMBRIDGE
The Pitt Building, Trumpington Street, Cambridge, United Kingdom
EDITIONS DE LA MAISON DES SCIENCES DE L'HOMME
54 Boulevard Raspail, 75270 Paris Cedex 06, France

CAMBRIDGE UNIVERSITY PRESS
The Edinburgh Building, Cambridge CB2 2RU, UK   http://www.cup.cam.ac.uk
40 West 20th Street, New York, NY 10011-4211, USA   http://www.cup.org
10 Stamford Road, Oakleigh, Melbourne 3166, Australia
Ruiz de Alarcón 13, 28014 Madrid, Spain

First published 2000

Printed in the United States of America

Typeface Palatino 10/13 pt.   *System* DeskTopPro$_{/UX}$ [BV]

A catalog record for this book is available from the British Library.

Library of Congress Cataloging in Publication Data
Berkowitz, Leonard, 1926–
Causes and consequences of feelings / Leonard Berkowitz.
p. cm. – (Studies in emotion and social interaction)
Includes bibliographical references and index.
ISBN 0-521-63325-7. (hardcover). – ISBN 0-521-63363-X (pbk.)
1. Emotions. 2. Affect (Psychology) I. Title. II. Series.
BF531.B45   2000
152.4 – dc21
                                    99-040249

ISBN 0 521 63325 7 hardback
ISBN 0 521 63363 X paperback
ISBN 2 7351 0849 X hardback (France only)
ISBN 2 7351 0850 3 paperback (France only)

Contents

Acknowledgments

I am greatly indebted to all of the researchers who, with great insight and ingenuity, seek to determine just why people come to feel good or bad and how this positive or negative affect can influence one's memory, judgments, decision making, and behavior toward others. Testing our commonsense suppositions and everyday beliefs regarding the causes and consequences of feelings, or even daring to develop and investigate often novel theoretical formulations intended to account for these effects, has benefited all of us: me, the readers of this book, and I hope, many of those who want to understand better the whys and wherefores of human behavior. I owe much in particular to Gordon Bower, Bob Zajonc, and Joe Forgas, whose research and thinking contributed greatly to my own ideas, and am also grateful to my colleagues at the University of Wisconsin–Madison, Richie Davidson and Joe Newman, who taught me much and in one way or another encouraged me to think carefully about emotions.

Leonard Berkowitz
Madison, Wisconsin
August 1999

Introduction

To be fully human is to have feelings. Can we imagine being alive and not feeling happy at our success on a daunting task or not being sad if a loved one dies tragically? Are there people who have never become angry at learning that someone has wronged them or who haven't enjoyed a concert or an exciting game or a cooling drink on a hot day or who haven't been frightened by a sudden danger? Surely, unless there's some serious neurological problem, to live is to experience pleasure or displeasure, happiness or sadness, anger or fear or contentment.

This book is concerned largely with the causes and, especially, the consequences of positive and negative feelings: How our thoughts, judgments, memories, and interactions with others can be affected as a result of experiencing pleasure or displeasure. You will see that our emotions, our moods, and even our physical sensations can distort our judgments, alter what ideas occur to us and what we remember, and affect our behavior to those around us. Many of these influences are quite surprising and certainly far more complicated than most people generally expect. More important in this pragmatic age, feelings can lead to error. The best way to minimize the mistaken judgments and/or erroneous decisions and/or faulty recollections that feelings can produce is to understand the nature of these effects and the conditions under which they arise.

This book will attempt to summarize what is known about the causes and consequences of good and bad feelings. Neurologists, cognitive neuroscientists, and psychophysiologists have taught us a great deal about emotions and feelings, and the interested reader would do well to delve into their writings on these topics. But we can also obtain valuable insights from the research and writings of psychologists and other behavioral scientists.

I'm not claiming that we have only recently gained an adequate understanding of how feelings operate. Astute observers of humankind have discussed their possible influences at least since the times of the ancient Greeks, and much of what they said holds up under close scrutiny. Still, it's worth noting that many of the comments and analyses offered in generations past are in substantial disagreement and that we can't find consistent guidance in the classic writings. More than this, as you will see, some of the most popular notions of feeling effects are, at best, oversimplified, and others are wrong, at least at times. With feelings being so pervasive and so significant in our daily lives, we would do well to understand what impact they have.

Before proceeding further, however, I should be clear what is involved in the term *feeling* as this word is used here. In this book feeling is synonymous with conscious affect. It encompasses experienced emotions but covers other kinds of sensations as well. Many psychologists have a rather narrow conception of emotions. They prefer to think of emotions as having fairly specific causes and targets (for example, most emotion theorists say we're angry at someone or happy about something). In order to minimize confusion, then, I will only speak of feelings and will give this term a broad meaning that includes emotional experiences, moods, and even physical sensations.

One implication of this far-ranging notion is that feelings can arise in a variety of ways. Sometimes they're produced by definite events in the outside world (such as the joy arising from a victory); at other times they result from highly noticeable physical sensations (such as the pleasure of sex or the discomfort created by being confined in a hot, humid room). But as a growing body of research has now shown, feelings can also be aroused by stimuli of which we're not fully conscious – details in the situation that we've actually detected but at such a low level of awareness that we don't consciously realize that we have encountered them.

To give you a brief taste of some of the interesting findings psychologists have obtained in their studies of the many and varied causes of feelings, I'll say a little more about this last-mentioned nonconscious stimulation. When Oatley and Duncan asked people to describe times when they had been happy, sad, angry, and afraid, they found that in a number of cases the respondents did not know what had provoked the emotion.[1] The persons reporting these "free-floating" feelings apparently had responded to certain cues (or signals) in the surrounding world even though they did not consciously know to what they had reacted. This probably is what happens when people are anxious or even somewhat irritable on entering a particular situation and don't know why they have these feelings. From this book's perspective we would say that they don't have unconscious feelings; feelings for us here are conscious experiences. It's better to say, instead, that the processes by which the feelings are produced are nonconscious. The next chapter will discuss this further as we consider how feelings are generated.

It's also important to recognize that however feelings are aroused, their representation in our mind, our conscious experience, is often a mental construction based to a certain extent on the awareness of bodily changes. This is certainly not a new idea. Over 100 years ago the great American philosopher-psychologist William James held that emotional experiences grow out of the bodily reactions to some significant occurrence. One passage in his 1890 masterwork *Principles of Psychology* is well known as a convenient summary of James's theory:

> *Common sense says, we lose our fortune, are sorry and weep; we meet a bear, are frightened and run; we are insulted by a rival, are angry and strike. The hypothesis here to be defended says that this order of sequence is incorrect . . . and the more rational statement is that we feel sorry because we cry, angry because we strike, afraid because we tremble.*[2]

I think it's fair to say that most contemporary investigators of human emotion now accept the essentials of James's theory: Bodily sensations have a major role in emotional experience. This may seem to be a rather unremarkable idea, but it has some very important implications. Thus, very much in line with James's conception, we now know that the bodily sensations produced by making the muscular movements characteristic of a particular emotional state can give rise to the feelings that are typically experienced in that state. The stereotypic upper-class Englishman who keeps a "stiff upper lip" and remains impassive when confronted by serious problems might actually lessen the feelings of distress he would otherwise experience. Chapter 2 will summarize some of the evidence for this kind of bodily feedback effect and will suggest some of the conditions that make it more or less likely.

In accord with James's thesis, my view is that people's experienced feelings are formed largely from their bodily reactions to the emotion-instigating stimulation. The mind integrates the bodily sensations along with other associated mental representations, with this mental construction being guided partly (but not entirely) by previously acquired conceptions of how one customarily feels in a certain class of situations. To make this more concrete, suppose that Joe is faced by a bully who has just insulted him. Joe's body reacts quickly: His heart beats faster, his face becomes hot, his mouth clamps shut and his brows draw together, his fists clench. Joe also might recall other times when he had been insulted and the feelings that he had experienced on these occasions, as well as the stories he had read, seen, and heard about angering occurrences. He also thinks of himself as angry. Joe's mind integrates all of these inputs, guided to some degree by his conception of what anger is like, and forms the anger experience. Joe feels angry.

I've said a number of times that this book will be concerned largely with the consequences of the hedonic nature of affective states. You can see this in the title: *Causes and Consequences of Feelings*. It's reasonable to ask whether this focus on feeling valence doesn't omit other important aspects of feelings, other qualities that might also have a significant influence on thoughts and actions. Think of fear and distress. Can we appropriately group them together because of their hedonic similarity – both are unpleasant – at least for the purposes of interest to us in this book? Chapter 1 will show that we can characterize any given affect, to a great extent, in terms of both its valence and its intensity. Both fear and distress are felt as negative, but fear is often experienced as more intense than distress. Nevertheless, because both of these states are affectively unpleasant, can we disregard their differences at times, and ask only what are the effects that both have in common, indeed, that all negatively valenced feelings produce?

But of course, affective states have qualities other than their valence and intensity, and these other qualities can sometimes have an influence on what thoughts come to mind and what actions are undertaken. Thus, at least partly because of the specific physiological reactions that occur in these emotions, anger is typically experienced as a "hot" feeling, whereas many persons say they feel "cold" when they are afraid. The consequence is that anger and fear don't always affect judgments and actions in the same way. Anger is generally associated with approach inclinations but fear is usually linked to an urge to avoid the perceived danger. In keeping with the rather specific nature of anger, I'll show you later in the book that anger doesn't always have the same impact on thought processes, such as the use of stereotypes, as other unpleasant feelings.

In spite of these exceptions, however, we will look mostly at the consequences of a feeling's hedonic nature (or valence). This means I won't have anything to say about specific feelings (or emotions), such as envy, elation, or disgust. You can find interesting and provocative discussions of specific affective states in many textbooks on emotions, such as those by Carlson and Hatfield, Izard, and Lazarus.[3] This book seeks only to report the findings obtained by psychologists, usually social psychologists, in their carefully conducted investigations of the causes and consequences of feelings, and as I have noted, most of the studies of interest to us here have dealt only with the effects of feeling valence. Even with this perhaps limited coverage, however, you'll see that there is a substantial body of research and that a great deal can be said about what has been learned.

Let me give you some brief examples.

Take the matter of the accuracy of eyewitness testimony. Suppose a person is walking down the street when two automobiles collide only a few yards in front of her. She has a strong emotional reaction. Will the intense sensations she feels affect her memory of what happened? And more particularly, will her recollection of the event be accurate if she is called on to testify in court? You will see later, in Chapter 3, that the answers to these questions are much more complicated than you probably believe. Emotionally aroused people may actually have a very good memory for the central features of the emotional occurrence, although their memory of the more peripheral details in the situation can suffer. The witness might be quite accurate in her report, say, of how the cars were traveling and yet be in error about other aspects of the situation, such as how many bystanders there were on the nearby sidewalks.

Let's turn to a much more controversial matter. Quite a number of psychologists, psychiatrists, counselors, and other mental health specialists have claimed that sexually abused youngsters frequently repress their memories of an adult's shocking mistreatment of them. If prior traumatic incidents are frequently vividly and easily recalled – and this is often the case for children, as for adults – why is childhood sexual abuse (supposedly) readily buried in the unconscious so that it cannot be recalled until much later in life? We'll take up this question in some detail in Chapter 4 when we consider the impact of stress on memory.

Although certainly not as controversial, there are also surprises in the research on the effects of pleasant moods. Happy feelings can also influence our judgments, decisions, and actions in unexpected and complicated ways. In general, don't we believe that good moods promote all kinds of good things – that people will work harder, think more clearly, and make better decisions when they're feeling good rather than bad? We would expect this, but life isn't quite this simple. Research to be reported later will show you that happiness can sometimes have undesirable consequences.

Then too, consider how positive and negative moods might affect susceptibility to persuasion. Most of us generally suppose that a communicator is most likely to be convincing when the audience is in a good mood. But here too, as you will see in Chapter 6, this is a much too simple expectation. For one thing, the audience members' positive feelings might actually make them indifferent to whatever high-quality, though complex, arguments are contained in the message. Some studies have suggested that when people are feeling happy they are apt to be fairly lazy mentally, so they don't think actively about the information they obtain.

The book is divided into four parts. In the first section, Chapter 1 will begin with a survey of attempts to identify the underlying dimensions along which the various affective experiences can be placed. This review will consider, among other things, the relationship between positive and negative feelings: Are they the opposite ends of a single bipolar continuum or are they independent dimensions? After this, the chapter will look at the varied causes of feelings, starting with relatively automatic influences in which thought does not play a major part. Chapter 2, the second half of this first section, will continue the discussion of the causes of feelings. It will look at the effects of cognitions, including appraisals and attributions, but then will turn to the noncognitive role of bodily reactions in generating feelings.

The next major section of the book is concerned with the impact of feelings on memory. Chapter 3 will first introduce some important concepts and then will provide an overview of the associative network analysis of how feelings can influence memory. Among other things, this review will look at the controversial problem of mood-dependent memory – whether memory is affected by the degree of similarity between one's mood at the time certain information is first encountered and the mood later when an attempt is made to recall the information. Following this discussion, the chapter will begin our discussion of the effects of stress on memory by considering the accuracy of eyewitness reports: To what extent are eyewitnesses' recollections of what they had seen impeded or even distorted by the feelings that the event had aroused in them? Chapter 4 will then extend this examination of possible affect-induced memory distortions by reviewing the controversy regarding the effects of personal traumas. Here we will be particularly interested in the argument about repressed memories. What evidence is there that children who had been victimized by adult abusers often defensively block their memories of the disturbing occurrences from conscious awareness?

The third section of the book has to do with affective influences on ways of thinking. Chapter 5 will focus on the effects of feelings on judgments and decision making, and in covering this topic will introduce you to the most important theories regarding the influence of affective states on cognitive processes. These theoretical analyses will be extended and even modified somewhat in Chapter 6, where we will turn to the effects of feeling on persuasion and task motivation. As I indicated earlier, in reviewing these affective influences we will look at the intriguing findings regarding the effects of a good mood. But in addition, we will consider whether communicators can enhance the acceptance of their proposals by frightening the people in their audience.

Finally, Chapter 7, which comprises the fourth and last section, will take up the influence of feelings on social behavior, notably helpfulness and aggression. Here you will see how good moods can promote magnanimity to others and that bad feelings are apt to bring out the worst in people. Although you may expect findings such as these, you may be surprised at the pervasiveness of these effects, as well as the conditions that keep them from occurring.

I've now given you just a brief sampling of the topics to be covered in this book and the ideas that will be developed as we go along. Feelings permeate our daily lives, and we certainly wouldn't want to do without them. Yet few of us have more than a seriously incomplete understanding of how feelings come about and how they may influence what we think and do. Part of what we believe we know is fairly valid, grounded as it is in our daily interactions with others. But much of what we also think we know about feelings can be incorrect, at least by being an overly simplified conception of how feelings actually operate. This book will try to take you on a voyage of discovery so that you can gain a better understanding of a major part of your life.

Before we embark on this journey, however, let me tell you about some of the conventions I will follow in organizing the material. First of all, even though I will refer to research throughout the book, some studies will be reported in more detail, generally because I will discuss them at some length. These relatively important investigations are identified for you by being indented and printed in italics. I will also occasionally indent and italicize other especially important material. In addition, to make the book more readable, the research references appear in the form of notes at the end of the book.

PART I

The Nature and Origin of Feelings

1. Feelings: Their Nature and Causes

This book deals largely with the ways in which people's feelings influence their thoughts, memories, judgments, and actions. In the next two chapters, though, we will be concerned with the nature and origin of feelings: generally speaking, how feelings are experienced and what aspects of the situation give rise to these experiences.

As I indicated in the Introduction, when I use the term feeling in this book I'm not necessarily thinking of emotion as the latter concept is usually understood. Although there are exceptions, most psychologists basically conceive of an emotion as a complex sequence of responses to a personally relevant stimulus. These reactions occur throughout the brain and body and include cognitive evaluations, bodily and neural changes, motor impulses, and emotion-related thoughts, as well as a particular feeling. Moreover, psychologists usually regard emotions as being focused on a certain object or issue. In this sense, we're happy about something or afraid of something or envious of someone. In this book, however, the word feeling is synonymous with affect and refers only to conscious experience rather than to the full constellation of emotional reactions. Furthermore, a feeling may or may not have to do with a particular object or issue or happening. People might have good feelings as the result of a specific event: perhaps because their team won a game or because they did well on an assigned task. But affect can also be produced by vague, barely noticed, or even subliminal occurrences, such as a warm, sunny day or a familiar, pleasant melody. This latter type of general, object-less feeling is sometimes called a *mood*. Many students of emotion think of a mood as being somewhat different from the relatively more focused emotion: It is an affective state that typically is fairly long-lasting, often at a relatively low or moderate level or intensity, and generally objectless and free-floating.[1]

We can also say that we are interested primarily in what Russell and Feldman Barrett have recently termed *core affect* rather than in *prototypical emotional episodes*. A core affect is the feeling that a person experiences consciously at the moment and may or may not be focused on any particular object or event. Prototypical emotional episodes, on the other hand, are much more complex. Typically they are concerned with a specific object or event, real or imagined, so that they embrace affect but also include appraisals of the activating target, related ideas, and behavioral inclinations. For Russell and Feldman Barrett, a mood is a "prolonged core affect without an object or with a quasi-object."[2]

But whatever is involved in the feelings, whether they are part of a relatively complex emotional episode or not, and however long-lasting they may be, this book, generally speaking, does not distinguish among them except in regard to their valence (whether they are pleasant or unpleasant). However specific the cause or focused the target, I will regard them all as affective states and will be concerned with the consequences of the feelings that are experienced.

The Nature of the Affective Experience

What Are the Dimensions of This Experience?

We seem to have a great variety of emotional feelings. When they're angry, many people say they feel hot, whereas they're apt to describe themselves as cold if they're afraid. Many of us report having a lump in our throats when we're sad, but we are highly unlikely to have this sensation when joyous. Nonetheless, even with these differences, a number of researchers have argued that affective experiences can be meaningfully described in terms of only a relatively small number of dimensions, and they have attempted to identify these underlying common aspects of feelings.

In their investigations, they usually first ask the participants to rate either their feelings or their understanding of a set of emotion-related stimuli (such as words having emotional connotations or pictures depicting emotion-arousing events). These ratings are then usually analyzed to determine whether some of them cluster together. For example, when people report feeling happy, do they also tend to say they are content or excited? When a person is described as sad, is she also apt to be rated as distressed or passive? Is an emotional event regarded as depressing also said to be agitating and/or sleepy or scary?

Employing this kind of methodology, more than a generation ago several factor analytic studies identified 6 to 12 separate clusters of affective experiences. These were supposedly the basic dimensions along which emotional feelings varied and included such qualities as the degree of "felt sadness," the degree of "felt anxiety," the magnitude of "felt anger," and the intensity of "pleasurable feelings." More recent research indicates, however, that many of these clusters are not independent of each other but tend to occur together in larger groupings. Indeed, it's now generally agreed, when the affect ratings are subjected to careful statistical analysis, they are often found to vary along only two (or perhaps three) separate dimensions. In other words, we can describe feelings to a substantial (but not complete) degree in terms of their particular location in an area circumscribed by these two independent axes.

Russell and Feldman Barrett propose, quite reasonably in my view, that it is the core affects, the feelings that are currently being experienced, that can be located within the circular area, the *circumplex,* formed by these independent dimensions. The more complex prototypical emotional episodes, being packages of feelings, appraisals, ideas, and behavioral tendencies, can be organized in a variety of different ways, perhaps in a hierarchical as well as a dimensional structure. For example, the prototypical episode of sadness conceivably could be regarded as a superordinate category involving, among other things, the more subordinate core feelings of sadness and depression. It may well be, then, that those investigations that uncovered a multiplicity of affective dimensions obtained these findings at least partly because they employed emotional stimuli fraught with meaning, such as pictures. These relatively complex social stimuli could have brought to mind prototypical emotional episodes rather than activating only the "purer" core affects.[3]

This structural conception can be quite useful in describing a substantial part of people's affective reactions to the situations they are in, and it seems to be valid across a broad range of linguistic cultures.[4] This doesn't necessarily mean, however, that psychologists are in complete agreement as to just what are the two (or possibly three) underlying dimensions.

Pleasure-Displeasure and Active-Passive. For many investigators, such as Russell, our thinking about affect terms, and the experiences associated with these words, is largely, but not entirely, centered on two basic bipolar dimensions: *pleasure-displeasure* and *active-passive* (the latter dimension sometimes also labeled *active-sleep* or *activation-deactivation*). Calling this view a *circumplex model* of affect, Russell places affective experiences on a circle, with pleasure set arbitrarily at 0° and displeasure set opposite at 180°. (Because pleasure and displeasure are at opposite poles of a single continuum, this type of conception is also often termed a *bipolar model.*) The active-passive dimension is perpendicular to this valence dimension, so that arousal is at 90° and sleepiness at 270°. Think of these dimensions as marking off four quadrants, as in the top half of Figure 1.1. According to one of Russell's studies, the words *astonished* and *delighted* are typically regarded as being in the northeast quadrant because both have to do with a mixture of arousal and pleasure. However, astonished is high on arousal but is only slightly pleasant, whereas delighted is high on pleasure but is only somewhat aroused. *Afraid* and *distressed*, on the other hand, are both in the northwest quadrant, but although both of these affective terms are associated with relatively high arousal and displeasure, the participants in this research thought of afraid as connoting a somewhat higher arousal level than distressed.[5]

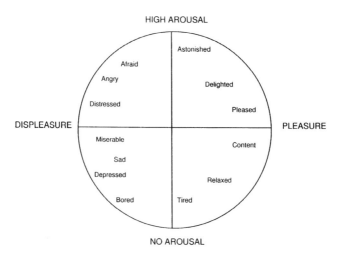

Figure 1.1 Scaling of affect words on the Russell circumplex model (modified from Russell, 1980, p. 1169).

Positive Affect and Negative Affect. In 1985 David Watson and Auke Tellegen published a different but also well-known formulation of the underlying dimensions of affective experience. On the basis of the statistical analyses of people's self-reported moods they had conducted, they stated that feelings could be organized in terms of the affective structure summarized in Figure 1.2. There are four basic bipolar dimensions spaced 45° apart, they maintained: (1) High to Low Positive Affect, (2) High to Low Negative Affect, (3) Pleasantness to Unpleasantness, and (4) Strong Engagement to Disengagement.[6]

In this scheme, as you can see, *blue* and *sad* are at the extreme Unpleasant end of the Pleasantness-Unpleasantness dimension rather than being located at the polar end of the High Negative Affect dimension, and extremely high Positive Affect is better indicated by *elated* than by *happy*. (I'll say more about this later.) The last dimension I listed, having to do with degree of engagement, is apparently similar to the Arousal-No Arousal dimension in Russell's model, but otherwise, the 1985 Watson–Tellegen analysis evidently disagrees with Russell's scheme in an important respect. It tells us that an extremely unpleasant feeling isn't necessarily very high on the Negative Affect dimension; the Pleasantness-Unpleasantness and Negative Affect dimensions are correlated to a good degree but, according to Watson and Tellegen, they aren't identical aspects of feelings.

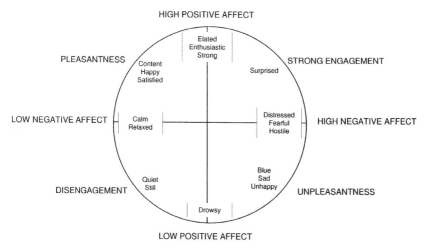

Figure 1.2 Positive-negative structure of affect (modified from Watson & Tellegen, 1985).

Later research, again based mainly on analyses of self-reported feelings, convinced Watson and his associates that the essentials of the original Watson–Tellegen conception are correct, although they also pointed out that the exact nature of the affective structure will vary from one situation to another. Their findings seem to be clearest, they noted, when the feelings have to do with one's current, momentary experience rather than with one's mood over, say, an entire day. The later analyses also led the Watson team to suggest that the various feelings are organized somewhat hierarchically. The highest and most general aspect of feelings has to do with how pleasant or unpleasant they are. Then, below this on the hierarchy, are the feelings' location on the positive and negative affect dimensions. Finally, the specific, discrete affects are even further down, at the lowest level of the affective hierarchy.[7]

This last-mentioned observation about the generality of pleasant-to-unpleasant feelings is obviously consistent with Russell's identification of pleasantness-unpleasantness as a major aspect of affective experience, and I'll soon return to this important agreement. But for now, let's look at the feature of the 1985 Watson–Tellegen formulation that had attracted the greatest attention and that was the principal focus of the investigators' research: the proposal that positive and negative affect are largely independent dimensions.

In 1985 Watson and Tellegen characterized these two dimensions in this manner:

> *The first factor, Positive Affect, represents the extent to which a person avows a zest for life. The second factor, Negative Affect, is the extent to which a person reports feeling upset or unpleasantly aroused. . . . [O]nly the high end of each dimension represents a state of emotional arousal (or high affect), whereas the low end of each factor is most clearly and strongly defined by terms reflecting a relative absence of affective involvement. . . . [These factors] are independent, uncorrelated dimensions. . . .*[8]

Both the Russell and Watson–Tellegen factor analytic interpretations of the affect data can be defended, mathematically speaking (as all of these researchers have acknowledged). And moreover, each conception can be helpful in interpreting particular findings. Consistent with the Russell bipolar model, for example, certain kinds of bodily reactions seem to be associated with affective experiences on the pleasure-displeasure axis, whereas other bodily responses vary with position on the activation (or arousal-sleep) dimension.[9] However, because it seems contrary to common sense, and even everyday language, to hold that positive and negative feelings are independent aspects of affective experience, I'll focus mainly on evidence supporting the Watson–Tellegen conception.

Sometimes, for instance, an emotional occurrence produces both good and bad feelings. An employee who has just retired after long years of work might be both happy and somewhat anxious about his new freedom from company routines. Positive and negative affect can arise together, just as the Watson–Tellegen model proposed. Watson, Tellegen, and their colleagues also pointed to other research results. In one investigation, Zevon and Tellegen asked 23 men and women to rate their mood on a 60-adjective checklist at specified times each day for 3 months. After carrying out factor analyses of the ratings made by each of these people, the researchers concluded that most of the participants had rated their feelings largely in terms of the two dimensions of positive and negative affect. Further attesting to the apparent independence of these two factors, when the investigators combined the data for all of the people in their sample, they found that relatively high positive affect scores were distributed over a wider range of days than were high negative affect scores. Strong negative feelings evidently were a more extreme and more unusual reaction than strong positive affective experiences.[10]

Studies of persistent individual differences also point to a separation between positive and negative affective systems. Strong extroverts are typically disposed to have relatively intense positive feelings, whereas extreme neurotics are apt to be high in negative affect. Some people evidently are inclined to be in either a good or bad mood a great deal of the time, much as if their psychological makeup is dominated by either a positive or a negative affect-generating reaction system. In line with these observations, when Berenbaum and his associates examined the ratings university students made of their sad, angry, and fear moods every day for 6 weeks, the investigators found not only that these negative moods were relatively stable over this time period, but also that the experience of any of the negative feelings during the first 3 weeks was a good predictor that other negative moods would arise in the second 3 weeks. Some persons' feelings apparently are controlled largely by a psychological and/or neurological system generating negative moods.[11]

Research on the biology of emotion also seems to call for a clear separation of pleasant and unpleasant feelings. The physiological mechanisms involved in positive affect are often different from those operating when there is a negative experience. Davidson's important studies of brain activity testify to such a difference. Activation of the left frontal cortex is generally associated with pleasurable states, whereas unpleasant affect is typically linked to high electrical activity in the right frontal cortex. Adding to this evidence, facial muscles can also reflect the valence of an affective state. The zygomatic muscles that pull the lip corners up and back are usually activated by pleasant feelings, but the corrugator muscles that draw the brows together and downward become active when affect is unpleasant.[12]

Cacioppo, Gardner, and Berntson went further along these lines. Thinking of the pleasantness-unpleasantness dimension as having to do primarily with tendencies to approach or avoid external stimuli, they argued that there are separate positive and negative affect systems, which they termed *appetition* and *aversion systems*. However, they maintained, because the person cannot approach and withdraw at the same time, but must do one of the other, there is a single bipolar response system concerned with actions ranging from strong approach to strong withdrawal (i.e., from positive to negative).[13]

Nevertheless, even with all of this evidence, the original Watson–Tellegen formulation has some serious conceptual problems, as Larsen and Diener noted in their thoughtful review of these different models. Look at the axes Watson and Tellegen had named Positive Affect and Negative Affect in Figure 1.2. Low Negative Affect is defined by such terms as *calm* and *relaxed* – words that virtually everyone would say have a somewhat pleasant connotation. This particular pole seems to have more to do with low arousal or a low state of activation than with unpleasant experience. Similarly, ask yourself why happy is somewhat below the High Positive Affect pole, and why sad and unhappy are said to be less extreme on the High Negative Affect dimension than, say, hostile or jittery. The answer should be clear. In both of these latter cases, words that suggest a lower level of arousal are lower on the given dimension. As Larsen and Diener commented, the Watson–Tellegen dimensions "reflect composites of hedonic valence and high activation."[14] Experiences at the end of the High Positive Affect axis in the Watson–Tellegen formulation do not represent all positive experiences but only those that are pleasant and also highly activated or aroused. Similarly, those experiences at the High Negative Affect extreme in this formulation don't represent all unpleasant experience but only those involving strong arousal as well as strong displeasure.

There was another problem besides the combination of valence and strong arousal level at the high ends of the Watson–Tellegen dimensions. Many people had been puzzled by the terms used in 1985 to mark the low ends of these continua – for example, that *calm* and *relaxed* indicated low Negative Affect. To overcome these difficulties, the Watson–Tellegen group now maintained that their two dimensions have to do with Positive *Activation* and Negative *Activation* rather than with Positive Affect and Negative Affect. These constructs, they said, are unipolar, not bipolar, in nature, and it is the high poles of these dimensions that are important, not the low ends. According to this newer view, a low level on one or the other dimensions reflects "the absence of a particular kind of activation rather than the presence of a given affective state" (such as calmness or relaxation). So what we now have are two theoretically distinct *biobehavioral systems*, one that can bring about strong positive feelings and the other promoting the activation of intense negative affect.[15]

Reconciling the Russell and Watson–Tellegen Conceptions

What can we say about the bipolarity of affect? Are positive and negative feelings the opposite ends of a single continuum or not? The Watson–Tellegen and Russell positions are now moving closer together than they were commonly believed to be in the past. I've already noted the Watson–Tellegen group's latest proposal that the various feelings exist in a hierarchical structure, with the most general feature of these affects being their degree of pleasantness-unpleasantness. As Watson and Tellegen put it in another paper, "A general bipolar dimension of happy versus unhappy feeling states emerges at the apex of [the affect] hierarchy, attesting to its pervasiveness in self-rated affect." Russell and Clark have welcomed this view, observing that on this central issue they and Watson–Tellegen are in agreement.[16] It is meaningful to say, as I have done throughout this book, that a very important (but not all-important) aspect of any given feelings is its valence, that is, how pleasant or unpleasant it is.

Then too, if we keep in mind the Watson group's new characterization of their postulated two independent dimensions as Positive Activation and Negative Activation (rather than as Positive and Negative Affect), we can see that the two research groups are, in actuality, also not far apart on this matter. In accord with the attempted reconciliation offered in 1992 by Larsen and Diener, both sets of investigators agree that when Watson and Tellegen were talking about positive feelings, they had in mind affective "states that were both pleasant and activated (such as enthusiasm)" and that excluded "happiness and serenity and the like." And similarly, the negative affect of concern to Watson and Tellegen had to do with strongly activated negative states "such as panic or nervousness" and did not include such low-level states as melancholy.[17]

Some research results obtained by Diener and his associates are relevant in this connection. On examining how undergraduate students rated their feelings at times when they experienced an emotion, the investigators found that a strong, definite mood of a particular valence (such as decidedly happy or decidedly sad) was rarely accompanied by intense affect of the opposite valence. In other words, people do not have both strong positive and strong negative feelings simultaneously. Those who are in a very bad mood are unlikely to have strong pleasant feelings of any kind at that time. The full-fledged activation of one of these affect systems evidently inhibits complete activation of the other system at the same time. However, if a person is experiencing only relatively weak pleasant or unpleasant feelings on any given occasion, he or she could also have any level of the other type of affect. And so, low levels of bad feelings can occur together with some degree of pleasant feelings.[18] The man I mentioned earlier who was both happy and anxious about his retirement from work probably wasn't exceedingly happy; his pleasure wasn't strong enough to keep him from also feeling anxious.[19]

In sum, there's reason to think that positive and negative affects aren't always as independent of each other as the original Watson–Tellegen model had held in 1985. We sometimes can have a mixture of pleasant and unpleasant feelings but, at other times, an intense feeling at one end of the pleasure-displeasure axis seems to prevent affective experiences at the other extreme on this dimension. Keep in mind, though, that this latter affective incompatibility usually occurs within a narrow time span; it is only when strong feelings of one kind exist that intense feelings of the other type are ruled out at that time. If we were to look at people over a range of hours, days, or longer, we might not find this same incompatibility. A person obviously might feel good on one occasion and be in a bad mood later. Indeed, some people are prone to have both intensely positive and intensely negative feelings but, of course, not at the same time. They characteristically react strongly to emotion-arousing incidents, so that they're very happy when something good happens and very unhappy on another occasion when a bad event occurs.[20]

Some Questions About the Circumplex Conception

Another feature of both the Russell and 1985 Watson–Tellegen models of affect that has caused considerable controversy is their assumption of a circumplex structure. Watson and Tellegen have now expressed misgivings about this assumption, but Russell and his colleagues still believe that a circumplex structure fits the available data well.[21] Let's consider some of the questions that have been raised about the circumplex idea.

Are Affects Continuous or Are They Separate from Each Other?

I noted earlier that circumplex models essentially hold that the different affective concepts around the circle are not distinct, bounded categories, but rather are continuous and more or less flow into their adjoining neighbors. A number of theorists take issue with this continuity view, at least with regard to emotional states, and propose discrete categories of emotional experience. One researcher[22] has indicated, for example, that some of our affective terms can be grouped together into higher-order, relatively distinct categories. When this psychologist reanalyzed the data from one of Russell's circumplex studies, he concluded that at least four somewhat separate segments can be identified within the circle: sleepiness, distress, anger, and sadness. It could be that we create some distinctions in our conceptions of the various affective experiences and don't see all of these experiences as being only continuations of each other along the circumplex axes.

Niedenthal has gone even further in arguing along these lines. She and her colleagues maintain that we have a strong tendency to group together those objects and/or events that evoke the same specific feelings in us independently of their valence. This is especially so, they say, when the feelings are those that are involved in the commonly regarded basic emotions such as happiness, fear, anger, and sadness. For example, we are very apt to think that all those things that make us happy are members of the same conceptual category even if they seem very different and generate happiness in different ways. One implication of this, as Niedenthal and her collaborators have demonstrated, is that an emotional state's influence on information processing often depends more on the distinctive nature of that state than on its pleasantness-unpleasantness alone. Thus, sad persons are especially likely to recognize words having a sad connotation relatively quickly but aren't necessarily likely to be fast in recognizing anger-related words, even though both sets of words are negative in nature.[23] I'll have more to say along these lines later.

Distinct Differences Among Affective States. There certainly can be more to affective experience than just pleasure-displeasure, activation-deactivation (or activity-passivity), and intensity. We've already seen that people at times think of a number of emotional feelings as distinctly different categories of experience rather than only as sensations varying along such continuous dimensions as their arousal level and how pleasant-unpleasant they are. The affective states usually have other qualities as well that help to distinguish them from each other. A fair amount of research has now identified these additional qualities, but I'll highlight some of the main features by telling you about findings obtained in an important cross-national investigation reported by Klaus Scherer and Harald Wallbott.[24]

First, because many different bodily systems contribute to the affective experience, Scherer and Wallbott decided to summarize the bodily reactions using concepts taken from the psychophysiology literature. Sometimes, they noted, when we're emotionally aroused we have ergotropic symptoms, sensations emanating principally from the cardiovascular and muscular systems, such as alterations in breathing rate, increased heart rate, muscle tension, and perspiration. Or we might have trophotropic symptoms, such as a lump in the throat, stomach troubles, and cold or hot feelings. All of these are specific sensations, more detailed than just being unpleasant and/or intense to some degree.

In this study, Scherer and Wallbott and their collaborators asked university students at 37 universities on every inhabited continent to describe their feelings when they are joyous, angry, afraid, sad, disgusted, ashamed, and guilty. Although there were some differences among the countries in the reported physiological symptoms, motor expressions, and subjective feelings of these emotional states, supporting the social constructivist position discussed later, the cross-national similarities in how the emotional states were experienced were far greater. Scherer and Wallbott tell us that, across the countries, fear and anger were accompanied by a stronger arousal of ergotropic sensations, such as the sense of an increased heart rate and muscle tension, than were joy and sadness, with fear having a greater arousal level than anger. On the other hand, the participants indicated that there were stronger trophotropic sensations in joy than in either fear, anger, or sadness. Felt temperature differences were especially notable. As we all know, anger is frequently regarded as a hot emotion, and someone who is easily provoked is often said to be hot-tempered or hot-headed. Well, very much in line with this characterization, the participants typically indicated that they felt hotter when they were angry than when they were afraid, sad, or joyous. By contrast, the students tended to report feeling cold when they were afraid or sad.

It could be argued, of course, that the similarities across the broad range of countries involved in the study don't necessarily prove that the emotional sensations are biologically determined; after all, the people taking part in the investigation were all university students, and many of them could have acquired the same ideas from the mass media as to what the different emotions feel like. Nevertheless, Scherer and Wallbott were impressed with how closely the participants' descriptions of their sensations correspond with what is known about physiological changes in the various emotional states. According to these writers:

> Given the correspondence between experimental studies using psychophysiological measurement and our self-report data, it seems premature to claim that self-reported reactions only exist as socially constituted representations in our heads. . . . The evidence, then, seems to support theories that postulate both a high degree of universality of differential emotion patterning and important cultural differences in emotion elicitation, regulation, symbolic representation, and social sharing.[25]

Whatever the principal sources of people's affective experiences, culture or biology, how can we reconcile the dimensional and discrete-category views of emotional feelings? I would argue that both positions are correct to some degree. We're frequently aware of the unique nature of whatever affective state we're experiencing on that occasion, but at times the particular feeling's location on the circumplex dimensions becomes very important. On these occasions, what matters to us is how good or bad we feel, whether we feel active or passive, and the intensity of the feeling.[26] This being the case, much of our discussion in the later chapters will be especially concerned with the effects of pleasant and unpleasant feelings, although we will occasionally also refer to more specific, more distinctive affects as well.

How General Are the Models of Affective Experience? There's one other question that I should bring up at this time: Do these models, whether of the Russell or Watson–Tellegen variety, fit people's affective experiences in cultures other than our own? For some students of emotion the answer is "probably not." Theorists taking a social constructivist stance generally maintain that emotions are shaped by culturally acquired beliefs, or schemas, and aren't biologically determined. They say that societally shared conceptions tell us what, if any, emotion is produced by a certain kind of situation, and how each emotional state is experienced and expressed. In societies said to possess a culture of honor, as a case in point, shared beliefs are quick to define many different kinds of unpleasant encounters with others as personal challenges or even threats to one's honor. Furthermore, the culture of these societies teaches its members that they should become angry at these perceived affronts, and it prescribes retaliation as the appropriate response. Strong versions of this perspective contend that the affective experience one has in an emotional state is also constructed on the basis of the culture's expectations as to what one should feel under particular circumstances. If emotional feelings are as malleable and as readily influenced as this type of reasoning assumes, affective experiences could conceivably be organized along lines other than those posited by the circumplex models.

However, contrary to such an extreme view, I've already noted that Russell's circumplex structure "has been essentially replicated across a wide variety of linguistic cultures." In addition to occurring in native speakers of English in the United States and Canada, it has been found in the self-reported emotion ratings of Chinese, Croatians, Estonians, Greeks, Israelis, Japanese, Poles, Swedes, and Gujarati.[27] In the absence of any clear contrary evidence, it does seem that the model we've been discussing fits people's emotional ideas and experiences all over the world.

Psychological Theories About the Origins of Affect

You might think it's obvious why people feel happy or unhappy: They're put in a good mood when something pleasant happens and feel bad when they have an unpleasant experience. This is only a commonplace observation, but still, you may be surprised at the great number of ways in which this principle is manifested. In general, many different factors can determine whether we feel pleasure or displeasure. I'll briefly spell out a number of these influences, ranging from the simple to the more complex, and highlight their implications for the study of feelings as we go along. To organize this discussion, I'll first take up external stimulation that can affect our feelings more or less independently of what we do. Then I will turn to more internally controlled factors, those having more to do with the effects of our own behavior.

Affect-Generating External Stimulation

Natural Pleasures. Quite a few of our pleasures and displeasures are relatively simple in that they arise through mechanisms that are not only built into us but that also operate very early in life. Humans, much like other animals species, are typically pleased by sweet foods and liquids but find bitter-tasting substances unpleasant. They also often enjoy gentle tactile stimulation, such as the feel of a soft woolen blanket, but are disturbed by abrasive, painful rubbing of, say, sandpaper on the skin. Our biological heritage probably also leads us to like warm, sunny weather and maybe even certain kinds of rhythmic sounds.

Research psychologists studying emotions have at times varied their subjects' feelings by making use of such pleasant or unpleasant situational stimuli. As a notable example, in one of their investigations of the influence of mood on judgments, Schwartz and Clore found that many of us feel better on bright, sunny days than when the skies are overcast. The university students they interviewed in sunny weather reported being happier than the students who were questioned on rainy days. Certain sound patterns can also be pleasant or unpleasant, perhaps because of cultural learning but maybe also partly because of our biological heritage. Think of the old saying that "Music soothes the savage breast." Well, a pleasant melody might not entirely eliminate a person's strong anger, but it might at least improve his mood if he has no strong feelings before the music starts. And conversely, unpleasant music that grates on our nerves could well create negative feelings. Although there clearly are individual differences in these effects, music is such a reliable influence on mood states, for a short time anyway, that quite a few experimenters have used musical selections to shape their subjects' feelings. Other investigators have even used music to induce a short-lived depressive mood. In much the same vein, aesthetic considerations can also affect our feelings, again maybe for both cultural and biological reasons. Whatever the explanation, our mood can improve if we find ourselves in an attractive room or it can suffer if the room is a mess, affronting our aesthetic senses. Some experiments have thus influenced participants' feelings by varying the appearance of the laboratory room.[28]

Associations with Earlier Affective Experiences. Sometimes our feelings are aroused by reminders of an earlier affective experience. We see or hear something that automatically recalls this previous experience to mind and thereby activates, to some degree, the feelings we had on that occasion. The situational detail, often termed a *cue*, has this effect because of its association with an earlier emotional event. Behavioristically inclined psychologists would say that the reaction developed through classical conditioning, the process in which the cue (the conditioned stimulus) becomes paired with the stimulus (the unconditioned stimulus) that originally evoked the emotional reaction. Because of its association with the original emotion elicitor, this cue evokes the feelings that had been aroused earlier.

The psychological literature provides many demonstrations of this kind of conditioning. The participants in one experiment heard a neutral sound just before they received some insulting comments. After repeated pairings of this tone with the unpleasant remarks, the sound alone evoked the visceral reactions characteristic of an emotional disturbance.[29] We have even more dramatic examples of this phenomenon in many phobias, in which a person is exceedingly fearful of a certain kind of situation even though, objectively speaking, there is no real danger. Consider stage fright or a strong fear of lightning. The conditioned stimulus (such as the sight of a watching audience or of a thunderstorm) is somehow connected in the individual's mind with a dangerous or anxiety-provoking occurrence, so that this stimulus now automatically activates the bodily reactions and feelings that the original threatening event produced.

Several experiments have relied on the association of a stimulus with emotion-arousing events to generate specific feelings. In experiments employing the guided imagery procedure, the researchers basically ask the participants to think of an earlier incident in their lives when they were in a particular emotional state – say, happy or sad or angry. The memories the participants bring to mind are the cues evoking the affect they experienced during that earlier incident.[30] The widely used Velten mood induction procedure, published in 1968, is conceptually similar. Here the participants are given a series of 50 (or, originally, 60) statements, one at a time, and are asked to think about each of them. In one series the statements are increasingly depressive in tone: After beginning with the fairly neutral sentence "Today is neither better nor worse than any other day," the series continues with statements such as "I feel rather sluggish now" and then goes on to much more morose ideas such as "I want to go to sleep and never wake up." The other, elated (or happy) series also starts with the neutral sentence but then goes on to happier ones, such as "I do feel pretty good today," and concludes with the elated statement "God, I feel great!" More often than not, according to published research, the ideas and memories activated as the participants think about each statement serve to evoke the associated feelings.[31]

Does Familiarity Breed Contempt? The Mere Exposure Effect. Let's go further and extend this discussion of positive and negative happenings. As I suggested earlier, you may be surprised at the kinds of events that are pleasant to us. Consider the role of familiarity. Although we sometimes are told that "familiarity breeds contempt," we also know that we often develop a greater liking for things we encounter again and again.

Familiarity can be pleasant. Think of the Eiffel Tower, the Art Nouveau structure that now symbolizes Paris and even all of France. The tower is now viewed quite fondly by most Parisians, but a storm of protest greeted the structure's completion in 1889, and it was widely condemned as an "unforgivable profanation of the arts and a slap in the face for a nation which had previously upheld the banner of civilization. . . ." However, as the years passed, attitudes toward the Eiffel Tower became much more favorable, and it's now more likely

to be seen as a "friendly giant." Had its growing familiarity contributed to this attitude change? Maybe, as one psychologist put it,

> *Because of its tremendous height, the tower was ubiquitous and inescapable
> and hence was likely to be seen day after day. According to one long-standing
> hypothesis, familiarity leads to liking, and perhaps attitudes toward the tower
> changed simply because it became a familiar part of the landscape.*[32]

There is indeed evidence that familiarity often breeds liking rather
than contempt. This is actually a fairly old idea in psychology, one
that has been discussed at least as far back as the early years of the
twentieth century, but its best support comes from research initiated
by Robert Zajonc.

Zajonc's thesis is both simple and sweeping: The greater the repeated exposure to a novel situational stimulus, the more favorable
will be the attitude toward that stimulus, with the liking increasing
logarithmically – in a positively decelerating curve – as the number of
exposures rises. It is the increased exposure alone, the mere exposure
to the stimulus, and not what happens during the encounter, that
leads to the more positive attitude. In his initial 1968 monograph
advancing this proposition, Zajonc pointed to a number of supporting
observations. For one thing, more frequently used words usually are
more favorable than less frequently employed words. This relationship holds for the rated liking for the words as well as the positivity
of their meaning, and also exists in several languages, including Rus-
sian and Urdu. We can also see the frequency–liking relationship in
quite a few experimental studies: When people are repeatedly presented with certain neutral stimuli, whether these are nonsense words
or unfamiliar Chinese ideographs or musical selections or even pho-
tographs of people they don't know, they typically develop a more
positive attitude toward the stimuli they encounter most often. In one
clever and newer variation on this theme, research participants were
shown two photos of their own face and were asked to indicate which
they liked better. One photo was the usual kind of picture, showing
how they looked to others; the other photo was their mirror image –
the way they saw themselves when they gazed into a mirror. As the
investigators had expected, because the participants were much more
familiar with their mirror image than with the way they appeared to
others, it was the mirror-image picture that they preferred.[33]

Findings such as these are remarkably general and have been duplicated widely with "nationals of dozens of different countries, sons

of alcoholics, amnesics, dieters, chicks, ducklings, goslings, and many other species. . . ." In fact, Zajonc has quoted two other researchers who "claim that the mere exposure effect is the one solid sociopsychological effect that is found without exception across various cultures."[34]

At this point, you might be wondering about monotony and boredom. Suppose a simple musical jingle is repeated over and over again. Won't we get tired of it, maybe even annoyed? Two points can be made in answer to such a question. First of all, the repetition-induced increment in liking for the novel stimulus will slow down more rapidly the simpler this stimulus is. In comparison, our appreciation of a relatively complex melody will continue to increase for a longer time as it is repeated. And then too, we may become bored with the presentation situation rather than with the repeated stimulus itself. If the situation is varied in some way or if one waits for a while after the repeated presentations so that the boredom-fatigue diminishes, Zajonc says there is a very good chance that we will see the usual mere exposure effect.[35]

Recent research has now gone well beyond these demonstrations of the generality of the mere exposure phenomenon. Most notably, a growing number of studies have now shown that the effect occurs even when the presented stimulus is not detected consciously. To mention only some of the evidence for this, in two of their experiments Murphy, Monahan, and Zajonc presented Chinese ideographs to their participants either one or three times, with each exposure so brief (4 milliseconds) that these people weren't sure what they had seen. In two other studies the exposure duration was much longer (1 second), so that the ideographs were clear. The speed of the exposure didn't matter as far as the mere exposure effect was concerned. Whether the participants could consciously detect the ideographs or not, the more frequently presented ideographs were better liked than those that were shown less often. Subliminal influence isn't limited to relatively simple and largely meaningless stimuli such as ideographs; it can also arise with pictures of actual persons.[36]

Findings such as these contradict one explanation for increased liking with repeated exposure. The pioneering psychologist E. B. Titchener proposed long ago that we have "a glow of warmth . . . a feeling of ease, a comfortable feeling" when we recognize something familiar. It's the sense of familiarity that supposedly is gratifying. However, research tells us that the mere exposure effect arises even when there is no conscious recognition, no sense of familiarity. Why does this come about? Zajonc offers one possibility. We know that virtually every species has an orienting response when a novel stimulus is suddenly encountered; the organism's automatic nervous system is quickly activated, much like going rapidly on the alert, ready for almost anything to happen. Zajonc suggests that this orienting response subsides as the once novel stimulus appears again and again. The organism relaxes, so to speak, and it is this relaxation that is pleasant.[37]

This last observation is very important for us here because we're focusing on the sources of feelings. Zajonc emphasizes that the mere exposure effect is affective in nature and isn't due to a cognitive change. Several lines of research testify to this affectivity. Monahan, Murphy, and Zajonc reported that people exposed to five repeated presentations of Chinese ideographs were in a better mood for a short time afterward than were other persons who saw the ideographs only once. This happened, moreover, even though the stimulus presentations were so brief (5 milliseconds) that they were difficult to see.[38] In the Murphy, Monahan, and Zajonc studies mentioned before, the investigators found that the pleasure generated by the repeated presentation of the Chinese ideographs diffused to add to the good feeling produced by subliminal pictures of happy facial expressions. In these experiments, the happy pictures evidently induced a positive feeling only when they were viewed at a level below conscious awareness, perhaps because the participants weren't suspicious of the photos they couldn't see consciously. This automatically produced feeling was then intensified by the automatically engendered pleasure arising from the repetitions of the Chinese symbols.[39]

Comparisons with the Expected. Let's now turn from the repeated appearance of previously neutral stimuli, as in the mere exposure effect, to the repeated attainment of rewards. Do we get more and more pleasure from the gratifications we obtain again and again? The mere exposure thesis tells us, you will recall, that the increase in pleasure with repetition is a decelerating curve. This seems to be the case with the repetition of a particular gratification as well. Suppose that Jill is a stockbroker in a large investment firm and earns $300,000 a year. This high income is exceedingly pleasant at first, but as she earns the same pay year after year, she becomes accustomed to this level of reward.

The level of pleasure she feels tends to diminish with the repetition. In psychological terminology, this customary income level had become Jill's adaptation level, the level of this kind of event to which she had become accustomed. This level became relatively (but not completely) neutral for her on the pleasure-displeasure dimension. Putting this another way. Jill had come to expect the $300,000 income, so over time she gained less and less pleasure at receiving it.[40] In general, certain events that at first make us quite happy tend to evoke less positive affect after they have taken place repeatedly. Much the same reaction can occur with the repetition of somewhat unpleasant events that aren't physically painful. Here too, as the slightly to moderately negative event is experienced again and again, there is a decline in the negative affect after each occurrence.

Another complication now enters the picture. An adaptation level serves as a comparison standard in judging a later stimulus of the same kind. Furthermore, the reaction to the later event depends on how far it is from the comparison standard on the relevant stimulus dimension. Psychologists have noted that after people have adapted (become accustomed) to a certain level of a particular kind of stimulation, when they encounter a new stimulus that is of the same type but is at a clearly different level, there is apt to be a contrast effect in the judgment of this new event; it's difference from the comparison standard is perceptually exaggerated. And so, if people are used to lifting weights no heavier than 20 to 25 lb, they'll believe that a 40-lb weight is much heavier than it actually is.

This kind of contrast effect can also enter into affective experiences. If you're asked to think of the happiest time of your life, according to one study there's a good chance that you'll think of a happy event that took place soon after an unpleasant incident. The great difference between the happy event and the preceding negative occurrence made the clearly positive incident seem very good indeed.[41] You might have heard the saying that one cannot enjoy intense happiness unless one has also experienced strong unhappiness. Maybe this is because positive happenings are enhanced by contrast with unpleasant events. And, of course, this same contrast phenomenon undoubtedly would influence Jill's reaction to an unexpected rise or decline in her income. Where she might be relatively indifferent to a small increase (or decrease) in her pay, she would be greatly pleased (or displeased) by a more substantial change.

Reactions to One's Own Actions

Self-Competence. So far I've focused mostly on how externally derived occurrences can evoke pleasant or unpleasant feelings. We'll now turn to affective reactions to one's own behavior. This too is a complicated matter, and at the risk of oversimplifying greatly, I'll touch on only a few considerations.

To start, none of us are surprised that people are happy when they get what they want and displeased if they fail to satisfy their desires. We have to add to this simple idea, however. The pleasure produced by goal attainment is usually greater when the goal is reached by one's own actions than when it is due to an outside agency. Moreover, the pleasure is particularly keen if the goal was regarded beforehand as challenging but still reachable. The good feeling created by seeing oneself as competent adds to the joy of goal attainment. Conversely, being responsible for failure to reach the goal can be especially unpleasant.[42]

Research psychologists wanting to manipulate their subjects' mood have sometimes followed this basic reasoning. In a number of experiments designed to test the effects of positive or negative feelings, university students were first given a test supposedly assessing their intellectual ability and soon afterward were told that they had done either well or poorly on the test. Because most of them wanted to believe that they had good intellectual ability, they were typically happy at the favorable report or unhappy about the negative feedback.[43]

Self-Attention Influencing Affective Intensity. All in all, the thesis here is that the pleasure (or displeasure) people experience on getting what they want (or on failing to satisfy their desires) is greatly affected by their understanding of how this result came about, especially their interpretation of the part they believe they themselves played in bringing about the outcome. Their perception of themselves can even influence how they will feel when something decidedly unpleasant occurs. I'll have more to say along these lines in the next chapter, but right now, let's consider analyses of how people's awareness of themselves can affect the intensity of their reaction to emotional events.

More than 2,000 years ago, we're told, a saying was written in gold on the Temple of Apollo at Delphi: "Know thyself." Many of us do try to follow this admonition, as psychologist Daryl Bem noted. In company with other psychological theorists, he has argued that we're not always clear about what we are feeling or what motivated us to behave as we did, and that, having this uncertainty, we want to understand ourselves. Perhaps more than other theorists, however, Bem suggested that we seek this self-knowledge by basing inferences about our feelings and motives on whatever evidence we might have. In particular, just as we might guess other people's emotions and motives from observations of their behavior, we infer our own feelings and motives from seeing what we do under the given circumstances.

> *Individuals come to "know" their own attitudes, emotions, and other internal states partially by inferring them from observations of their own overt behavior and/or the circumstances in which this behavior occurs. Thus, to the extent that internal cues are weak, ambiguous, or uninterpretable, the individual is functionally in the same position as an outside observer, an observer who must necessarily rely upon these same external cues to infer the individual's inner states.*[44]

To give you an example of what Bem had in mind here, suppose that two men, John and Jim, are in a physician's office awaiting a painful inoculation. Although the two men are equally ill and both would be helped by the treatment, the physician tells John that it's desirable for him to have the injection but that he doesn't have to undergo the treatment and can refuse it if he so wishes. John then decides to refuse the painful inoculation. At the same time, however, Jim is not given the choice and is informed that he must have the injection. Now let's imagine that you ask each man to say how afraid he is at that moment and get frank answers. Who is more fearful? Assuming that both men are uncertain of what they are feeling in this somewhat ambiguous situation, Bem's conception predicts that John would experience more fear. John presumably would infer that he's quite afraid because he saw himself refuse the inoculation, and as a result, he consciously feels afraid. Jim, on the other hand, did not observe himself avoid the treatment and can only guess what he's feeling from his vague inner sensations.[45]

In the hypothetical case just described, John presumably was more fearful than Jim because of the inference he had made about his actions (his refusal to be inoculated) in the given situation. Another factor might also have contributed to John's fear: In thinking about himself, John was giving considerable attention to his internal sensations, the sensations automatically generated by the perceived threat.

This high level of self-awareness could have intensified his feelings. According to Michael Scheier and Charles Carver, when people focus their attention on the affect they are experiencing at that time, they are apt to heighten this feeling.

In the early 1970s, Shelly Duval and Robert Wicklund advanced their self-awareness theory, holding that heightened attention to oneself tends to increase adherence to one's salient ideals and behavioral standards. An impressive body of research supports this contention. Whatever the manner in which people become highly conscious of themselves – whether by viewing their reflection in a mirror, seeing a camera focused on them, writing about themselves, or even becoming highly conscious of how they are different from everyone else nearby – they then also (1) become more aware of whatever important attitudes and values they have that are relevant to the situation they are in and (2) seek to act in keeping with these attitudes and values to the extent that they are committed to them.

Carver and Scheier went on from there. In one study, Carver selected participants who either favored or opposed the use of electric shocks in psychological experiments and then, later, placed all of them in a situation in which they were to punish another person with shocks whenever that individual made a mistake on an assigned task. Some of the participants were led to be highly aware of themselves as they carried out their instructions by being seated in front of a large mirror. The results showed that the self-attentive participants adhered more closely to their previously expressed attitudes regarding the use of electric shocks than did their counterparts in the no-mirror condition; those who favored the use of shocks were most punitive to their peer, whereas those opposing this methodology were least punitive.[46]

Scheier and Carver then extended this research even further to deal with the effects of self-awareness on strong feelings. They argued that just as heightened attention to oneself increases awareness of salient attitudes and values (that is, strongly held attitudes and values that come to mind because of their relevance to the immediate situation), this self-consciousness promotes awareness of the dominant feelings in the situation and thereby intensifies these feelings. Several of their studies tested this reasoning. In one of them, either a happy or a depressed mood was induced in the subjects using the Velten procedure described before. Half of the men and women saw their reflections in a mirror as they read the Velten statements, whereas the mirror was reversed for the other participants so that there was no reflection. All of these people then rated their mood. Figure 1.3 summarizes how good the participants felt on average in each of the experimental conditions.

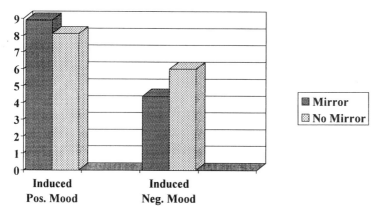

Figure 1.3 Effect of attention and induced mood on level of positive feeling (data from Scheier & Carver, 1977, Experiment 3).

As the researchers had expected, the people who were highly aware of themselves had the strongest feelings. More specifically, they had the most positive mood when they read the positive statements in front of the mirror, but were much less happy when they saw their reflection as they read the negative statements. The self-attention produced by the sight of themselves intensified their mood.

Scheier and Carver then demonstrated how general this phenomenon was. Some people are often highly conscious of themselves. In their mind's eye, so to speak, they seem to look at themselves much of the time, as if they are outside themselves observing what they are doing. Using a questionnaire measure assessing this tendency, which they called private self-consciousness, Scheier and Carver selected subjects who scored either high or low on this personality characteristic. When they later showed their male students pictures of emotional scenes, they found that the highly self-conscious participants were most strongly affected by what they saw. Those men who were highly aware of themselves, this time because they habitually observed themselves, were happiest after seeing photos of attractive women and were saddest after looking at pictures of gruesome atrocities. Much the same point can be made about pain. There's good evidence that paying attention to one's pain often intensifies it.

Besides influencing feelings, heightened attention to oneself can affect how one acts when disturbed. Research gives us an illustration. If people are afraid of a possible danger for some reason, those who are highly aware of themselves at that time, either because something (such as a mirror) has drawn their attention to themselves or because they are typically very self-conscious, are most likely to behave in a fearful manner.[47]

At the start of this section on the origin of affect, I referred to the commonplace idea that people are pleased when they reach their goals and are displeased when they fail to fulfill their desires. I then discussed a number of other considerations that complicate this simple proposition. In their most recent, and very ambitious, analysis of self-regulation, Carver and Scheier have added yet another complication that is somewhat in line with self-awareness theory. To give you an idea of what they have in mind, think back to Jill, the stockbroker. You'll recall that her income has been high but fairly constant for the past several years. Jill is very intent on succeeding in the financial industry and wants to earn a great deal of money as a mark of this success. We can say that Jill is within striking distance of her financial goal but isn't sure that she is making definite progress toward reaching it.

Carver and Scheier now maintain that when people are engaged in goal-relevant activity, their attention often turns inward, activating an "action monitoring" system in their minds that assesses progress toward the goal. Consciously or unconsciously, this psychological action monitoring system uses whatever standards are available and appropriate in the situation to determine whether the person is getting closer to the goal or is further away from it than before. Contrary to our commonsense suppositions, however, Carver and Scheier suggest that this action monitoring system is not primarily responsible for whatever pleasure or displeasure arises at that time. Rather, they propose, the affect experienced is actually due to yet another monitoring system: one sensing the rate of progress toward the goal. This second system presumably judges whether the person's progress toward the goal is fast enough relative to the rate the person expected or desired. If the approach to the goal is faster than expected or desired, pleasure is felt; conversely a slower improvement rate produces negative affect. Theoretically, in our hypothetical example, Jill would not experience any affect, positive or negative, if she thought she was moving toward her financial goal only at the rate she expected, and she would be unhappy if she thought she wasn't moving fast enough.

Research by Hsee and Abelson indicates how people's satisfaction with their progress toward their goal is affected by the rate of progress. In their first study, they asked university undergraduates how they would feel about certain changes in their progress toward a desired outcome. The participants were responsive to the rate of movement. If we extrapolate the findings of this study to Jill's case, she would rather see herself as definitely moving toward her financial goal than constantly earning the high income she desires. And more obviously, she would prefer rapid rather than slow progress toward her goal. Furthermore, judging from the findings, if Jill thought her income could be reduced, she would prefer earning a lower income over a period of time than undergoing the frustrating experience of having her present high pay suddenly decline to the same low level.[48]

2. More on the Causes of Feelings
Appraisals and Bodily Reactions

After examining the nature of affective experiences, the previous chapter considered a number of factors that lead to these feelings. We can also think of the influences affecting emotional states in a broader way. Generally speaking, psychologists sometimes talk about two types of emotion theories: those that emphasize central processes, primarily involving cognitions, and the more peripherally oriented formulations giving much more attention to the role of bodily reactions. This chapter will look at both of these approaches to emotional experience. It will begin with an examination of several cognitively focused theoretical schemes indicating that people's understandings determine the specific nature of the feelings they have when they are emotionally aroused. Then the chapter will turn to the study of how certain skeletal-muscular reactions can influence specific feelings.

To illustrate the differences between these two different approaches, let's start with the passage from William James's pioneering 1890 book on psychology cited in the Introduction.

> *Common sense says, we lose our fortune, are sorry and weep; we meet a bear, are frightened and run; we are insulted by a rival, are angry and strike. The hypothesis here to be defended says that this order of sequence is incorrect ... and that the more rational statement is that we feel sorry because we cry, angry because we strike, afraid because we tremble. ... Without the bodily states following on the perception, the latter would be purely cognitive in form, pale, colorless, destitute of emotional warmth. We might then see the bear, and judge it best to run, receive the insult and deem it right to strike, but we should not actually feel afraid or angry.*[1]

Thoughts Determine Feelings

The Two-Factor Theory: Arousal and Cognitions

The Schachter Theory. Although James's proposal seems to contradict the fundamental assumptions of the cognitive approach to emotions, at least one cognitively oriented theorist believed James was right in an important respect. Stanley Schachter, an exceedingly influential social psychologist in the decades following World War II, held that bodily reactions are involved in the genesis of an emotional experience – but only in a very general undifferentiated way. Here I'll summarize the basic ideas he and Jerome Singer published in their 1962 paper presenting this analysis.[2]

Schachter's conception is sometimes termed a *two-factor theory* of emotion because it stressed the role of two determinants: bodily reactions and cognitions about the physical sensations. For Schachter, the physiological changes produced by the emotion-instigating occurrence are initially detected only as a diffuse, neutral arousal state. Theoretically, cognitions then intervene to shape the specific feeling out of these vague sensations. The person's attributions, beliefs about the cause of the arousal, are especially important in this shaping. What if we see a bear, as in James's example? Schachter's theory would say that our initial reaction is an affectively neutral excitement. However, because we realize it was the dangerous bear that aroused us (that is, we attribute our internal sensations to this threat), we rapidly conclude that we are experiencing fear, and then we do feel afraid and may even act in a frightened manner. Positive emotions presumably develop in essentially the same way: Diffuse sensations are attributed to a positive occurrence, and positive feelings then arise.

The picture is a bit more complicated when the arousal source is ambiguous. In this case, the theory says, the person will seek to explain his or her sensations and will attribute the arousal to whatever cause seems likely. The actions of other people in the same situation presumably are very important in identifying this cause and thus defining what was happening. Once the attribution is made, then, the diffuse arousal is molded into specific feelings.

The two-factor theory of emotion prompted an impressive number of studies in the years immediately following its publication. Except in one respect that I'll get to soon, this research has not been kind to Schachter's formulation. A number of investigators failed to replicate the Schachter and Singer results, even when they attempted to duplicate the essentials of the original procedure. Take, for example, the two-factor theory's assumption that people often are very susceptible to social influences in deciding what emotion they are experiencing. When Marshall and Zimbardo could not replicate the Schachter and Singer findings, they proposed that "our true emotions may be more rationally determined and less susceptible to transient or whimsical situational determinants than has been suggested by Schachter and Singer."[3]

Yet, the negative evidence doesn't invalidate all of the theory's reasoning. When Reisenzein surveyed the research bearing on Schachter's analysis, he concluded that the findings supported the two-factor model's basic idea that attributing one's arousal to a particular source can shape the emotional experience, at least under certain conditions.[4] It's important to elaborate on this point.

Misattributions. You'll recall the Marshall and Zimbardo comment, cited just before, that emotions often are not as susceptible to transient situational determinants as Schachter and Singer had supposed. Nevertheless, there are occasions when a transient situational influence can have a considerable impact on emotional experience. The two-factor theory suggests that this is especially likely when people are physiologically aroused for some reason that's not altogether clear to them. Uncertain as to the cause and nature of their physical sensations, they may then misattribute their feelings to a nonemotional cause and, as a consequence, may decide they are not having an emotional experience. An early experiment by Ross, Rodin, and Zimbardo is a well-known demonstration of this effect.

> At the start of this study, the female university students were frightened by being told that they would receive electric shocks later in the session. First, though, they were to work on two different puzzles while being bombarded by noise. Before they began this task, however, they were also informed that they would not be shocked if they solved one of the puzzles correctly but would be paid money if they solved the other puzzle.
>
> The attribution-shaping information was then introduced before the women began work on the puzzles and before the noise started. All of the women were told that the noise would have certain side effects. For half of the participants, the supposed side effects listed were the usual sensations people experience when they are afraid, such as a pounding heart, shaky hands, and a sinking feeling in the stomach. If these persons then had the feelings characteristic of fear as they worked on the puzzles, they presumably would attribute their

sensations to the noise and thus wouldn't think of themselves as afraid. The noise-created side effects listed for the remaining women were sensations not linked to fear, such as ringing in the ears. If they felt their hearts pound and their hands shake, theoretically they wouldn't think it was the noise that was causing these feelings because the noise (they were told) didn't produce these effects. They might then conclude that they were afraid and act frightened.

The noise bombardment then began, and the researchers recorded how much time (in the 3-minute period) the women spent on each puzzle – the one that could keep them from being shocked and the one that could bring them money. The investigators expected that those who could attribute whatever threat-induced bodily sensations they had to the noise (in the Attribution-to-Noise condition) would be less fearful than those who could not make this attribution (in the No Noise Attribution condition). Figure 2.1 shows the percentage of the participants in each of the two attribution conditions who spent more than half of the time on a given puzzle. As you can see, the researchers' prediction was upheld. Fully 60% of the subjects who attributed their sensations to the noise spent most of their time trying to earn money rather than avoid the possible shock, as if they weren't especially fearful. By comparison, the great majority of the subjects who weren't able to assign their sensations to the noise evidently were more fearful and devoted their time mostly to avoiding the possible shocks.[5]

We have to be clear, however, that this misattribution effect occurs only under limited conditions, much as the previously mentioned comment by Marshall and Zimbardo indicates. It's not always possible to alter people's emotional experience by getting them to attribute their arousal to an innocuous unemotional source. In the earliest mis-

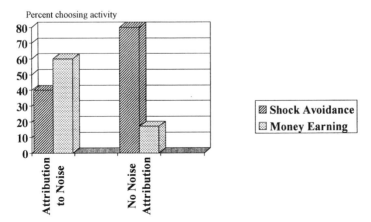

Figure 2.1 Predominant activity chosen by frightened subjects as affected by the attributed source of bodily sensations (data from Ross et al., 1969).

attribution experiment, as a case in point, Nisbett and Schachter first aroused either low or high fear in their subjects; the participants were told they would soon receive a series of electric shocks, but some were assured the shocks would be fairly weak, whereas others were informed the shocks would be quite painful. The researchers then attempted to convince some of the subjects in both of these fear-level conditions that the physical sensations they now felt were actually due to a drug they had just taken. It turned out that this misattribution procedure was effective only for those who were not very fearful. Having been told that the shocks to come would be weak, they had only mild bodily reactions to this information and could therefore readily attribute their sensations to the drug. As a consequence, they presumably didn't think of themselves as fearful and tolerated a good deal of mild electric stimulation when it came. By contrast, those persons who had been informed that the shocks would be very painful, and who thus become exceedingly frightened, were not especially tolerant of the mild shocks when these were delivered. They presumably knew what their strong feelings were due to – the threat of the painful shocks they would receive – realized they were fearful, and acted accordingly.[6] We can say, then, that our attributions modify the specific nature of our emotional experience only when the bodily sensations involved in this experience are relatively ambiguous and we aren't sure just why we are aroused.

Differentiating Among Emotional States. My discussion of misattributions up to now has considered how beliefs about the cause of an existing physiological arousal can alter the specific experience of this already established but ambiguous bodily state. Nowadays, though, attribution theory is used mainly to account for the generation of emotional states, not for how they might be modified. But the underlying idea is much the same in both cases: It's the meaning of an event that determines what emotion we feel, and this meaning, attribution theory says, is greatly dependent on our judgment of how the event arose.

One of the leading proponents of this view, Bernard Weiner, has given us a good example of how attribution theory explains the differences among various emotional states. To illustrate his formulation, suppose you've just learned that someone you know, Stan Jones, died today in an automobile accident. Basing his analysis on studies of ordinary persons' causal thinking, Weiner held that the way you will react emotionally to this news depends largely on three considerations: (1) What do you believe is the locus of the cause? That is (in attribution terminology), do you think some factor internal to the principal person caused the event to occur or was this causal factor external to this person? Did Stan Jones himself bring about the accident in some way or was it due to other factors in the surrounding situation, such as another driver, a slippery street, a mechanical problem with his car, and so on? (2) Somewhat related to this internal/external dimension but conceptually distinct is the question, How controllable was the cause? Was it possible for someone to instigate the occurrence deliberately or, conversely, intentionally keep it from happening? Do you think Stan could have done something to prevent the accident? If the accident happened because he took his eyes off the road he could have influenced the event, but he had little control if it was primarily the other driver's fault (uncontrollable external cause) or if he had a heart attack at that time (uncontrolled internal cause). (3) Finally, how stable is the perceived cause? Is it temporary or relatively long-lasting?

Weiner and his colleagues have shown that people consider these three matters in differentiating among pity, anger, and guilt. And so, according to their findings, you would pity the people involved (Stan Jones and his family) if you thought the bad event (Stan's death) was the result of uncontrollable factors, but you would be angry if you attributed the event to a controllable external cause. You presumably would be angry with the other driver, for example, if you believed this person had caused the accident and could have kept it from happening. Finally, on learning of the unhappy event, you would feel guilty if you thought that you yourself had been responsible for Stan's death and had had sufficient control to have prevented the accident.[7]

Appraisals

We now come to a related but somewhat different theoretical conception, one also emphasizing the importance of an incident's meaning. To introduce this particular reasoning, let's start with a contrasting line of thought: William James's example of the individual running away from a bear. According to James's theory, you'll recall, the person's fear experience grows out of his or her bodily reactions in fleeing from the danger. This conception was roundly criticized by many psychologists, including Magda Arnold, widely recognized for her influential writings on emotion two generations ago. Where James had said only that we run from the bear because of our "ideas" about this animal, Arnold noted that James "really presupposes an appraisal that the bear is harmful . . . that this bear means danger for us. . . ."

Arnold stressed the overriding importance of such an appraisal in her encyclopedic survey of research on the emotions published in 1960. An appraisal, she said, was "the direct, immediate, nonreflective . . . [and] automatic" judgment about one's relationship to a particular object or situation, and it was this appraisal rather than the bodily reactions that gave rise to the emotional experience. For Arnold, this appraisal was more than just an interpretation of what was happening; it also involved an assessment of personal significance. Arnold held that an emotion will not be aroused unless the object or situation is appraised as having a personal meaning, as being personally desirable or undesirable. As you can see, the appraisal idea gives greater explicit attention to the personal significance of an occurrence than does standard attribution thinking.[8]

Commonalities and Differences. The appraisal concept was soon taken up by many other psychological researchers, and the great majority of psychological analyses of emotion now incorporate this perspective. Not surprisingly, though, these analyses are not identical in detail.

Richard Lazarus is probably the appraisal theorist closest to Magda Arnold both historically and conceptually. Like Arnold, he focused on people's considerations of their well-being, and also, somewhat as Arnold did, he differentiated between primary and secondary appraisals. Lazarus regarded appraisals as operating in a two-stage process. The primary stage presumably first determines what relevance a given occurrence has for the person's goals, especially those involved in relationships with others. If the event is thought to be personally relevant, this primary appraisal then judges whether it is consistent or inconsistent with goal attainment. Returning to our earlier hypothetical example, suppose someone hears of Stan Jones's death in the auto accident. His primary appraisal is to consider what bearing the event has on his own wants and needs and whether Stan's death is beneficial or harmful to the satisfaction of his desires. In the next step, the secondary appraisal, the person further analyzes the critical incident and, in doing so, establishes a more differentiated emotional experience. In this process, he determines (1) accountability, who is responsible for the event, and thus who should be the target of any attempts to cope with the situation; (2) his ability to cope with the occurrence physically and psychologically; and (3) what he expects in the future as a consequence.

Lazarus says these aspects of an appraisal can be considered by themselves, at the "molecular level," but they can also be viewed, at the "molar level," as part of a more general theme. Because appraisals in Lazarus's formulation basically have to do with the person's relationships with others, sets of molecular-level appraisals can be grouped together in *core relational themes*. Thus, in the case of the emotions generated when someone is harmed (such as in Stan Jones's death), the core relational theme for anger is other blame, and the molecular-level appraisal components have to do with whether the event is seen as (1) goal relevant and (2) inconsistent with goal attainment and with whether (3) another person or situation is held accountable. The core relational theme for sadness, on the other hand, is irrevocable loss or helplessness about the loss. An occurrence producing sadness theoretically grows out of molecular-level appraisals of the incident as (1) goal relevant, (2) inconsistent with goal attainment, (3) being such that there is little perceived ability to cope with the problem, and (4) giving rise to the expectation of an inconsistency with future goal attainment.[9]

Other appraisal theorists have proposed sets of basic dimensions that people are assumed to employ in assessing the significance of the events in their lives. Although I can't provide a detailed survey of these different formulations here, some of their commonalities and differences are worth noting. Many of them hold (with Lazarus) that the appraisal process operates in several stages, first a rather general assessment and then a more detailed examination. Many assume that the event in question is specifically evaluated for its pleasantness. This particular aspect is sometimes kept separate from the degree to which the occurrence is viewed as conducive to goal attainment. Also, virtually all of these formulations contend, along with Weiner's attribution theory, that one of the most important aspects of the appraisal has to do with the perceived *agency*, the degree to which the cause of the event is seen as internal or external to the person or object of main interest in the situation. This particular dimension is generally regarded as being involved in differentiating among anger, sadness, and guilt; anger arises, it's usually said, when people experiencing an unpleasant occurrence assign agency to someone else. Many appraisal analyses also maintain that the incident is judged for its *legitimacy*, that is, whether or not it conforms to accepted norms of propriety.

There also are some substantial differences among the various appraisal analyses. For example, Scherer is the only major theorist in this area who believes that events are assessed for their novelty. And more than most of the other theorists, he also emphasizes the ongoing rather than static nature of the appraisal process. In his view, the person engages in a series of "checks," first for novelty, then for pleasantness, next for how relevant the situation is to the person's goals, and so on. Also adopting a somewhat different stance, Stein and Levine give more attention than other appraisal theorists to people's judgments of whether a lost goal can be reattained or not. For them, anger results when we lose a desired state of affairs or cannot reach it but believe there is a possibility that we can get it in the future, whereas sadness stems from the perception that the goal is irretrievably lost.[10]

Given all of the different appraisal dimensions that have been proposed, it's reasonable to ask, along with Scherer, whether there is a minimum number of factors that most people consider in assessing an event's significance. Several studies have attempted to answer this question, but I'll mention only one of these, partly because it also investigated the possibility of cross-national differences.[11]

> *Mauro, Sato, and Tucker asked almost 1,000 students at universities in the United States, Japan, Hong Kong, and the People's Republic of China to recall episodes of various emotional states, report how they had felt at those times, and answer specific questions about how they had appraised the emotional situations. These latter appraisal questions reflected 10 dimensions that had been proposed by Smith and Ellsworth, Roseman, and Scherer.*
>
> *On statistically analyzing the questionnaire responses from the four different countries, the researchers concluded that their participants had judged the emotional incidents mainly in terms of seven dimensions:*
>
> 1. Pleasantness: *how pleasant the situation was because it was seen as fair and* the participant *was in control of what happened.*
> 2. Certainty: *how certain, predictable, and understandable the situation was.*
> 3. Effort: *how much effort was thought to be required in the situation and whether there were any obstacles to goal attainment.*
> 4. Other control: *the extent to which others were perceived to be in control of events.*
> 5. Appropriateness: *the perceived appropriateness of the participant's feelings in the situation.*
> 6. Circumstances control: *the extent to which the event was caused by circumstances beyond anyone's control.*
> 7. Attention: *motivation to attend to or ignore the occurrence.*

The analyses also indicated that there were surprisingly few differences from one country to another in terms of where each emotional state was located on each of these appraisal dimensions. Anger, for example, was generally regarded as moderately unpleasant and fairly high on other control, and fear involved both unpleasantness and uncertainty. One of the few national differences had to do with the extent to which sadness was linked to the situation's control by others. In fact, the researchers reported that "appraisals of control over events are responsible for most of the observed cultural differences" in the emotional states' location on these dimensions. The Chinese typically regarded other people as the cause of sad occurrences, whereas in the United States, sadness was more frequently thought to be the result of circumstances beyond anyone's control.

"Taken together," Mauro, Sato, and Tucker concluded, "these results suggest there may be a set of pan-cultural basic dimensions of appraisal that are important for emotions and that, across [these] cultures, similar appraisals on these dimensions result in similar emotions."[12]

Questions and Problems. With appraisal theories of emotion attracting so much attention, these conceptions inevitably have also drawn a number of criticisms. Again, we cannot present a detailed discussion of the objections that have been raised and the problems that have been highlighted, so I'll touch on only a few of the issues.[13]

Some of these issues have to do with the methodology employed in the great majority of investigations in this area. Most appraisal studies asked the participants to remember specific emotional experiences and then asked them how they had judged the significance of these episodes. Another procedure was to give the subjects brief descriptions of hypothetical emotion-arousing events, with these descriptions deliberately establishing variations along certain appraisal dimensions. The participants then had to indicate what emotions they or some other person would experience in the given situation. Much less frequently, a few investigations required people to report on the appraisals they made in naturally occurring situations such as a college examination or a political incident.[14]

We have to wonder whether, in all of these studies, the participants were reporting their everyday theories of how emotions were generated rather than the psychological processes that actually took place. As Parkinson and Manstead noted in their important critique of appraisal theorizing, this uncertainty is especially great in those investigations inquiring into recalled emotional reactions. These writers pointed out that, for the findings to be valid, the research subjects must have encoded their emotional appraisals at the time of the remembered incident in a form that permitted ready recall later. However, appraisal advocates generally agree, with Arnold, that people often make many of their assessments rapidly, automatically, and with little if any conscious thought. Assuming that this is so, the participants may not have had the easy or even complete access to their unconscious appraisals that the appraisal methodology presupposes.

> . . . The issue then becomes one of whether these reconstructed appraisals could ever be accurate representations. It seems possible that they are based instead upon commonsense causal schemata . . . for emotions, which may also be tailored by participants to fit with the implicit model of emotions suggested by the demand characteristics of the experimental instructions.[15]

Another problem has to do with the actual causal status of at least some of the appraisal dimensions identified in the research. The investigators have generally assumed, of course, that appraisals lead to the emotions. Several psychologists, such as Parkinson and Manstead, as well as Frijda, have argued, however, that on some occasions causality conceivably could have operated in the opposite direction. Think of the previously mentioned effort and attention dimensions proposed by Smith and Ellsworth and also found by Mauro and his colleagues. Rather than people's effort and attention shaping their specific feelings, people in an already existing emotional state might believe that they have to exert effort to cope with the incident and/or pay attention to what is happening. In fact, it's been shown that moderately negative affect often promotes closer attention to events in one's surroundings and more careful thought about these occurrences than does positive affect.[16]

Anger gives us a more surprising example of this causal direction problem. Appraisal theories and common sense are united in saying that anger results from blame. We presumably believe that someone else or some other thing is the cause (agent) of an undesirable state of affairs if we are to become angry. However, contrary to this widely shared supposition (and very much in tune with my own theorizing, summarized in Chapter 7), Frijda suggested that anger might at times motivate an attempt to attach blame, that is, find an agent responsible for the unpleasant occurrence. We can cope better with a distressing situation if we think we know who or what caused it. Here too, there is supporting evidence. In several experiments, Keltner, Ellsworth, and Edwards induced either sad or angry feelings in their subjects and showed that the angry persons then became more likely than their sad counterparts to believe that other people were responsible for what had happened to them. Anger had created a readiness to attribute agency to others.[17]

Are Cognitive Processes Always Responsible for Emotions? The last dispute I'll take up here has to do with the role of noncognitive processes in the generation of emotions. In 1980 the eminent psychologist Robert Zajonc, whom I introduced in Chapter 1, published a provocative article that sparked a great deal of discussion and controversy. Zajonc argued that cognitions and emotions operated as separate systems and that many affective reactions are governed by processes that do not involve information processing and understanding. Basing his contention largely on his research on the mere exposure phenomenon (discussed in Chapter 1), in this and later papers Zajonc maintained that we can come to like something, or even develop pleasant feelings, without the intervention of our cognitions.[18]

Lazarus objected to Zajonc's clear separation of emotion and cognition, insisting that emotions cannot be experienced unless there is cognitive activity. For an emotion to be aroused, he held, "people must comprehend – whether in the form of a primitive evaluative perception or a highly differentiated symbolic process – that their well-being is implicated in a transaction, for better or worse."[19]

Psychologists are now pretty well agreed that the dispute here is largely about definitions: how one defines cognition and emotion. But even so, there's no easy solution to the problem. The term *cognition* has different meanings to different psychologists. Whereas some restrict this construct to processes involving higher brain structures, particularly the neocortex and hippocampus, others say that even relatively primitive subcortical regions of the brain, such as the amygdala, evaluate the biological significance of situational stimuli and thus are involved in cognitive operations. We also have different definitions for the concept *emotion*. Zajonc's meaning was broad, encompassing affective preferences and general feelings of pleasure and displeasure, whereas most appraisal theorists contend that Zajonc is dealing primarily with unfocused feelings or moods and not real emotions.[20]

A Possible Resolution. The resolution of this controversy may require an eclectic stance similar to that taken recently by Scherer. In one of his latest writings, Scherer has limited the scope of appraisal theorizing. It doesn't deal with "free-floating moods, preferences, reflexive pain reactions, or emotional memories," he noted, but rather is concerned only with "full-blown emotions." I would add that appraisal theorizing is relevant only for those emotional states whose cause is salient to the people having the experience. Scherer also suggested adopting a multiprocess approach to emotions (although he preferred to talk about multiple levels of information processing). Building on Howard Leventhal's multilevel process theory of emotion, Leventhal and he proposed that the stimulus checks involved in Scherer's appraisal formulation can develop from three levels of processing: (1) the *sensorimotor* level having to do with the automatic, even reflexlike, activation of expressive-motor programs by external stimuli and internal changes of state, (2) the somewhat more cognitive *schematic* level within which sensorimotor processes are integrated with the simplified, general prototypes of emotional situations, including the feelings typically aroused in these episodes, and (3) the highly cognitive *conceptual* level involving abstract propositions or rules about emotions that are stored in memory.[21]

Whether or not we incorporate Scherer's appraisal model into this multilevel formulation, it might be that physical pain's activation of aggressive urges occurs at the sensorimotor level, that phobias (such as stage fright) involve the schematic level, and that appraisal rules operate at the conceptual level. At any rate, a growing number of theorists now believe that the appraisal perspective cannot account for all emotion-related phenomena.[22] Many of our emotional reactions clearly result from our assessments of the situation we are in. Yet our feelings, thoughts, and even memories can also be affected by processes outside the appraisal realm, and a comprehensive analysis of emotions must deal with these processes as well. We'll now turn to one nonappraisal-related matter: the effect of bodily reactions on feelings.

Effects of Skeletal-Motor Reactions

At the start of this chapter I referred to William James's thesis that people's bodily reactions, such as skeletal-muscular movements, can shape the specific nature of their emotional experiences. We run from a danger, he said, and we become afraid. But although this idea is today frequently linked to James's theory of emotions, it actually was expressed before the end of the 19th century when James wrote his classic book on psychology.

In one scene of Shakespeare's play *Henry V*, the king urges his soldiers on as they prepare to attack the French at Harfleur:

Stiffen the sinews, summon up the blood . . .
Then lend the eye a terrible aspect; . . .
Now set the teeth and stretch the nostril wide
Hold hard the breath and bend up every spirit
To his full height.

King Henry clearly believed that his men would become fiercer if they "imitate[d] the action of a tiger" and adopted an aggressive facial expression and posture.

The Bodily Feedback Thesis

However, as well known as this excerpt from Shakespeare's play has been over the centuries, a scholarly review by Adelmann and Zajonc tells us that scientists didn't turn their attention to the possible effects of skeletal-muscular movements on emotions until the middle of the 19th century when two French physiologists, apparently writing independently, suggested that bodily movements can influence feelings and thoughts. But the statement we know best today was published about a decade or so later by Charles Darwin in his 1872 monograph *The Expression of Emotion in Man and Animals*. "The free expression by outward signs of an emotion intensifies it," Darwin maintained. "On the other hand, the repression, as far as this is possible, of all outward signs softens our emotions."[23] Muscular movements supposedly can modulate an emotion, strengthening it by openly displaying the movements characteristic of that particular emotional state and weakening it by restraining this overt expression. William James agreed with Darwin. "Refuse to express a passion, and it dies," he said in his 1890 book *The Principles of Psychology*, and "Whistling to keep up courage is no mere figure of speech." But whereas Darwin seemed to talk only of bodily movements affecting an existing emotional state, James went further by arguing that bodily changes are the direct cause of the emotional experience.

Critics, especially the great physiologist Walter Cannon, objected to James's focus on the role of the internal organs (the viscera) in producing the emotional experience. They noted, among other things, that the viscera are generally too insensitive and respond too slowly to be the basis of often rapidly developing and quickly changing emotional feelings. In actuality, however, James believed the skeletal musculature also played an important part in creating these feelings (although his 1890 formulation did place much more emphasis on autonomic reactions than did his original 1884 version). Showing this, even in his later discussion he asked his readers, "Can one fancy the state of rage and picture no ebullition in the chest, no flushing of the face, no dilation of the nostrils, no clenching of the teeth . . . ?" For James it is the total complex of physiological and muscular responses to an "exciting event" that gives rise to the particular emotional experience, not the visceral changes alone.[24]

Although a few theorists offered somewhat similar conceptions in later years, as Adelmann and Zajonc have reminded us, this line of thought had relatively little impact on psychology until the 1960s and 1970s. At that time, Silvan Tomkins and then Carroll Izard proposed that emotional feelings were initiated primarily by feedback from the facial muscles to the central nervous system. In Tomkins's words, "Important as [inner bodily responses] undoubtedly are, we regard them as of secondary importance to the expression of emotion through the face . . . the face expresses affect, both to others, and to the self, via feedback, which is more rapid and more complex than any stimulation of which the slower moving visceral organs are capable."[25]

This *facial feedback* conception continues to be important in the study of emotions, although proponents of this general line of thought have broadened their theorizing in the past two decades or so. They now recognize that a wide variety of bodily responses, including muscular reactions in other parts of the body, can also "feed back" to the central nervous system and thereby influence one's emotional experience significantly. As a case in point, in his latest theoretical statement, Izard holds that sensorimotor processes throughout the body – in the central nervous system, facial expressions, and posture, as well as in instrumental behavior and muscle action potentials – all contribute to the activation of emotions.[26] The present section will not be as far-ranging as this, however, and will deal exclusively with the effects of voluntary movements of the facial and body muscles that are usually involved in the open expression of emotional states. But even with this relatively narrow focus, the discussion here will refer to the bodily feedback conception because this is the label generally employed in the psychological literature.

Theoretical Issues. One possible way of reconciling the cognitive appraisal approach with the bodily reaction-feedback conception is to follow the lead offered by Darwin in the quotation presented earlier. Maybe muscular reactions (and other bodily sensations) only modulate the emotional state that had previously been activated by an appraisal, intensifying this state if the emotion-related muscular movements are expressed overtly or softening the emotion if the outward signs are repressed. Researchers sometimes refer to this possibility as the *weak version* of the bodily feedback hypothesis.

The much stronger, and more extreme, form of this hypothesis holds that bodily reactions initiate as well as modulate the emotional experience. This notion, typically not embraced by traditional cognitive appraisal theorists, has been propounded most notably by such researchers as William James, Silvan Tomkins, Carroll Izard, and, most recently, James Laird.[27] It is obviously important to determine if there is any empirical support for the strong form as well as the weak form of the bodily feedback conception.

Evidence for the Weak Version of Feedback Theory. Generally speaking, the best tests of the weak form of the bodily feedback conception can be found in those experiments in which the subjects are exposed to an emotion-arousing stimulus and then are induced either to move or to inhibit the movement of the muscles usually associated with that emotion. One of the studies conducted by Lanzetta, Cartwright-Smith, and Kleck is a good example.[28] As instructed, the participants in this experiment sometimes attempted to minimize the outward expression of pain when they received an electric shock; at other times they responded to the shocks with an open and perhaps even exaggerated display of emotion. Observers indicated that the acting was altogether convincing. Measures obtained after each shock trial showed that the subjects' pose had influenced their reactions to the electric shocks. Over all of the shocks the subjects received, immediately after acting as if they hadn't received a shock, they reported having experienced less pain, and also were less aroused physiologically, than after they had responded in an exaggerated manner. The participants' muscular reactions, showing their feelings or repressing them, had affected their emotional experience soon afterward, much as Darwin and James had postulated. Furthermore, this influence apparently was more than a self-delusion.

Although there have been occasional failures to confirm these body feedback effects, an impressive number of experiments have yielded supporting results. The overall pattern, it's fair to say, indicates that the voluntary muscular responses usually associated with an emotional state, in the face and/or other parts of the body, often intensify the emotional experience.[29]

Interestingly, in at least one of the later experiments, the findings show that the feeling-influencing motor reactions need not be pronounced or even visible to outside observers. McCanne and Anderson trained their female subjects both to suppress and to heighten the tension in certain facial muscles: those associated with smiling and, separately, those involved in frowning. As a consequence of this training, the tension in the specified muscle group could be recorded electromyographically but wasn't detected by watching judges. When the participants then were asked to imagine pleasant and unpleasant emotional scenes over a series of trials, suppression of the activity of the "smile" muscles lessened the pleasure they felt in thinking of the happy events, and suppression of the "frown" muscles reduced the distress produced by imagining the negative scenes. Restraining the activity of one's facial muscles apparently can soften the emotional experience even when this restraint is carried out very subtly.[30]

Did the Participants Know What Their Muscle Movements Meant? Although the evidence just reviewed is consistent with the arguments advanced by Darwin, James, and others, discussions of this research have raised some important methodological and theoretical questions that we should consider here. One of them has to do with whether the participants in these experiments were aware of the psychological meaning of the muscles they were asked to move or to restrain. Even though the researchers (such as McCanne and Anderson) hadn't told the subjects that they were to look happy or sad and didn't identify the psychological meaning of the particular muscle movements, maybe the participants had realized they were making a smile or a frown, or whatever the expression represented. There could then have been two possible consequences. One, they might have then deliberately modified their ratings of their feelings to conform to what they believed the investigators expected of them (the experimenters' supposed demands). Or two, the thought of the meaning of their muscle movements, such as the thought that they were smiling or looking sad, could have been responsible for their resulting feelings, not the muscle movements themselves.[31]

A number of experiments carried out since the 1980s address this problem. In these investigations the subjects were exposed to some kind of emotion-generating stimulus, as in the earlier studies, but then they were required to adjust certain facial or body muscles in such a way that they undoubtedly were unaware of the psychological meaning of these movements. This was the case, almost surely, for the subjects of the ingenious experiments devised by Fritz Strack, Leonard Martin, and Sabine Stepper.

> *Supposedly because they were in a study of how physically impaired persons might carry out various activities, the men and women participating in the first experiment by Strack and his colleagues were asked to do a variety of things with a pen. Some of them were to hold the pen in their nondominant hand, others were to grasp it tightly with their lips, and the remaining subjects were to hold it gently with their front teeth so that their lips didn't touch it. Holding the pen in the teeth moves the facial muscles associated with smiling, whereas this smiling expression is inhibited when the pen is grasped with the lips. The pen-in-hand condition can be viewed as a relatively neutral control group.*
>
> *At any rate, after the participants had used the pen in a variety of ways (to support the study's ostensible purpose), such as to draw a line between numbers printed on a page, they were shown several cartoons. Still keeping the pen in the designated position, they rated how funny each cartoon was to them. The condition differences on these ratings were consistent with the facial feedback hypothesis even though the subjects hadn't realized the emotional meaning of their facial movements: The people who had adopted the smiling expression regarded the cartoons as funnier than did their counterparts in the nonsmiling-lips condition. The pen-in-hand group's ratings fell between these two extremes.[32]*

Another possible question is whether muscular responses in parts of the body other than the face also contribute to the emotional experience. We saw earlier that William James, among others, believed this experience grew out of a wide variety of bodily changes, whereas other theorists have claimed that the face is the primary source of the sensations generating the emotional feelings. The most recent studies tend to support the broader view. These investigations have demonstrated that changes in body posture can also influence emotional reactions – as long as these body movements are the ones associated with typical emotional states. Stepper and Strack, for example, found that university students who were told they had done well on an assigned task reported feeling less proud of their performance when they had been seated in a slumped rather than an upright or neutral posture at the time they were informed of their success. A slumped posture, of course, is characteristically linked to feelings of failure and depression. Adopting this "depressive" position evidently interfered with the development of pride at the news of the success. Similarly, in another study, when students were threatened by news of a coming examination, those whose legs and shoulders had been deliberately placed in a relaxed position experienced less stress than did others who had been made to adopt a tense posture.[33] The way the participants sat apparently had activated the emotion-related thoughts and feelings usually linked to that body posture.

Another problem has to do with the emotional state that presumably is generated by facial and bodily movements. Looking at the studies that had been conducted up to the mid-1980s, Winton pointed out that they hadn't really demonstrated any emotion-specific effects. The experiments typically contrasted only two kinds of emotion-expressive movements (whether in the face or the body): one associated with a positive emotion, such as a smile, and another linked to a negative state, such as a frown or a slumped position. It could be, then, Winton observed, that the muscular changes employed in these feedback experiments had only produced variations along some pleasant-unpleasant dimension, and hadn't created the specific emotional experiences postulated by James, Tomkins, Izard, and the other feedback theorists.[34]

This certainly was a reasonable point at the time. However, more recent investigations indicate that muscular actions can indeed give rise to specific emotional effects. One such study was conducted by Jo and Berkowitz.

> After the women in this experiment talked individually about either a neutral or an emotion-arousing incident (in the latter case, one that had made them either angry or sad), they were asked to squeeze a small device at a particular level of force. What's especially important here is that the hand squeeze was either sufficiently strong so that the subject made a tightly clenched fist or was fairly loose and not very fistlike. With her hand in the instructed position, each woman spoke for several minutes about how she had felt at the time of the recalled episode and then rated her present feelings. Because a clenched fist is frequently associated with angry feelings, the question here was whether this tightening of the hand muscles would heighten the anger activated by the recollection of the anger-arousing incident without also strengthening other unpleasant feelings such as sadness.
>
> Figure 2.2 summarizes the mean condition ratings on the measures of felt anger and felt sadness after controlling for the participants' scores on these measures at the start of the session. We can see, first of all, that, as expected, the women who had talked about the angering incident while making a tightly clenched fist reported having the strongest angry feelings at present. The fist clench had no such intensifying influence on the ratings of felt sadness in this

anger-recalling condition or on those who had spoken of a sad event. Equally important, the women recalling the sad occurrence actually were saddest if they hadn't tightened their fist, much as if a clenched fist was incompatible with sad feelings. (Although this isn't indicated in the figure, it's also worth noting that there were no reliable differences between the fist-clenched and non-fist-clenched groups on any of the feelings indices when the subjects talked about an emotionally neutral event.) All in all, then, the muscular movements in the hand that are frequently associated with anger had a specific effect, heightening an existing anger experience without intensifying felt sadness.[35]

Evidence for the Strong Form of Feedback Theory. A number of studies have now found that the voluntary muscle movements usually involved in an emotional state can initiate as well as modulate the experience of that emotion. Zajonc, Murphy, and Inglehart have given us some interesting demonstrations of this finding that may surprise you. In a series of experiments they found that even the facial movements made by speaking certain kinds of words can influence people's affective reactions. In one study, native German speakers were asked to read a number of stories aloud. Some of these stories were replete with words requiring them to make movements with their mouths and lips that were just like the facial expression of disgust, whereas the other stories had few such words. The great majority of these persons liked the stories inducing the "disgust" expression less than

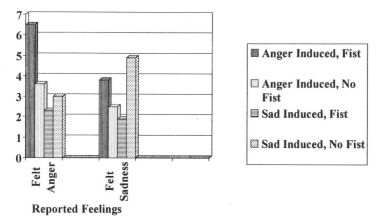

Figure 2.2 Effect of hand condition on reported feelings after mild anger or sadness was induced (data from Jo, 1993). These are adjusted means after preinduction feelings were held constant.

the other stories. They also regarded the former as less pleasant, even though the two kinds of stories were virtually identical in content.[36]

Still, these studies hadn't addressed the question of emotion-specific effects. Other investigations, however, did look into this matter, along with the possible initiating function of bodily movements. Duclos, Laird, and their colleagues asked whether body postures and facial expressions could generate feelings. The second of their series of studies is especially notable for us here.

> *Supposedly because this was an investigation of "brain hemisphere activity during various tasks," the subjects in this experiment adopted three different postures without being told what these poses represented. In one posture, that characteristic of fear, the participants kept their heads facing forward as they leaned their upper bodies backward while twisting them slightly and dipping one shoulder – much as if a sudden danger had unexpectedly appeared. Another posture, generally associated with sadness, required them to fold their hands in their laps, drop their heads forward, and let their bodies sag. The third posture was the anger pose; they placed their feet flat on the floor, clenched their hands tightly, and leaned their bodies forward. After each pose was held for a brief period, the participants rated their feelings at that time.*
>
> *The results were very much as the Laird team had predicted: Even though the mood ratings were fairly low, the subjects' strongest reported feeling after adopting a given pose was the mood that was characteristically associated with that posture. The pose manipulations obviously didn't have exactly the same meaning for every person; Figure 2.3 reports the findings for those participants who did associate the specified posture with the intended feeling. As you can see, the subjects indicated that they had felt the most fear when they were in the fear posture, rated themselves as saddest after adopting the sad pose, and had felt angriest after they had been in the anger posture.[37]*

All in all, then, this research indicates that emotion-associated body movements as well as facial expressions can initiate at least some kinds of emotional experiences, even if only at a low level of intensity.

Emotion-related muscular movements can affect our thoughts as well as our feelings. According to the research of Keltner, Ellsworth, and Edwards mentioned earlier in this chapter, you'll recall, we tend to make different attributions when we're sad than when we're angry. Sadness heightens the chance that we'll attribute our life circumstances to outside situational forces, whereas when we're angry we're more apt to regard some person as responsible for what happens to us. Extending this point further, the researchers demonstrated that these differences in causal attributions can also be produced by getting people to adopt either a sad or an angry pose in their face and body.[38]

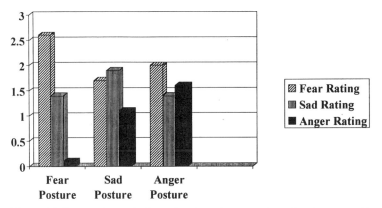

Figure 2.3 Reported mood after adoption of an emotion-related posture (data from Duclos et al., 1989, Study 2). Data exclude subjects for whom posture manipulation was not successful.

When Posing an Emotion Doesn't Generate the Feeling. Considering all this research evidence, there appears to be quite good support for the strong as well as the weak version of the body reaction thesis. But another issue still causes uncertainty: We sometimes act as if we're angry or sad or afraid, adopting the posture and facial expression of this emotional state, but we don't experience any feelings. Why don't we feel angry or sad or frightened on these occasions? Or as William James himself had asked, Why is it that "we can all pretend to cry and not feel grief; and feign laughter without being amused"?[39]

For James the likeliest answer to this question is that most emotion simulations evoke only a few of the bodily changes that are usually produced when an emotion is aroused naturally, and these at only a weak level. His explanation wasn't altogether right. Much of the research just reviewed, especially the findings reported by McCanne and Anderson, demonstrate that even slight and subtle emotion-related muscular movements in the face, hands, and body apparently can elicit or modify emotion-related feelings and thoughts, at least to some degree.

Interfering mental activity may also counter whatever (largely weak) effects are produced by the enacted emotional expressions. To explain what I have in mind here, I'll refer to the associative-network conception of memory that I will discuss more fully in Chapter 3. This formulation provides a good way to explain both the bodily feedback effects and the occasional failures to see these muscular influences on feelings. Simply put, this theory holds that the skeletal-muscular movements characteristic of a particular emotional state tend to activate automatically those ideas and feelings that have frequently arisen in this emotion, and thus that have been frequently associated with these particular bodily movements. We might say that this is a "default effect" that occurs when little attention and thought are given to what one is doing; the bodily movement effect unfolds automatically. However, as a number of cognitive theorists have noted, when people pay attention to their very-well-learned routine actions, a cognitively controlled regulatory process often begins to operate. Thoughts then come to mind; the persons might wonder what is happening, what reactions are appropriate, and try to react accordingly. Some such process might take place when we simulate being in a certain emotional state. We may not feel grief when we pretend to cry and may not feel amusement when we feign laughter primarily because we're paying considerable attention to what we're doing and how we're actually feeling. This inner-directed attention and the interfering thoughts that come to mind could well lessen the automatic effects of the emotion-related facial expressions and postures.

An experiment conducted by Jo and Berkowitz supports this possibility. In this study, the participants who were led to make an angry frown were significantly harsher in their evaluations of a job applicant than were others who had been induced to smile – but only when their attention was drawn away from their feelings. The manipulated facial expression did not have this effect when the participants had been made highly aware of their feelings before they judged the applicant. In fact, those persons who were led to be highly conscious of their feelings even seemed to bend over backward not to let their affective state influence what they said about the applicant.[40] I'll say much more about this apparent correction (or regulation) effect in later chapters. But at any rate, we're apparently unlikely to see the kinds of bodily feedback effects postulated by James, Tomkins, Izard, and Laird when people are highly attentive to their bodily sensations.

Some Theories About Bodily Feedback Effects

Even with all of the investigations of the bodily feedback conception just summarized (and the many more that could also have been cited), we still aren't altogether clear about just why movements of certain groups of muscles influence the emotional experience. Researchers have advanced several different types of theories, but space limitations don't allow a comprehensive review of all of these interesting formulations. Instead, we'll confine ourselves to two types of analyses that appear to be fairly general in their applicability.[41]

The Associative Network Conception. The most general of these theoretical schemes is the associative network perspective on emotions. As I noted earlier, and will discuss in greater detail in the next chapter, this approach basically regards each emotional state as a network of components that are linked together associatively. The anger state in the adult, for instance, is presumably a collection of certain kinds of feelings, ideas, memories, and physiological reactions throughout the body including skeletal-muscle motor patterns. Because these different parts of the syndrome are associated with each other in the nervous system, the activation of any one component theoretically tends to excite the other components as well in proportion to their degree of association. From this point of view, it is by no means surprising that certain kinds of muscular movements in the face, hands, and body tend to activate certain kinds of feelings, thoughts, and even some specific physiological reactions; if these muscular movements are the ones usually expressed in a given emotional state, their performance will tend to activate the other components of this state as well.

Levenson, Ekman, and Friesen have provided some evidence in line with this analysis. They tell us, for one thing, that the movement of particular groups of facial muscles gives rise not only to specific emotional feelings but also to distinctive, emotion-specific autonomic reactions. Furthermore, and this is also important for the associative network conception, the more closely the manipulated facial muscle movements resemble natural expressions of emotion – so that, we can say, more of the emotion-expressive motor pattern is activated – the stronger is the activation of the associated autonomic processes.[42]

Other findings are also consistent with this conception of emotions as associative networks. Consider the study mentioned before by Keltner, Ellsworth, and Edwards. They demonstrated that people tend to have some of the thoughts typically linked to anger and sadness when they adopt the facial expressions that are also characteristic of that state. Making a sad (or angry) face seems to activate the kinds of ideas that are associatively connected to sadness (or anger). Another line of research is also easily understood in associative terms. John Cacioppo and his colleagues noted that when people obtain or consume a desired object, such as food, they often flex their arms in bringing this object closer to them (so that it can be enjoyed and/or eaten). By contrast, the arm is typically extended away from the body in order to push away an unattractive object. The researchers therefore hypothesized that arm flexion movements would be generally linked with positive experiences, whereas arm extensions would tend to have a negative meaning. In keeping with this reasoning, when the participants in a series of experiments were asked to indicate their attitude toward various neutral stimuli (Chinese ideographs or nonsense words) shown to them, the stimuli that had been presented as they made arm flexion movements were better liked than the stimuli that were shown when they carried out arm extensions.[43]

Although we cannot say more about this associative network approach here, one final point should be made. This analysis doesn't indicate that the activation of a particular component in the emotion state network will necessarily result in open manifestations of the other components. As we saw earlier, making a sad face doesn't always give rise to sad feelings. Because of certain situational conditions, other thoughts and psychological control mechanisms can intervene at times to mask or even weaken the reactions associated with the activated network component.

The Self-Perception View. James Laird, one of the leading investigators of bodily feedback effects, has advanced a very different explanation of how these voluntary muscular movements influence the emotional experience.[44] In line with Bem's self-perception perspective (discussed in Chapter 1), Laird says this experience is essentially constructed by the person as the result of self-perception – self-observation and interpretation. He regards depth perception as a good analogy. People use a variety of subtle cues to infer that an object they are viewing exists in three dimensions, and they aren't always consciously aware of the indicators they're employing to make this inference. Somewhat similarly, according to Laird, we automatically and nonconsciously also use subtle cues from our bodies, as well as from the surrounding situation, to form our emotional experience.

Laird is sympathetic to the appraisal theories of emotion formation. Nonetheless, he emphasizes that his formulation is broader in scope and considers more than causal attributions. We may become angry partly because we think someone has deliberately wronged us (our appraisal). But, in a variation of William James's bodily reaction thesis,

Laird adds that our anger experience also grows out of our detection of our bodily reactions, especially our emotion-related muscle movements.

Laird has devoted considerable attention to individual differences in what cues have a major role in the formation of the emotional experience. He believes some persons are consistently apt to be very responsive to their self-produced bodily reaction cues. Perceiving these cues and highly aware of their bodily reactions, these individuals are the ones who are most likely to experience the feelings associated with emotion-related facial and bodily movements. And these cue-responsive persons are even likely to have a fairly good memory for information whose content is consistent with their facial expressions. So, when they were induced to smile in one experiment,[45] they were more likely to recall previously encountered information that was humorous rather than anger-provoking in nature.

An experiment reported before highlights the consistency in these "self-produced cue users." After the participants in this study had gone through the various bodily postures (described earlier), they were induced to adopt both "smile" and "frown" facial expressions. The subjects whose feelings were most responsive to this facial manipulation also tended to be the ones whose feelings had been greatly affected by their bodily postures. Perhaps these findings can be appended to William James's previously cited comment about the effects of running away from a bear. Many of us might feel only a very low level of fear because we run, but apparently there are some persons whose running would result in their experiencing a good deal of fright.[46]

PART II

Feelings and Memory

3. Influences of Feelings on Memory

Writing in the first century of our common era, the Greek biographer Plutarch marveled at the accomplishments of memory. "What wonders it performs in preserving and guarding the past." Memory is truly wonderful, and yet we all know that memory can also be imperfect. We forget much of what we have experienced and at times even prune and reshape our recollections in accord with our wishes, beliefs, and thoughts of the moment. The present and following chapters will examine still other influences that can distort our memories – our feelings.

Introduction

Before going further, it will be helpful to introduce some terms that psychologists typically employ when they discuss memory. When Plutarch made his comment about the wonders of memory, he was generally referring to people's ability to be consciously aware of their past experiences. Many researchers refer to this as *declarative memory*, the ability to recall particular facts or events. We will be concerned with this kind of memory in much of this chapter, such as when we're considering the accuracy of an eyewitness's memory of a witnessed crime. However, people can also remember some things that do not involve specific pieces of information: notably the skills they acquired in the past, such as how to ride a bicycle, swing a golf club, or shift gears when driving a car. This is often termed *procedural memory*. In addition, psychologists frequently distinguish between *explicit* and *implicit memory*, essentially a difference based on how memory is accessed. Explicit memory obviously has to do with the recollections a person brings to mind when deliberately trying to remember some fact or occurrence. Again, a good example is an eyewitness attempting to remember what she or he had seen earlier. But sometimes past experiences can affect people's thoughts, feelings, or actions without their conscious awareness of this influence; it's very much as if these experiences are now remembered implicitly, unconsciously, even though there is no conscious attempt to bring them to mind.

Psychologists often study implicit memory by means of priming procedures. An experiment by Bargh and Pietromonaco will give you an idea of how these procedures are often carried out. The researchers first showed their study participants a series of words at very fast rates of exposure, so fast that the words could not be consciously recognized. What's important is that in some cases many of the words in the series had hostile connotations. Although the people seeing them were not consciously aware of the words' meanings, the frequently presented hostile words were still able to activate hostile thoughts in these participants' implicit memory systems so that they were primed to use these ideas under appropriate circumstances. As a consequence, when they were given ambiguous information about a stranger soon afterward, they formed a distinct negative impression of him.[1]

Implicit memory is much more than a laboratory phenomenon. It can play a very important role in the aftereffects of highly emotional events. Psychologist Daniel Schacter, a notable explorer of implicit memory, illustrated this influence by telling a story about a Vietnam veteran who participated in a Fourth of July holiday parade several years after returning home. He was driving a jeep in the parade when some children tossed a lit firecracker under his vehicle. "The sudden noise initiated a terrifying flashback wherein he felt and acted as if he were once again [being attacked by the North Vietnamese]." He jammed his foot down on the jeep's accelerator "in a frantic attempt to flee from the 'enemy' and, moments later, crashed."[2] The veteran had retained an implicit memory of a traumatic wartime experience that was suddenly reawakened by the exploding firecracker, even though he consciously knew he was safe at home. The next chapter will say more about this phenomenon.

But to get back to the different kinds of memories, researchers do not agree on whether they are rooted in different neurological processes or what their exact relationships are or even whether other distinctions are advisable. Nevertheless, for our purposes, and simplifying somewhat, we'll regard declarative knowledge as being associated with explicit memory and procedural knowledge as being associated with implicit memory.

In considering the impact of feelings on memory, this chapter will begin with an examination of how mood can influence the content of one's recollections. We'll focus largely on whether feelings tend to activate affectively congruent declarative memories. Many of you will not be surprised to hear that people who feel good are likely to have happy memories when they're asked to think of their past lives and that those who are in a bad mood are apt to recall unhappy events. But how general are these tendencies? Aren't there times when sad or depressed persons try to make themselves feel better by steering their memories in a positive direction? And there's a seemingly related matter. A friend of mine has told me that when his wife is angry with him, she is very likely to think of other occasions in which he had also offended her. Is this apparent activation of the woman's implicit memory a common phenomenon? When we're in a particular mood, are we especially apt to remember automatically other incidents that occurred earlier when we were in the same kind of mood? And if this tendency does exist, how can it best be explained psychologically?

The last section in this chapter will be concerned with the effects of stress on memory, and, more particularly, how emotional stress might affect the accuracy of eyewitness reports. This is obviously a matter of great practical importance in our legal system. People are frequently aroused emotionally by a crime or serious accident that they just happen to see. Do the strong feelings they experience affect the accuracy of their later reports to the police and/or the validity of their testimony in court trials?

I will point out that psychological research has not always come up with the same answers to these questions. We will then try to resolve these different findings by considering a number of factors that might govern just how feelings can influence eyewitnesses' memory. This discussion will identify some conditions determining when stress lowers the accuracy of these recollections and even when it might lead to better than normal memory.

The following chapter will further analyze the effects of highly disturbing feelings by taking up the controversy regarding recovered memories of long-past childhood abuse. As the reader may know, a number of adults claim that they now remember having been molested by their caretakers when they were young children – long after they had forgotten these disturbing occurrences. Their contention, more often than not, is that their long-repressed unwanted childhood experiences had suddenly been recalled years later. *Repression* is a complicated and even a somewhat ambiguous concept. Most often it has to do with the idea that the human mind frequently protects itself against dangerous thoughts, desires, and experiences by repressing them – by hiding these unwanted ideas, urges, and feelings from consciousness, although they supposedly are still alive and active somewhere in the brain. But although many mental health professionals, as well as popular literature, movies, and TV, express little doubt that repression occurs, not a few memory researchers are skeptical about whether it occurs as readily and extensively as is commonly supposed. Furthermore, more and more psychologists and psychiatrists now prefer to employ the concept of *dissociation* rather than repression in their interpretations of seeming lapses in memory. They basically hold that the trauma can be recorded in the person's implicit memory without being available to her or his explicit memory. The two memory systems are said to be dissociated, as presumably had occurred in the case of the Vietnam veteran mentioned earlier. Whatever the interpretation, though, we will look at the argument and see what memory researchers have learned about the possibility of recovered memories of past disturbances.

Influence of Feelings on Memory Content

In the early 1900s, when psychologists first began to investigate how feelings influence memory, many of them asked whether pleasant events were better remembered than unpleasant ones. This question was typically prompted by Freud's concept of repression, on the oversimplied assumption (as will be discussed in the last section of this chapter) that the repression mechanism tends to keep unpleasant memories from conscious awareness. And so, supposedly consistent with the idea of repression, this early research typically found that people are somewhat more likely to recall the good rather than bad things that had happened to them earlier in their lives.[3]

We don't know, however, what mood the participants were in when they brought up their recollections, and we can't say how their feelings at that time affected what they reported. A number of psychologists have therefore deliberately induced either a positive or a negative mood in their research participants and then have tested to see how these people's memories were influenced by this newly established feeling. As just one example, here is an experiment reported by Snyder and White:

> *The female university students in this study were first induced to be either happy or sad and then, seated individually in the laboratory, reported events that had taken place in their lives the week before. These descriptions were then rated by independent judges as to whether they were happy or sad in nature. Figure 3.1 gives the average number of happy and sad incidents that were recalled by the happy and sad participants. As you can see, the happy subjects reported more happy than sad experiences, whereas the sad women described more sad than happy occurrences.*[4]

To explain this finding, I'll rely primarily on Gordon Bower's theoretical analysis of how people's feelings can influence their recollections. A number of psychologists are troubled by some aspect of this formulation, and Bower himself has modified some of the details of his conception over the years. Nevertheless, Bower's research program, initiated in the late 1970s and spelled out in a series of papers published from 1981 to the 1990s, has had a major impact on the study of the influence of feelings on memory. Any review of the psychological literature in this area would be seriously incomplete if it omitted consideration of his theorizing. In addition, I believe that Bower's theoretical scheme has exceedingly important implications for the study of emotions generally and can help integrate several seemingly different sets of findings. Without delving into the theoretical and methodological intricacies of Bower's research, I'll summarize his

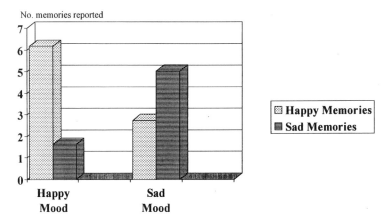

Figure 3.1 Number of happy and sad memories reported under a happy- or sad-induced mood (data from Snyder & White, 1982, Experiment 1).

most relevant analyses, citing studies selectively to illustrate how his formulation accounts for many of the ways in which people's feelings affect what they remember of earlier events.[5]

Bower's Associative Network Theory of Feeling Effects

In common with other theorists, Bower found it useful to conceive of memory as a collection of mental networks, each of which consists of pieces of information that are linked together associatively. To state this idea in more concrete terms, suppose we encounter a particular stimulus – for instance, a barking sound. Our initial response is to identify the stimulus, and so, a number of possibly appropriate concepts, such as "dog," will come to mind. These concepts will awaken a variety of memories, presumably because activation spreads from each of the now operating ideas to other items of information in our memory store, with this spread being proportional to the degree of association between the ideas. Therefore, if Jane classified the sound as a dog's bark, the thought "dog" might remind her of the friendly collie she had as a child. Joe might think of the sound as a bark, but for him, the concept "dog" brings to mind the vicious watchdog that had bitten him when he was young. For Jane the chain of associations is "bark–dog–nice collie who was fun," but in Joe's case it is "bark–dog–dog who scared me." Let's call each of the concepts (or each item of information) a *node* in the memory network.

Bower added to this general line of reasoning by proposing that any distinct emotion, such as joy or depression or anger, can also be regarded as a node in the memory networks. Each of these emotion nodes, in turn, he held, is linked associatively not only to a pattern of physiological reactions and expressive-motor responses, but also to a generalized description in memory of the types of situations that had evoked the emotion in the past and also to a general set of ways of responding when experiencing that emotional state. It's important to recognize here that for Bower the postulated network is semantic, that is, it consists largely of verbally encoded concepts (such as "dog" or "collie" in Jane's case) and conceptions of prior occurrences. Moreover, the emotion nodes are said to be typically linked in verbal terms to past events from one's life (e.g., for Jane the concept "collie" is connected to the mental proposition "the collie was fun"), as well as to conceptions of how one acts when a particular emotion is aroused.

Most important of all, along with other theorists, Bower also proposed that activation can spread in all directions through this semantic network, depending on the strength of the associations linking the various concept/nodes together. When the concept "dog" comes to Joe's mind, he is reminded of scary animals, and this particular memory might then activate the fear node, leading to activation of other fear-related thoughts and memories and perhaps even to a feeling of fear. These thoughts, memories, and feelings aren't always strong enough to be fully conscious, but nonetheless, as in the case of implicit memories, they may be sufficiently active in the person's mind to influence what he or she subsequently will think, feel, and do. Similarly, the activation of a particular emotion node can spread activation to the other memory structures with which it is connected. Psychologists say that the emotional feeling *primes* these other memories, that is, heightens their availability for conscious use. In Joe's case, the arousal of fear might well make him remember, even if only at a low level of awareness, past occasions when he had become frightened and might even bring to mind relatively general conceptions of scary things and situations, including dogs.

Let's now spell out the implications of this formulation in somewhat greater detail. I'll start with the case I mentioned earlier of the wife who always brought up her husband's supposed shortcomings whenever she was angry with him. Why did she, in her fury, always remember how the man had frustrated her in the past? One good possibility is that her angry feelings at that particular moment matched the angry feelings she had experienced before when her husband had disappointed and frustrated her. For our purposes here, let's make this a case of declarative memory (as if the woman had at that time deliberately tried to recall her husband's past behavior). According to Bower's network theory, memory for any given material is dependent to some extent on how closely one's feelings at the time of attempted recall of this material match one's feelings at the time the material was learned.[6] The degree of similarity between the feelings at the time of learning and those at the time of recall is crucial in this *mood-state dependent* remembrance.

It's a somewhat different situation when the material to be recalled had not aroused any feelings at the time it was first encountered but does have an emotional meaning. Imagine that you're a student in a class on cognitive psychology. To demonstrate the phenomenon we're now discussing, the instructor presents the concept "attitude" and asks the people in the class to quickly choose a word beginning with the letter *p*. Three possibilities are *poor, positive,* and *pessimistic*. Let's also suppose that you're in an especially good mood for some reason. If you're similar to many of the students who had taken part in a study using this procedure,[7] there is a good chance that the first word that occurs to you of these three possibilities will be *positive*. The happy mood you're in has facilitated the recall of information having much the same meaning as your feelings at that time. Putting this *affective* (or *mood*) *congruence in recall* in theoretical terms, activation can spread in the memory network from a particular emotion node to other memory structures that are linked to it semantically. As a consequence, memory is best for that material whose meaning is affectively congruent with one's present mood.

Supporting Research

Mood-State Dependent Memory. Bower basically regarded the mood-state dependent effect as just one kind of context effect, a phenomenon long known in the study of memory. If we first encounter a particular bit of information within a certain context, it often is easier to recall that material later when we are in the same situation, or at least a notable part of that situation. A British experiment carried out more than a generation ago gives us a dramatic example. Interested in the memory capacity of deep-sea divers, Godden and Baddeley required their subjects to learn lists of words either on the beach or when submerged under 15 feet of water. The beach or the water was the context within which the learning occurred. The investigators then tested the subjects' recollection of the words in the same environment as before or in the opposite setting. There was a context effect: Whether the words had first been learned on land or underwater, memory was about 40% better if the recollection was tested in the same environment as the initial learning.[8] The presence of the same surrounding stimuli apparently helped the subjects remember what they had learned earlier in that setting.

Bower believed that one's mood could serve as such a context cue. Our feelings at the time we pick up a particular piece of information are a prominent part of the situation in which we learn that material and thus become associated with that information. If we have the same feelings later, these sensations could then activate this particular material in implicit memory. And so, in an early study by Bower and his students, the participants could best remember what they had learned earlier when their mood at recall matched their mood at the time of the initial learning.[9]

Bower placed great emphasis on mood-state dependent memories in his first papers on semantic network theory. However, although other investigators occasionally published findings showing this effect, when Bower later tried to replicate his initial results, he found he was unable to do so, and he began to doubt that mood-state dependency was as pervasive as he first thought.[10]

More recent research, though, especially by Eric Eich at the University of British Columbia, has demonstrated that affective-state dependency in memory is a real phenomenon that can be obtained reliably under certain specific conditions.[11] One such condition has to do with the intensity of the feelings. Eich's findings indicate that people's memories are affected by their feelings to the degree that these feelings are strong and fairly stable. Bower and others have made the same point. Another important factor has to do with the source of the information that is subsequently to be remembered: People's current feelings are especially likely to help the recollection of earlier information acquired in the same feeling state if that earlier information had been generated by their own thinking rather than delivered to them by an external source. And so, if Jane feels bad right now, she is especially apt to remember what ideas she had previously when she had also been in a bad mood. It could be that self-generated information is more strongly linked to a particular emotion node than material acquired from the outside. The later reactivation of that emotion node is then more likely to bring the former, self-generated information into conscious awareness.

Another factor affecting the extent to which mood-dependent memory will be found has to do with the nature of the recollection situation. In Eich's words, "mood dependent effects are more likely to emerge when [memory] retrieval is tested in the absence than in the presence of specific, observable cues or reminders."[12] Getting back to Jane and her unpleasant mood, suppose we ask her to remember events from her adolescent years in a situation that is full of things that remind her of the happy times she had experienced as a teenager. Because they are so prominent at this time, these salient situational cues could readily cause Jane to recall the pleasant incidents rather than the negative events we otherwise might have expected her to remember. However, if Jane is asked the same question about her adolescence in the absence of any such reminders of pleasant times past, she is more apt to display affective dependency and recall unhappy incidents.

Interestingly, Eich now believes mood-dependent memory is such a pervasive phenomenon that it even plays a role in other instances of context-dependent memories. Think back to the context effect found in the Godden and Baddeley experiment mentioned before; the subjects could best recall the word lists they had learned earlier when the physical setting they were in (i.e., being on land or underwater) was the same as that in which they had initially learned the words. Well, according to one of Eich's recent papers, the similarity in the subjects' feelings over the two occasions may have been more important than the physical similarity between these occasions.[13]

Mood-Information Affective Congruence in What Is Remembered. Semantic network theory also holds, as noted earlier, that one's current mood can also affect what is recalled independently of the present feeling's similarity to an earlier mood. The theory tells us that as the mind searches memory for previously acquired information that may be relevant to a particular situation, its search may be biased in favor of the kind of information that has the same affective meaning as the prevailing mood state.

To make this clearer, here is another experimental procedure that has demonstrated mood congruence in recall. A researcher asks the people in her study to memorize each of the words she will present to them. Included in the list, in random order, are words having negative connotations (such as *sad*, *worried*, and *troubled*) as well as words having a pleasant meaning (such as *happy* and *elated*). After the memorization period, the researcher places the participants in a particular mood state – let's say either happy or sad – and then asks them to recall as many words from the list as they can. There's a good chance that the people in the study will remember more words whose meaning is consistent with their present feelings than words whose meaning is not in accord with their mood. For instance, if they're happy at the time, they're likely to have a better memory for the words they learned earlier that have happy connotations.[14]

Although there have been occasional exceptions, which we'll discuss later, most of the published experiments have generally confirmed the semantic network theory expectation: Mood-congruent memory is fairly common. We can see this in a survey of pertinent studies conducted by Matt, Vazquez, and Campbell.[15] Employing

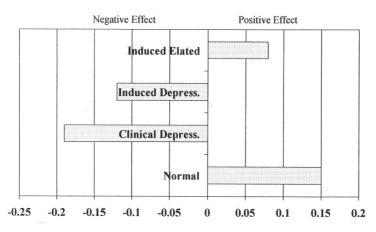

Figure 3.2 Mean effect size in studies of mood congruency in various groups (data from Matt et al., 1992, Figure 1). Positive effect = recall favors positive material. Negative effect = recall favors negative material.

meta-analytic statistical procedures, these psychologists basically pooled the relevant memory experiments published between 1975 and 1988 in order to determine how substantial were the differences in the recall of material having a positive meaning compared with the recall of negative-connotation material. Figure 3.2 summarizes some of their major results.

One question they addressed was whether normal persons have affectively biased memories. It was noted earlier in this section that ordinary people generally tend to have a somewhat better memory for earlier events they found pleasant than for previous incidents that were unpleasant to them. The bottom row in Figure 3.2 indicates how general this pattern is; besides being more inclined to remember earlier pleasant rather than unpleasant events, normal people are also more likely to recall previously encountered information having a positive meaning rather than a negative one, even when this material is not directly linked to an emotion-arousing experience. All in all, it appears that most persons have more positive than negative memories, not because they have repressed their unpleasant experiences but because they are often in a good mood.[16]

Clinically depressed persons, on the other hand, have a very different memory pattern. As can be seen in the second row from the bottom in Figure 3.2, they typically have a better memory for negative than positive information; their memory bias is congruent with their characteristic negative mood. Much the same congruency in memory has been found in a more recent study in which the participants scored either high or low on a standard measure of depressive tendencies. Here too, those with high scores (who were relatively depressed but not clinically so) had a better memory for negative than positive words, and displayed this congruence in both explicit and implicit memory.[17]

This pervasive trend toward mood congruency in memory is also apparent in laboratory experiments in which researchers deliberately manipulated their subjects' mood state, as can be seen in the top two rows of Figure 3.2. In all of the studies of this type reviewed by Matt and his colleagues, people in whom a depressive mood was induced tended to have better recall of negative rather than positive material, whereas their happier counterparts were more likely to remember positive rather than negative information.

Influence of Feeling on Attention and Learning

Bower's theoretical account of how feelings can affect what people recall from their past goes well beyond the influence of one's present mood on the content of memory. He also noted that feelings can have an impact on what is learned from the surrounding situation, at least partly because feelings can steer attention. Putting this quite generally, Bower and other investigators have concluded that affective states can influence what information is extracted from the surrounding environment. People experiencing a particular emotion tend to give a disproportionate share of their attention to information that seems to be consistent with their feelings.[18] And so, those persons who are fairly happy most of the time are apt to pay considerable attention to things and events having a happy meaning for them.

How far can we extend this idea? Does it apply, for example, to sad people? Wouldn't we expect sad or depressed persons to avoid focusing on negative matters and, instead, seek out information that might alleviate their bad mood? Well, even sad or depressed persons often exhibit this affective-attentional congruence, according to a number of studies. One investigation, of several that could have been cited, was published by Forgas and Bower.

In this experiment, the male and female subjects were put in either a good or a bad mood by being misled about how well they had done on a preliminary test;

then, seated before a computer screen, they were asked to read a series of statements describing a stranger. In line with the notion of affective-attentional congruence, the happy subjects spent more time looking at the positive information about the stranger than about the negative information, whereas the unhappy subjects took more time to read about the stranger's negative qualities.[19]

There may well be a specificity in this kind of attentional bias that is worth pointing out. Much of the research on effects of feeling has been guided, explicitly or implicitly, by the circumplex model assumption discussed in Chapter 1, which states that the most important aspect of an affective experience is its valence, that is, how pleasant or unpleasant it is. However, although a feeling's valence is often significant, Chapter 1 also pointed out that people often distinguish among a number of their affective states; in their minds, they at times may construct different categories of feelings. Paula Niedenthal, one of the leading proponents of this categorical conception of emotional states, argues that attentional congruence is frequently more a function of affective-category matching than of valence matching. That is, we detect most readily those stimuli whose meaning closely matches the specific feeling we are experiencing on that occasion. A sad person will tend to pay a good deal of attention to things that have a sad meaning and not necessarily to things having hostile connotations, even though both sadness and hostility are negatively valenced. Another example of this affective category matching can be found in one of the differences between anxious and depressed people. On the basis of her review of the evidence, Mineka has concluded that highly anxious people tend to give a great deal of attention to possibly threatening information, whereas depressed persons are likely to attend more to occurrences with a meaning of sadness or loss.[20]

We do more than just give greater attention to whatever information is in tune with our mood. We also tend to think about this congruent information more deeply, and in our minds we attach this material to a broader base of associated ideas so that it becomes more firmly rooted in our memories. In psychological terminology, the affectively congruent information is highly elaborated associatively. As a result, we learn better the information that is congruent with our current emotion. Adding to this, Bower also noted (as we will discuss further in the section on eyewitness memory) that emotionally arousing events are more firmly planted in our memories the more intense is this arousal.[21]

Influence of Feelings on Interpretations

When people recall an incident they had witnessed earlier, they are essentially reporting how they had encoded what they had seen, that is, how they had interpreted the event. This interpretation is what was stored in their memory, not the objective facts that an outside observer might have recorded. What's important for us here is that the people's feelings at the time they witnessed the occurrence could shape their interpretation of what they had seen and thus influence what they recall about the event. Semantic network theory holds that emotional states prime semantically related ideas. That is, if people experience a particular feeling, thoughts having the same kind of affective meaning are likely to come to their minds. These activated ideas may then color their interpretations of ambiguous occurrences. Someone who is angry at the moment, for example, will have hostile ideas. If another person acts in a seemingly strange manner toward him, this ambiguous behavior might well be viewed as unfriendly and it will be remembered as such.[22]

Some Additional Questions About Feelings and Memory

With all of this supporting evidence, it's important to realize that investigators have not always seen the mood congruency we've been talking about, either in state-dependent memory or in the recall of affectively toned material. Most puzzling of all, several studies have even found a trend toward incongruency in memory.[23] It's worthwhile to say something about these apparently unusual discordant findings because they suggest that factors other than those specified by Bower's semantic network theory could determine what effect emotions will have on memory.

Some Possible Regulatory Influences. In some cases, such as in the experiment reported by Isen, Shalker, Clark, and Karp, positive moods led to affectively congruent memories, whereas negative moods did not.[24] In this study, the male and female participants were placed in either a good or a bad mood by being given false information about their performance on an interesting game. When these people were then asked to recall as many words as possible from the list of words they had seen earlier, those who were feeling good because they believed they had won remembered more pleasant than unpleasant or neutral words. However, those who had lost and were feeling bad did not recall reliably more of the unpleasant than pleasant words. As the researchers put it, the results were asymmetrical; whereas the participants' positive mood had led to positive memories, the negative mood evidently had not biased the subjects' recollections very much at all. Isen later stated that this asymmetry is fairly common and that negative affect does not bring to mind negative material as strongly as positive feelings facilitate recall of positive information.

Although there are many reasons why negative feelings don't always prime (bring to mind) affectively congruent memories and thoughts, Isen and her colleagues have at times suggested that a mood regulatory process could have been at work. The idea here is that when many people are in a bad mood, they attempt to get out of this unhappy state by thinking positively and controlling their memories. And so, in the study by Isen, Shalker, and their colleagues cited before, the negative words conceivably might have occurred to the defeated subjects as they searched their memories, but these unhappy-meaning words might then have been pushed out of conscious awareness as the subjects tried to put themselves in a happier frame of mind.[25]

We have a puzzle here. Quite a few psychologists and other mental health specialists believe that many persons are inclined to engage in defensive avoidance of unhappy ideas and memories, especially when they are feeling bad. But given the fact that most published studies have found an affective congruence in memory under both positive and negative moods, as I pointed out earlier,[26] we're challenged to ask when this kind of defensive mood regulatory process comes into play.

One good possibility is that people differ in how defensive they are, how readily they attempt to ward off unhappy memories. So, if we sometimes fail to see negative mood congruence in memory in a study, this might be because the investigation happened to employ quite a few persons who were high in those defensive qualities. For example, many of the participants might have been high in self-esteem. People who think well of themselves generally believe they are "masters of their fate, captains of their souls." But in addition to being self-confident, they're typically motivated to preserve both their good opinion of themselves and their faith that good things usually happen to them. As a consequence, they may also be motivated to alleviate whatever distress they're experiencing at the moment. If they're in a bad mood, they may attempt to improve their feelings by searching out positive memories. Smith and Petty have demonstrated this self-esteem-induced regulatory process in a series of experiments at Ohio State University. The students in one of their investigations were first placed in either a bad or a good mood and then were shown a number of news headlines, some of which were positive and others negative in tone. When all of them were later asked to recall as many of the headlines as they could, those who were low in self-esteem generally exhibited standard mood congruence; the worse they felt, the more negative statements they remembered. The results were very different for those high in self-esteem; in these people, the worse their mood, the more positive were the headlines they recalled.[27]

There is another possible kind of regulation process that is somewhat more surprising and that might also influence what people recall when they're emotionally aroused. Consider the series of investigations carried out by Parrott and Sabini in natural settings as well as in the laboratory. Whether the participants' mood was affected naturally by the weather or was deliberately manipulated by experimental stimulation (such as by having them listen to happy or gloomy music), when these people were asked to recall a recent event, the first memory that came to mind tended to be affectively inconsistent with their feelings. The happy persons typically recalled a relatively sad incident, whereas their sadder counterparts generally reported a happier occurrence. The only study in this series that obtained memories congruent with mood was one in which the participants had been asked to try to sustain their mood. Can it be that people dredge up memories in line with their feelings only when they are consciously seeking to preserve these feelings?[28]

But then again, adding to the puzzle, in a later experiment, Parrott found that mood–memory congruence can occur even when people don't try to maintain their mood. In this experiment, the college student participants were first induced to be either happy or sad and then, after they had worked on several tasks, were told that the study was over and they could stop trying to sustain their present feelings. Even so, when the subjects were then asked to remember three events from their high school years, their recollections were congruent with their feelings; those who had been placed in a good mood tended to report events having both more positive affect and less negative affect than did their unhappier counterparts.[29] The subjects' moods led to affectively consistent memories even when they weren't trying to keep their existing feelings alive.

Although we don't have a clear-cut explanation for the mood incongruency obtained by Parrott and Sabini, I'd like to suggest a highly speculative possibility: Many of the people in the Parrott–Sabini research could have engaged in a regulatory process, but one directed toward being objective and accurate in what was said rather than toward the reduction of feelings. Several psychologists have now proposed that when people are motivated to be accurate in their judgments and self-reports but suspect that their statements could be susceptible to a possible source of error, they often tend to overcorrect for this possible bias.[30] If this kind of regulatory process had occurred in the Parrott–Sabini research, the participants had presumably realized (for some reason) that the memories they reported could have been affected by their feelings, and they then bent over backward so to speak, to correct for this possible biasing influence.

We cannot say, however, just why such a conjectured "overcorrection" occurred in the Parrot–Sabini studies and why it hasn't been seen more often. Mood congruency in memory does seem to be the normative pattern.

Nonverbal Influences on Affective Congruence in Memory

One final question to be addressed here has to do with nonverbal influences. As was mentioned before, Bower's theory holds that emotion nodes in the memory network can be activated by verbal symbols or even by physiological and/or motor reactions. The research summarized in Chapter 2 demonstrating that facial expressions and/or other bodily movements characteristic of a particular emotion can actually awaken the feelings and even some of the ideas normally associated with those emotional states is very much in keeping with this analysis. Here I'll add to this earlier discussion by taking up the question of whether the mere display of a facial expression typical of a given emotion can facilitate memories that are affectively consistent with that expression.

> *Laird, Wagener, Halal, and Szegda have published evidence in keeping with the associative network conception just summarized. In one of their studies, the researchers first asked their male and female subjects to move particular facial muscles in a specified manner. Although the participants weren't told the nature of these facial movements, they were the expressions characteristic of either fear or anger or sadness. Then, while maintaining the expressions, the participants listened to a series of emotion-related sentences and soon afterward tried to recall as many of the sentences as they could.*

The subjects' facial expressions influenced what sentences they recalled best, but especially in the case of those people whose feelings were most strongly affected by their expressions. Figure 3.3 summarizes the findings for this group. (The results were very similar for the other subjects but were not as strong.)[31]

Two aspects of the results are especially noteworthy. First, they demonstrate the mood congruency in memory. The best-remembered sentences were those whose meanings matched the nature of the participants' facial expressions at the time they heard the sentences. And second, the effects were highly specific. All of the sentences and all of the facial expressions were generally negative. This means that the associative connections that linked a type of sentence to a type of facial expression were not based on the mere unpleasantness of the sentence and expression. Rather, the connections were a function of how well a sentence's specific meaning matched the specific nature of the expression being held at that time.

Going a little further into this research, the reader should realize what is involved in the interpretation of the findings of Laird and his colleagues that I've offered. On first thought, these findings suggest that the subjects' facial expressions had influenced what they recalled because of the mood generated by their facial movements. This mood could have then led to the congruent recollections. It's also possible, however, that the bodily actions had given rise to these memories through a direct connection between the particular facial expression and memory structures having similar affective associations. Riskind

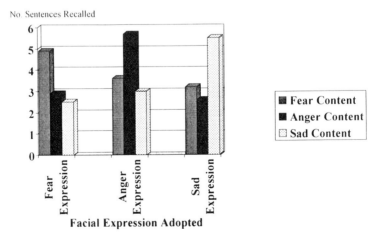

Figure 3.3 Number of sentences of each affective type recalled as a function of facial expression (data from Laird et al., 1982, Study 2). Data are for subjects whose feelings were strongly affected by facial expression.

has reported two experiments supporting this latter possibility. Varying his subjects' facial expressions and bodily postures, he found that the participants typically recalled happy events from their past lives faster when they had a happy expression and posture than when their bodily movements were sad. Furthermore, those adopting the expression and posture characteristic of sadness were quickest to remember past sad events. These effects were still present, moreover, even when the feelings produced by the bodily movements were held constant statistically.[32]

The implications seem clear: In line with associative network theory, memory is affected by the activation spreading from aroused emotion nodes to memory structures having a similar meaning. Specific memories may also be facilitated by the activation spreading through the linkages connecting particular emotion-associated bodily reactions to semantically related memory structures.

Feelings and Eyewitness Accuracy[33]

How Accurate Is Eyewitness Memory of Disturbing Events?

Stress Impedes Memory – Sometimes. According to a survey conducted a few years ago of psychologists who were interested in the accuracy of eyewitness testimony, the great majority of these experts believed that intense emotional stress often reduces memory accuracy.[34] Their views were undoubtedly based to some extent on common sense, but they also rested to a considerable degree on the results of a number of experiments. In these studies, employing many different kinds of stressful conditions, the disturbing circumstances tended to impede the participants' ability to recall information they had received.

In some of these investigations the stressful situation was only simulated. For example, the people taking part in an experiment by Loftus and Burns were shown one of two videotaped versions of a staged bank robbery. Both versions showed young boys playing in a parking lot. However, the more violent videotape ended with a brief scene showing one of the bank robbers suddenly shooting a boy in the head, whereas in the less violent tape the final incident was an equally brief portrayal of a neutral conversation in the bank. A questionnaire was then administered to all of the subjects to test their memory for information about the boys that had been provided in the videotape immediately before the concluding event (that is, before the shooting or the neutral conversation). According to the researchers, the people seeing the emotionally arousing occurrence, the killing, were less able to recall the important detail about the boys than were those exposed to the less stressful videotape. If we can assume that the sight of the killing had disturbed the viewers (as seems likely), this emotional scene apparently had impeded memory for information obtained just before the event. (It's important to note, however, as will be explained shortly, that there was no difference between these two conditions in the participants' memory for the physical characteristics of the robber or for what the bank teller was shown doing.)[35]

Other investigations established more realistic disturbances. In one of these, the children in a staged "crisis" condition suddenly heard a very loud fire alarm, after which a young woman entered the room and expressed concern about the possibility of a fire. For comparison purposes, the youngsters in the control condition only heard a loud radio and saw the woman come into the room and ask some innocuous questions. When both groups of children were later questioned about what had happened, those who had been exposed to the highly stressful "fire alarm" were less accurate in their reporting and less accurate in their recognition of the young woman. Essentially comparable results were found in even more realistic studies with adults. In an experiment conducted by Baddeley, servicemen on an airplane flight were deceived into thinking that a sudden emergency had developed. When the men were tested later, it was found that the frightening occurrence had reduced their memory of the instructions given them at the time.[36]

Because of findings such as these, and many other observations as well, about a generation ago a British committee established to consider what might be done about cases of wrongful conviction questioned whether guilty verdicts should be based only on eyewitness testimony. A jury's decision shouldn't rest solely on eyewitness' recollections, the committee believed, "unless the circumstances are exceptional or the evidence is corroborated by information from another source."[37]

Emotion Arousal Sometimes Promotes Memory. Although the British committee's recommendation is undoubtedly justified as a general principle, the research results just summarized are not the complete picture by any means. There evidently are times when emotion arousal facilitates rather than impedes memory. In one well-known review of the research in this area, about half of the studies actually found that stress led to more accurate recollections than was displayed by the nonaroused participants.[38] As in the experiments mentioned before, the investigations showing these memory-facilitating effects employed a variety of disturbing conditions. Sometimes the stress was produced by a false version of a threatening event, as in the Loftus and Burns experiment mentioned earlier. For example, when Yuille, Davies, and their associates exposed English police recruits to a simulated stressful situation, the recruits' later memories of many features of the event were both more accurate and more resistant to decay over time than were the memories of their nonstressed counterparts.[39]

Other studies using actual occurrences also found that emotional arousal didn't necessarily lessen the accuracy of the witnesses' recollections. In one such investigation, the researchers questioned people who had witnessed post office robberies 4 to 15 months earlier. The witnesses' remembrances seemed to be quite accurate in that they were corroborated by police records. Adding to this evidence of memory facilitation, in some of the studies heightened arousal even seemed to improve memory by reducing the witnesses' rate of forgetting what they had seen. Yuille and Cutshall have published a dramatic instance of such an emotion-strengthened memory. They interviewed people who had been bystanders 5 months earlier when a store owner shot and killed a man who had robbed him with a gun. Judging from how well the witnesses' statements in this later interview matched the original police reports of the incident, the investigators concluded that the people who had been under greatest stress, because they had been closest to the event, had the best memory for the details of what had happened. This finding is now not unusual. Recent research indicates that intense emotion arousal can indeed promote memory, apparently at least partly because of the activation of the beta-adrenergic stress hormone system during the emotional experience.[40]

Flashbulb Memories – Accurate in Some Ways. Some kinds of emotional memories seem to be remarkably persistent, and it's informative to consider them even though, strictly speaking, they don't have to do with eyewitness reports. Many people of my generation can still recall where we were when we learned of President John Kennedy's assassination. It's as if our brains had suddenly taken a picture of the scene about us when we heard the surprising and emotionally arousing news and had kept the image fixed in our memories. Brown and Kulik drew psychologists' attention to these vivid and seemingly well-preserved recollections more than a generation ago, referring to them as *flashbulb memories*.[41] According to these researchers, an unexpected emotional occurrence activates a special brain mechanism that fixes in memory whatever one sees and hears at that time.

However, as psychologists have looked more closely into this matter, they have discovered that these so-called flashbulb memories aren't necessarily accurate, well-preserved "pictures" of what had happened when the incident took place. Ulrich Neisser, well known for his important analyses of the operation of cognitive processes, has demonstrated that people's flashbulb memories can have serious errors even though these persons are absolutely certain that their recollections are right.

The day after the space shuttle *Challenger* exploded in flight, killing its entire crew, Neisser asked his students to record in detail what they had been doing and who they were with at the time they heard of this tragedy. Many of the same students were then contacted about 3 years later, and they again described the situation they were in when they had first learned of the explosion. When Neisser and Nicole Harsch then compared the respondents' two accounts, they found that the later reports coincided very closely with the original reports in only about 7% of the cases. For a full quarter of the sample, the later recollections bore no resemblance at all to what had initially been described. Even more surprising, the researchers found that there was no relationship at all between the students' confidence in their memories and how accurate their later recollections actually were. The people who were very sure of their memories were just as likely to provide wrong reports as those who were more uncertain. Indeed, some of these persons were so confident that their present memories were right that they weren't even shaken by evidence that their original reports were very different from what they now believed. A Danish psychologist, Steen Larsen, has reported similar observations of his own memory after Swedish Prime Minister Olof Palme was murdered in 1986. Immediately after he first heard the news, Larsen recorded where he was at the time and who was with him, and then several months later tried to remember the occurrence again. Although he believed he had a vivid recollection of what he had been doing at the time, Larsen found his memory was wrong in several important respects. He was now certain his wife had been with him when he had first learned of the assassination, but discovered he actually had been alone.[42]

All of this tells us that flashbulb memories of emotionally charged events may remain vivid over time, but (at the very least) we can't be sure that these recollections are completely accurate. Moreover, research indicates, contrary to the supposition of Brown and Kulik, that these memories are not generated by a special mechanism in the brain. According to one investigator, the undue confidence with which flashbulb memories are held is the major characteristic differentiating these memories from other, more ordinary memories.[43]

Reconciling the Seemingly Contradictory Findings

How can we reconcile these apparently opposing research results? Why have some studies reported that eyewitness declarative memory suffers under emotion arousal, whereas other investigations indicate that such arousal can have a facilitative influence? To answer these questions, we have to consider just what happens when people see or hear an emotionally charged event.[44] At the very least, if their memory is to be accurate, they first have to pay attention to the incident, and especially to its most important aspects. They then have to interpret (encode) it correctly and somehow fix it in memory. After this, of course, they have to be able to retrieve their mental representation of the incident from memory later on. Although something was said about attention in the preceding section, here I'll focus mostly on this matter because of its considerable importance to the question of eyewitness accuracy. I will then conclude this section with a brief comment about memory retrieval.

Attention and Level of Emotion Arousal. Psychologists have taken several different tacks in trying to explain how emotion arousal can influence attention. Their earliest accounts of the effect of stress on eyewitness testimony typically followed the so-called Yerkes–Dodson law, propounded in 1908, suggesting that people's memory for what was happening would be best when they were only moderately aroused. The bystanders presumably wouldn't pay sufficient attention to the details around them if their arousal level was too low, and their memories would be disrupted if they were very excited. Thus, it was argued, persons witnessing a highly stressful incident supposedly would be too strongly aroused to remember all of the details of the event correctly.

Several generations later, in 1959, Easterbrook offered a better analysis of how memory accuracy might suffer under intense arousal. This theorist proposed that one's level of internal excitation influences the range of cue utilization, that is, "the total number of environmental cues [informative details] in any situation that an organism observes, maintains an orientation towards, responds to, or associates with a response." Applying Easterbrook's conception, then, our performance is often poor under very low arousal levels because we notice too many different details and don't focus sufficiently on the most important matters. When we are extremely excited, however, we are so narrowly focused that we fail to attend to, and thus don't make adequate use of, some relevant information that is available but isn't prominent in the surrounding situation. Put succinctly, Easterbrook held that high arousal results in increased attention to central cues and decreased attention to peripheral ones.[45]

Psychological research has now identified a number of problems in these studies. Most notably, both the Yerkes–Dodson law and Easterbrook's hypothesis essentially assume that there is a single arousal continuum ranging from a very low level at one end (such as might occur in a deep coma) to extreme excitation at the other end (as in the case of great terror). Contrary to such a unidimensional position, many investigators now contend that there are different kinds of arousal, and that the specific neurophysiological arousal system operating at one part of the activation continuum (such as in the low level going from sleep to awakeness) probably isn't the same system that operates at other levels (such as during intense emotional stress).[46]

Another difficulty is that emotionally excited people sometimes are driven to do too much thinking about the troublesome situation confronting them. They might be greatly puzzled or challenged or threatened by what they have encountered so that their minds become flooded with thoughts regarding what is happening and what they should do. As a result, they might not adequately notice important aspects of the situation. We can't always tell, then, whether their failure to pick up relevant information from the surrounding situation is due to their intense arousal itself or to these interfering thoughts. An anxious individual's poor work on an assigned task could conceivably be caused at times by such disrupting ideas in that particular situation and not by an excitation-produced narrowing of attention.

But even with these problems, the Easterbrook proposition has been supported by a number of experiments and seems to have a substantial grain of truth.[47] Most important for our purposes, this notion is useful in understanding how memory can be affected by emotionally disturbing conditions. As Christianson has emphasized, how well people will recall what they see under stressful, emotion-evoking circumstances depends to a considerable extent on how central to the situation are the details being asked about.[48]

Central features are those that stand out, psychologically speaking, sometimes because they are perceptually prominent, sometimes because they have to do with the perceived cause of the occurrence, and sometimes because they're very important to the person. Whatever the reason for their centrality, these features are generally remembered best, whereas more peripheral, less important details tend to be more poorly recalled. The subjects who had witnessed the emotionally upsetting killing in the Loftus and Burns study cited earlier apparently couldn't recall the details about the playing boys very well because these were only peripheral matters. They had much less difficulty, however, in remembering the more central aspects of the situation, such as the bank robber's physical characteristics and the bank teller's actions. Similarly, in the previously reported study of people who had seen actual post office robberies, the witnesses' recollections of such central details as the robbers' actions, weapons, and clothing seemed to be better than their memories of more peripheral information regarding the date and time of the incident and the other persons also present. Extending this principle to flashbulb memories, the recollections of the central features of the dramatic event (the incident itself) are more likely to be accurate than the memories of the surrounding circumstances (such as who else was present or where the person was at the time).

This last-mentioned point brings up an important problem that might have occurred to the reader: In many situations we can't be completely sure which details are central and which are peripheral as far as the witnesses are concerned. And so we might ask whether Neisser's students, after they first heard of the *Challenger*'s destruction, were concentrating their attention primarily on the space shuttle and its crew or whether, at that time, they were still paying more attention to the persons with them than to the news story. We don't always know what the witnesses regarded as the central feature of the situation they were in.

This difficulty was eliminated in a series of five experiments reported by Christianson and Loftus.[49] In each of these studies, the subjects were quickly shown a series of slides depicting "what a person might see while leaving home on the way to work" (e.g., a table in the kitchen or a pedestrian on a sidewalk). The three experimental conditions in each of these experiments differed primarily in terms of what the participants saw in the middle (eighth) slide. In one group, the Neutral condition, this critical slide showed a woman bicycling on the street, with one car prominent in the foreground and a second car off in the distance. For the subjects in the Emotional group the surrounding scene and the two cars were the same as for the Neutral group, but this time the woman was clearly shown lying on the ground next to her bicycle with her head bleeding, much as if she had just had a bad accident. The assumption here was that the people exposed to this picture would be somewhat emotionally aroused. Finally, there was an Unusual version of the critical slide depicting the same street scene, but this time the woman was seen carrying the bicycle on her shoulder.

It is clear from the data, as well as from the nature of the slides, that in all conditions the woman was the central feature of the critical slide and that the car in the background was the more peripheral detail. Some of the findings also support the assumption regarding the emotion-arousing nature of the emotional picture: The subjects' ratings at the end of the session indicated that the critical scene shown in the Emotional condition was much less pleasant than the key scenes presented to the other two groups and that there was no difference between these latter two scenes in how pleasant they were judged to be.

The researchers assessed the accuracy of the subjects' memories by asking them about the color of the woman's coat (a central detail) and the color of the distant automobile (a peripheral detail). When they examined their data, they found that the conditions differed, as they had predicted, in the percentage of the participants in each condition who remembered both kinds of details accurately. Most of the persons shown the emotionally unpleasant scene recalled the central feature correctly, but only a small proportion of them had an accurate memory of the peripheral detail; having narrowed attention, the majority of the aroused people in this condition hadn't noticed this relatively unimportant feature. The data also showed that this difference wasn't due to the unusual nature of the occurrence because the people seeing the clearly unusual critical slide were just as unlikely to remember the central feature as the peripheral one.

Emotion-Strengthened Memory. Studies of memory for everyday happenings have demonstrated that emotion-arousing incidents are usually more apt to be recalled days later than are nonarousing events; this is often the case whether the events are pleasant or unpleasant. This better memory for emotional occurrences isn't necessarily due only to an arousal-produced focusing of attention on the incidents at the time they took place or to a greater length of time spent with the emotional events. The emotional excitement these incidents generated could also have contributed to the heightened memory. In general, as Bower has pointed out in his important analyses of the impact of feelings on memory, "events associated with strong emotional reactions tend to be well learned, and usually more so (within limits) the stronger the reaction."[50]

Two of Christianson's experiments document this effect. In these studies, he showed the participants either the disturbing or the emotionally neutral series of slides he had employed in his other research, but he made sure that the subjects spent the same amount of time looking at the critical scenes. Even so, Christianson found that the central features of the scene were retained better when the event was upsetting rather than neutral in nature. Other investigations employing a variety of procedures have obtained essentially comparable results.

There are a number of possible reasons for this emotion-strengthened memory. For one, it could be, as Bower suggested, that many persons tend to brood about the emotional events they experience. Going over these happenings again and again in their minds, they presumably keep the incidents alive in working memory for a considerable period of time, and thus better learn what they had seen. Whatever the exact cause, something apparently happens in the brain when an emotionally charged incident occurs that leads to a better memory for at least those features of this event that had attracted the most attention.[51]

Putting all of these findings together, we evidently cannot say that people witnessing an emotional occurrence will necessarily have a poor memory for everything they see. In fact, their memory for the central aspects of the stressful scene might be quite good. It could be, though, that their memory for peripheral details, matters to which they hadn't given full attention at the time, will be impaired. More-over, if an adequate understanding of the complex nature of the event requires an appreciation of some of these peripheral details, emotion-ally aroused witnesses may not have such an adequate understanding. We should also realize that the person's confidence in his or her memory isn't a good guide to how correct the recollection is apt to be.

Automatic Preattentive Processing and Implicit Memory. The memory ef-fects we've been discussing aren't dependent on our being consciously aware of the meaning of the witnessed event. In introducing the con-cept of implicit memory, I pointed out that we can be affected emo-tionally by certain features of the situation we're in even when we aren't fully aware of these details and can't say that we had noticed them. Think back to the Bargh and Pietromonaco experiment cited at the start of this chapter. You will recall that subliminally presented words having a hostile connotation led the participants to judge the target individual in an unfavorable manner. The words in this case were processed preattentively, one might say, priming (bringing to mind) hostile thoughts that colored the subsequent perception of the ambiguous stranger.[52]

In accord with this kind of subliminal effect, one of Christianson's experiments found that emotional stimuli presented so quickly that the witnesses weren't sure what they were seeing had much the same impact on memory as the same stimuli presented for a much longer time. On the basis of these and other results, Christianson (and other investigators) suggested that the central features of some emotional events are perceived and reacted to more or less automatically, with relatively little thought and examination. On these occasions, the viewers evidently grasp the emotional significance of these details nonconsciously and store them in implicit memory. Of course, if the witnesses were consciously aware of what had happened and had paid more attention to the situational details, they would have en-gaged in more elaborate and controlled information processing in which they would have given considerably more thought to what they saw and/or heard.[53]

Memory Retrieval. Finally, I want to say something here about memory retrieval. Psychologists have learned that the way people's memories are tested can determine whether we see an influence of feelings on memory: Feelings are more likely to affect our free recall of features of the emotional scene, such as when we are freely trying to tell others what we had witnessed during the event, than our recognition of situational details, such as when we have to identify a criminal in a police lineup. Free recall requires far more mental effort than mere recognition, and this extra mental activity is more susceptible to influence by feelings.[54]

4. Personal Traumas and Memory

The previous chapter closed with an examination of people's recollections of frightening events that, more often than not, had happened to other persons. We now extend this topic by looking at memories of traumas in which the individuals themselves were severely threatened. Chapter 3 noted that emotion-arousing occurrences, or at least their central features, are often remembered quite well. Our main question here is whether there is a similar heightened memory for traumatic episodes. In other words, how well do people recall incidents in which they themselves are endangered physically or psychologically?

Much of our focus in seeking to answer this question will be on the notion of *repression*, the idea that the human mind frequently blocks unwanted memories, urges, and thoughts from conscious awareness. Because we're dealing with memory, this chapter will say nothing about whether one's forbidden desires are kept hidden in the depths of the unconscious, and will only consider the possibility that the mind often defends itself against pain and anxiety by preventing the conscious recall of earlier traumatic events.

Although the notion of repression is widely accepted, by many mental health specialists as well as by a good fraction of the broader public, it is actually a controversial idea for quite a few research-oriented psychologists. Much of the argument is centered on the well-publicized contention that a substantial number of people have repressed the sexual abuse they suffered in childhood. The chapter will review some of the reasons why several prominent researchers are troubled by this notion and by the more general thesis that we unconsciously are apt to forget our personal traumas. Evidence will be cited showing that traumatic episodes are often remembered quite well, at times even too well. However, the chapter will also point to a few relatively well-documented cases of repression suggesting that painful memories can indeed be blocked out of awareness on occasion. We will also consider a somewhat different account of disturbed memories about traumatic incidents, one holding that there may be a *dissociation*, a failure to integrate the decidedly unpleasant experience into the declarative memory store. However, although they may prefer to use a different term, many of the proponents of this dissociation idea, like those favoring the concept of repression, believe that only conscious recollection (explicit memory) is affected. An implicit memory of traumatic events presumably still exists that can be expressed in bodily symptoms, dreams, and even disturbed behavior.

Are Traumatic Events Repressed?

Recovered Memories of Childhood Sexual Abuse?

During the 1970s and 1980s, scores of mental health therapists, books, newspaper articles, and television talk shows dramatically told of women who had only recently recovered their memory of past disturbances. In many of these widely publicized cases, some involving celebrities such as the TV star Roseanne Barr, the women reported how, as a result of counseling or psychotherapy, they now recalled being sexually molested by other family members when they were children. These stories seemed to tear open a curtain of massive denial, revealing shocking scenes that previously had been kept hidden. Thousands of fathers, older brothers, and uncles, and at times mothers as well, it would appear, sexually abuse the young girls in their families in a truly monstrous manner.

For a number of mental health professionals, "recovered memory" cases demonstrate that the family is by no means the protective haven our society assumes. Young girls are all too frequently the innocent victims of the adult males around them. In their book on repressed memories, Elizabeth Loftus and Katherine Ketcham quote the psychiatrist Judith Lewis Herman as maintaining that incest is a "common and central female experience" and the psychotherapist E. Sue Blume as claiming that "incest is so common as to be an epidemic." Other authorities estimate that one-fifth to one-third of all women were sexually abused in childhood. Even those who think these claims and statistics are exaggerated generally agree that child abuse is a serious social problem.[1]

However, as Loftus and Ketcham (and others in their camp) make clear, the controversy surrounding the recovered memory claims doesn't really deal with the question of how often children are sexually abused. Loftus certainly does not deny the reality of this victimization. She says she does "not want to see a return to those days, not so long ago, when a victim's cries for help went unheard and accusations of sexual abuse were automatically dismissed as fantasy or wish-fulfillment and shunted away into the backwaters of the public conscience." Rather, skeptics such as Loftus (a psychologist) and Richard Ofshe (a sociological social psychologist) dispute the contention that many women have repressed their memories of the sexual abuse they suffered as children. Some recovered memory advocates insist that these buried memories are exceedingly common. And so, in her popular book *Secret Survivors*, Blume holds that fully half of all incest survivors do not remember their sexual traumas.[2]

Is there good evidence that many persons have indeed unconsciously protected themselves from the painful recall of these disturbing events by keeping their memories of the incidents hidden deep within their minds? Or is it likely, as the skeptics propose, that a substantial proportion of the people claiming recent recall of the sexual abuse they suffered in childhood are actually reporting false memories based on suggestions and beliefs imparted to them by their therapists and the popular literature?

To highlight a number of the issues that will be of concern to us, here is a brief summary of an actual case:

> In 1989 a woman in California turned to a psychotherapist for help in overcoming her bulimia, an eating disorder characterized by repeated bouts of binge eating and self-induced vomiting. Although the woman hadn't considered herself to be a sex abuse victim, the therapist told the client's mother that 70–80% of bulimics had been sexually abused. In the course of her therapy, the woman then participated in weekly group sessions led by the therapist in which sexual victimization was discussed. Soon afterward the client said she was having memory flashbacks in which she fuzzily recalled her father abusing her sexually as a child.
>
> Wanting to follow up on these reports, the therapist asked a psychiatrist to inject the client with sodium amytal, a barbiturate once popularly termed a "truth serum," to see what the client would then recall. Under sedation, the

woman said she now remembered that her father had repeatedly raped her when she was between 5 and 7 years of age. Some time later, when the woman expressed some doubts about this abuse, both the therapist and the psychiatrist assured her that it was extremely difficult for anyone to lie while under the influence of sodium amytal.

At the therapist's recommendation, the woman confronted her father by accusing him of raping her. In spite of his denials, the client's mother then filed for divorce, the man's employer fired him from his high-salaried executive position, and the daughter instituted a suit against her father. In return, the accused father sued the therapist, the psychiatrist, and the medical center in which the sodium amytal interview had occurred, maintaining that they had helped his daughter to falsely construct the memories of his sexual abuse. The jury agreed with the father that the therapist and psychiatrist had not carried out their duties adequately and awarded him $500,000 in damages.[3]

What Is Repression?

Before we go further, we should try to arrive at a fairly clear understanding of what the notion of repressed memories entails. The usual idea, of course, is that repression occurs when the mind wards off recollections of painful (i.e., decidedly unpleasant) events. However, for Sigmund Freud, who made this concept a central part of his psychoanalytic theory, repression meant something different. Although his thinking changed to some extent over the years,[4] he basically held that anxiety-provoking experiences, and not merely unpleasant ones, were blocked from conscious recall. You may want to keep this point in mind, but here we will continue to talk about the failure to recall traumatic incidents in terms of repression (whether the events are anxiety- or shame-arousing or not) because this is the way many of the discussions are couched.

Although it's very difficult to establish a precise conception of repression that satisfies everyone, David Holmes has summarized the basic ideas that the recovered memory proponents generally have in mind when they use this term. According to Holmes, these writers think of repression as having three features: (1) there is selective forgetting of psychologically painful material; (2) this process is not under voluntary control but comes about automatically; and (3) the repressed material is not forgotten but is, instead, kept buried in the unconscious until the anxiety associated with the memory is removed.[5] The last-mentioned feature is very important. To expand on Holmes's point, the recovered memory can be said to have been re-

pressed if it is recalled after the presumably memory-blocking threat
or anxiety is alleviated.

Some Problems

Even if we have only a fairly general conception of what is involved
in repression, it's important to evaluate the claims of those who insist
that many women are unable to recall the traumas they suffered in
childhood. We can start this process by returning to the previously
summarized California case and looking at some of the issues it raises.

One issue has to do with the quality of the evidence on which some
of the assertions rest. For example, consider the therapist's contention
in this case that 70–80% of bulimics have been sexually abused. Quite
a few psychotherapists share this belief, but there's no good evidence
for it. When psychiatrists Harrison Pope and James Hudson examined
the best controlled studies they could find in this area, they concluded
that bulimic patients did not "show a significantly higher prevalence
of childhood sexual abuse than control groups. . . . Furthermore, neither controlled nor uncontrolled studies of bulimia nervosa found
higher rates of childhood sexual abuse than were found in studies of
the general population that used comparable methods."[6]

There is the same lack of adequate evidence for other supposed
indicators of repressed abuse. In her book, Blume informed her readers that women are likely to be the victims of repressed incestuous
experience if they have such characteristics as a "fear of being alone
in the dark; nightmares; poor body image; headaches; arthritis; adult
nervousness," and so on. But because some of these troubles (such as
headaches and arthritis) may have direct physical causes, and because
other characteristics in Blume's list can be indicative of many different
kinds of stress, or can even be caused by biochemical imbalances in
some instances, symptoms such as these are hardly satisfactory signs
of past sexual abuse. The American Psychological Association has
advised the public to beware of claims that certain specific symptoms
are indicative of childhood abuse:

> . . . *there is no single set of symptoms which automatically indicates that a
> person was a victim of childhood abuse. There have been media reports of
> therapists who state that people (particularly women) with a particular set of
> problems or symptoms must have been victims of childhood sexual abuse. There
> is no scientific evidence that supports this conclusion.*[7]

We can also have misgivings about the belief shared by the therapist and the psychiatrist in the California case that the injection of sodium amytal would enable the client to recover her repressed childhood memories. In actuality, and contrary to what the therapist told the woman, there is no such thing as a "truth serum" that can keep people from lying. No drug can guarantee that that the injected patients will refrain from telling falsehoods. Indeed, some experts believe that people under sodium amytal may be so suggestible that they will actually construct *pseudomemories*, false memories that cannot easily be distinguished from true recollections, in response to the physician's assumed wishes. They therefore urge psychiatrists to avoid asking leading questions during the drug-assisted interview.[8] One wonders if the psychiatrist in the California case had followed this admonition.

Similar doubts can be expressed about hypnosis. Many therapists seeking to uncover their clients' supposedly repressed memories employ hypnosis rather than sodium amytal to get through their clients' presumed memory block. They usually liken the mind to an unsleeping videotape recorder that faithfully records all sensations and stores the information in the person's subconscious. Hypnosis, they then say, facilitates the "playback" of this recorded information. Some hypnosis enthusiasts, going even further, maintain that people frequently can recall considerably more of their past when they are in a hypnotized state than when they are fully awake.

Controlled research casts considerable doubt on these claims. The "memory as videotape recorder" metaphor isn't at all consistent with our current knowledge of how memories operate. Although the examination of eyewitness memory in the preceding chapter indicated that certain details of a witnessed event can be accurately recalled, our remembrances of the incidents that happen to us are generally constructions established on the basis of our understanding of what took place and are not necessarily faithful reproductions of these occurrences. To put this another way, we generally store in our memories not the actual physical sensations we received, but the result of our attempt to understand these sensations. Furthermore, as we will soon see, the memory trace of this constructed understanding is extremely susceptible to alteration by later information.[9] To go on about hypnosis, however, there's little good evidence that hypnosis promotes the accurate recall of past events. It is also clear that hypnosis

leads to an increased responsiveness to suggestions, as well as a sus-
pension of disbelief and a lowering of critical judgment.

About a decade ago a panel of the American Medical Association's
(AMA) Council on Scientific Affairs (chaired by the world-famous
authority on hypnosis Martin Orne) reviewed the research on the use
of hypnosis to refresh recollections. These authorities noted that the
experiences people have when they are deeply hypnotized seem to be
very real to them. In fact, they're so realistic to some persons that
when Sigmund Freud first used hypnosis in his psychotherapeutic
practice, he believed his patients' hypnotically induced memories
were accurately recalled records of past events. In time, though, Freud
came to realize (in the words of the AMA Council) "that these remembrances reflected an emotional reality but were not necessarily historically accurate – rather, they were generally a combination of fantasies,
desires, and fears as well as actual recollections of a different period
of time."[10]

The Council basically came to the same conclusion. Reports claiming the historically faithful recovery of earlier memories are only anecdotal in nature. More careful investigations in the field and the
laboratory indicate that the hypnotic state can bring up inaccurate as
well as accurate information about the past. Patients may be convinced that the events they reported when hypnotized actually happened, but their recollections are too apt to be transformations of their
own prior beliefs and/or imaginings based on cues received from the
therapist, perhaps blended with accurate memories.[11]

Finally, there is one more issue highlighted by the California case
I've been discussing in this section: Claims of recovered memories can
affect people other than the client and the therapist. Because his
daughter had accused him of sexually abusing her, the father in the
California case lost his wife and his job. Many other people have also
suffered as a consequence of such accusations, all of them automatically presumed to be guilty as charged because someone believed she
had recovered her formerly repressed memories of childhood sexual
abuse.[12] Given the uncertainties and the possibility that innocent people might be hurt if the client's recollections are wrong, one would
think that therapists would be cautious in diagnosing repressed memories of childhood traumas. Unfortunately, quite a few of them are
quick to assume that their clients had been sexually molested when
they were very young, and some, such as the therapist we've been

discussing, even encourage their clients to believe this. I'll have more to say about this matter later.

Observations About Trauma and Memory

How Common Are Repressed Memories of Past Traumas?

As indicated earlier, we can assume that quite a few people have been sexually victimized by others in their family. This isn't the issue here. Rather, with Loftus and Ketcham and Ofshe and Watters, we're interested in whether repressed memories are as common as the believers in repression assume. If "one-fifth to one-third" of all women have been sexually abused in childhood, there should be many persons who avoid consciously remembering these traumatic events. Do our minds regularly and automatically prevent us from consciously recalling highly disturbing occurrences?

If we look at reports of the aftermath of exceedingly threatening experiences, far more often than not we find that these incidents are more apt to be remembered vividly than to be forgotten. Psychiatrist Lenore Terr has reported this in her description of the memories of children who had suffered an extremely frightening occurrence. Twenty-six youngsters from a small California town had been kidnapped at gunpoint while they were on their school bus and then were buried underground inside the bus for about 16 hours before they finally escaped. According to Terr, the children's recollections of the incident were brilliantly clear, "far clearer, more detailed, and more long-lasting than . . . ordinary memory."[13] Two critics of the recovered memory movement, Ofshe and Watters, have also noted that traumatized children often have vivid memories of the awful event. For instance, they pointed to a study of children between 5 and 10 years of age who had witnessed a shocking event – the murder of a parent. According to the investigator in this case, not one child repressed the memory of that tragic experience. To the contrary, all of the youngsters, in the words of Ofshe and Watters, evidently

> *had recurrent thoughts of the episode that often came back at unwanted and unexpected moments. Their intrusive memories occurred even though they reported they did not like to speak of the events and seldom had to talk about the experience to anyone.*[14]

Traumatized adults frequently also have intrusive memories of the horrifying occurrence to which they were exposed. In 1981 two sky-walks at the second and fourth floors of the Hyatt Regency Hotel in Kansas City suddenly collapsed, dumping tons of concrete and steel on people in the crowded lobby below. More than 100 people died and over 200 were injured. When a psychiatrist later interviewed about 100 of those who had been involved in the tragedy, as survivors, observers, or rescuers, he found that nearly 90% of them had repeated recollections of the terrible accident. Summarizing this and other cases, Schacter commented that "The most common post-traumatic symptom is unbidden recollection of the trauma."[15]

How Accurate Are Memories of Traumatic Events?

The reader will note that Terr's characterization of the kidnapped children's vivid memories is in line with the findings, reported in the preceding chapter, of arousal-engendered heightened recall. Keep in mind, though, that the previously cited research shows that stress typically leads only to better recall of central details, not necessarily all details. Moreover, as the disturbing incident recedes into the past, remembrances of even important aspects of the occurrence can be distorted. We can see this in an investigation of children's recollections of a sniper attack at an elementary school playground. When the youngsters were questioned 6 to 16 weeks after the shootings, the researchers found that many of their memories had changed even over this relatively brief period of time. Some children who weren't at the playground on that occasion falsely remembered being at the scene. More important for us here, those who had been in the line of fire tended, in their memories, to move themselves away from the danger and/or introduced a variety of other inaccuracies.[16]

Terr's study of the kidnapped schoolchildren also illustrates how memories of terrifying events can be mistaken in significant respects. Four to 5 years after the traumatic event, the psychiatrist interviewed most of the youngsters and found that although their recollections were vivid and detailed, there were sometimes striking errors and distortions in about half of the cases. Even those children whose memories had been accurate soon after the kidnapping made mistakes in the later interview. As Schacter remarked in discussing Terr's study, "even 'burned-in' traumatic memories are not immune to change over time." Ceci and Bruck have made the same point: "All experiences –

no matter how emotionally salient – are susceptible to distortion. . . . Survivors of death camps, of natural disasters, and of serious accidents all appear to have distorted aspects of their experiences, including such forensically significant aspects as the identity of an individual who gouged out their eye while in prison. . . ."[17]

In addition to finding no marked evidence of repression in horrific incidents such as these, writers who are skeptical about the claims of repressed-then-recovered memories often point to the frequent intrusion of pseudomemories in the victims' recollections of traumatic events. Loftus and other memory researchers have repeatedly demonstrated how malleable memory can be, how readily our recollections of an event can be distorted by subtle information encountered after the original incident.[18]

Because memory is so easily molded by extraneous influences, people exposed to highly disturbing occurrences sometimes remember things that did not happen and are totally convinced that they did take place. Neisser's investigation of flashbulb memories mentioned in the previous chapter found such pseudomemories. To give you an example, one of the students received the news of the *Challenger's* explosion while she was talking on the telephone, but 3 years later she insisted that she had heard the report in class.

False memories can also be created about occurrences involving oneself, as can be seen in two anecdotal reports. In the better-known of these reports, the famous child psychologist Jean Piaget said that one of his earliest memories, which he had long believed, was of an incident that supposedly had occurred when he was about 2 years old. In his mind's eye, he wrote, he could still see himself sitting in his stroller and being pushed by his nurse along the Champs Elysees when a man jumped on them and tried to grab him.

> . . . [M]y nurse bravely tried to stand between me and the thief. She received various scratches, and I can still see vaguely those on her face. Then a crowd gathered, a policeman with a short cloak and a white baton came up, and the man took to his heels. I can still see the whole scene, and can even place it near the tube station.

However, despite the clarity of the psychologist's remembrances, this event apparently had never taken place. More than a decade later, the nurse became more religious and confessed to Piaget's parents that she had made up the entire story. The boy evidently had heard of the supposed intended kidnapping as he was growing up and in his imagination had constructed a memory that he had projected into the past.[19]

Loftus and her colleagues duplicated this phenomenon by successfully implanting pseudomemories in young children. Her 1994 book coauthored with Ketcham gives us several anecdotal illustrations of this process, but one will suffice here. A mother, who was a student in one of Loftus's classes, had convinced her 8-year-old daughter that she, the girl, had been lost in a particular condominium complex 3 years earlier. The mother buttressed her untrue story with believable details. About 3 weeks later, a family friend interviewed the child, supposedly for an article on childhood memories, and asked about a number of real events from the girl's past (that had previously been identified by the mother), as well as about the made-up occurrence. The youngster had difficulty recalling the real incidents that had taken place 2 years before but was quite clear in "remembering" the untrue event. Guided by her conception of what had taken place, she even embellished her story with new details.[20]

Some psychologists have questioned whether these demonstrations of implanted memories are actually evidence that therapists or others created false recollections of childhood sexual abuse in their clients. One of these writers showed experimentally that suggestions are accepted and become false memories to the extent that they are plausible. She then argued that people wouldn't accept a therapist's claim that they had been sexually molested as young children unless the claim seemed plausible to them because of their own past experience.[21] However, to complicate matters even further, people who believe that false memories of sexual abuse can indeed be implanted by authority figures sometimes point to known instances of false confessions. Social psychologist Richard Ofshe has illustrated how this can happen. Ofshe had become intrigued by the case of a man, Paul Ingram, whose daughter had charged him with having molested her sexually and having been the leader of a satanic cult. Suspecting that Ingram had confessed to the charge only because of his repeated badgering by the police, Ofshe decided to test Ingram's memory by inventing a fictitious story. He told the man that his daughters and sons had reported that he, their father, had forced them to have sex with each other while he watched. The next day, when Ofshe spoke to him again, Ingram said he now recalled having done what Ofshe had told him, and in his retelling, he even embellished the event considerably.[22]

And so, the argument rages back and forth.

The studies cited up to now have provided few, if any, indications of repressed memories. But those who believe in this concept still have a way of disposing of this contradictory evidence. They can argue, with Terr, that we've been dealing with only single episodes. For this psychiatrist (as Loftus and Ketcham put it), "Only when a child is subjected to *continuing* [italics in the original] trauma or terror are the defense mechanisms stimulated, interfering with memory formation, storage, and retrieval."[23]

Adult Remembrances of Past Abuse

Some Documented Instances of Recovered Memories

David Holmes, whose definition of repression was described earlier, states that 60 years of laboratory research have not yielded any evidence supporting this concept.[24] Nonetheless, there are a few cases in which repression does seem to have occurred. Jennifer Freyd of the University of Oregon, who is generally sympathetic to the idea of repressed memories, tells, for example, of what had happened to Marilyn Van Derbur Atler, a former Miss America. According to this woman, her father had sexually violated her for 13 years until she went to college, but she had blocked all recollection of this abuse until the repression lifted in adulthood. However, her sister always remembered what her father had done. Another, and perhaps better-known, recovered memory case is that of Ross Cheit, a professor of public policy at Brown University.

Several months after Cheit started psychotherapy because of general dissatisfaction with his life, and while on vacation with his wife, he dreamed of a man who had been his camp counselor more than two decades earlier. Cheit thought about this person for a few hours and then, for the first time in over 20 years, recalled that the man had molested him. He hired a private detective, who helped him find the man in a small town on the other side of the continent, and, after many attempts, finally succeeded in reaching him by telephone. The man remembered Cheit and admitted having molested various boys. Although at first he said that he couldn't recall having abused Cheit himself, Cheit located other people who also reported having been the man's victim years before.[25]

One way out of the impasse we now seem to have reached is to look for evidence of repressed memories in adults who had actually suffered serious mistreatment as children. Are many of these persons unable to recall the abuse that had been inflicted on them?

The Williams Study

Linda Meyer Williams has given us one estimate of the relative frequency of repressed memories in grownups. In her notable investigation, she interviewed 129 women, mostly poor African Americans between 18 and 31 years of age, who had well-documented histories of having been sexually assaulted as children about 17 years earlier. Sixty percent of the cases involved genital penetration, and some type of physical force was employed in 62% of the events. Williams found that fully 38% of the women did not recall the specific documented abuse case, although two-thirds of these particular interviewees did remember another time when they were sexually molested. (Given Terr's previously mentioned insistence that continued or repeated abuse is most likely to be repressed, it should be noted that the target abusive incident was a one-time event for about 70% of the sample. We're not told how many of the women not recalling the incident had experienced more than one abusive episode.)

Contrary to the observations made by a number of clinicians, Williams did not find that physically forced abuses or assaults in which sexual penetration occurred were especially likely to be recalled. But the victim's closeness to the molester did appear to be very important. The women were least likely to say they remembered the documented abuse if the perpetrator was a family member or someone well known to them, and were most apt to recall the incident if the molester was more of a stranger. The researcher acknowledged that some of the abusive instances may not have been reported in her interviews because they simply were forgotten. But still, Williams believed that a good proportion of the unrecalled incidents had been repressed, particularly when the abuser was a relative. So, she concluded, "having no memory of child sexual abuse is a common occurrence. . . ."[26]

Loftus, Garry, and Feldman have questioned this conclusion. Space does not permit a detailed review of their critique, but two of their points are especially noteworthy. One had to do with whether the children actually had formed a memory of having been assaulted when the event occurred 17 years before. At least some of the youngsters might not have understood the meaning of their experience and therefore hadn't constructed a memory of an abuse to be stored in their minds. Many of the girls had not themselves reported being assaulted but were identified as victims by others.

The second, and major, point was that the failures to report the documented abusive incident could have been due to ordinary forgetting rather than an active repression process. Loftus and her associates cited findings from a variety of surveys showing that people can forget all kinds of things. Thus, over one-quarter of the respondents in one study failed to recall an automobile accident that had happened 9 to 12 months earlier even though someone in the car had been injured, and over 15% of those in another investigation did not remember a hospitalization 9 months after discharge. For the Loftus team, the Williams study presents no convincing evidence that failure to report the documented episode is anything more than this apparently ordinary forgetting.[27]

In his discussion of Williams's study, Schacter also suggested that many of her respondents could have forgotten the abusive incident, although he also thought it was conceivable that at least two of the women in the sample had experienced repression: These were people who had told the researcher that they had forgotten the abuse immediately after it had taken place. Still, Schacter wondered whether "The 'blocking out' [was] an automatic, unconscious act of repression or a conscious attempt to avoid thinking about a distressing event."[28]

Some Possible Resolutions

Psychogenic Amnesia

Several writers, including a number of recovered memory advocates, have suggested that it is preferable to use the term *amnesia* when speaking of trauma-produced memory impairment. We sometimes hear of people who have "lost their memory" because of a serious physical or perhaps even psychological blow that they suffered. This memory loss most frequently results from physical damage to the brain, but evidently it can also come about, although apparently rarely, through a severe psychological injury. In one instance, the survivor of an airplane crash was unable to remember the details. In another, and perhaps better-known, example, some soldiers facing death in combat forgot where they were. These memory deficits might have been the result of the brain's neurophysiological reaction to danger; an exceedingly stressful event often produces the release of certain neurochemicals in the brain that aid in coping with the stress but, when in excess, can also damage the hippocampus, a part of the brain involved in explicit memory.[29]

Although memory researchers generally accept the reality of psychogenic amnesia, both Loftus and Schacter independently doubt whether it's a good idea to use this concept in connection with the supposed recovered memory cases. The repression described in these latter instances seems to be much narrower and more sharply focused than the forgetting characteristic of amnesia. For Loftus, psychogenic amnesia "typically involves a relatively large assemblage of memories and associated affects. . . . A rape victim suffering from psychogenic (traumatic) amnesia, for example, might forget her name, address, and occupation in addition to the details of the assault. But the amnesia is typically reversible, and the memories soon return." Moreover, it's quite usual for the person to be aware of the memory loss. Individuals having repressed memories, by contrast, "allegedly lose not only the memory of the trauma but also *all awareness that they have lost it* [italics in the original]." The memory loss here, Loftus says, doesn't resemble the forgetting in the typical amnesia case. Furthermore, according to Schacter, "Many limited amnesias, in which people fail to remember a traumatic event such as committing a murder or being raped, are due to alcohol intoxication, brain injury, or even deliberate faking."[30]

Dissociation

Dissociation is another term that's often used in connection with trauma-affected memories. The notion here is that certain earlier thoughts, feelings, and experiences are somehow separated from, or not fully integrated with, other aspects of the individual's personality. Amnesia for past traumatic occurrences, according to the American Psychiatric Association's *Diagnostic and Statistical Manual* (4th edition) is a dissociative disorder, "an inability to recall important personal information, usually of a traumatic or stressful nature, that is too extensive to be explained by ordinary forgetfulness."[31]

The French psychiatrist Pierre Janet called attention to these dissociations about a century ago. To give you an example, one of his best-known cases was that of Madame D., a woman who had been very disturbed by the death of her mother. She had no explicit memory of her mother's passing, and yet, every once in a while, she had isolated but troubling images of her mother's appearance. These vivid memory fragments seemed to be so separate from the rest of her conscious thoughts and feelings that Madame D. referred to them as hallucinations. As Schacter tells us, Janet believed that in these and other similar instances, the patients having these dissociated experiences were "plagued by implicit memories of [traumatic] events they [could not] remember explicitly."[32]

In at least one important respect, Madame D.'s case resembles that of the Vietnam veteran I mentioned in the previous chapter when I introduced the idea of implicit memories. Although, unlike Janet's patient, the veteran was able to recall his past traumatic experiences, both he and Madame D. were troubled by occasionally intruding, implicitly remembered sensations and images linked to these earlier threatening incidents. Many people who have endured extremely disturbing occurrences also suffer from recurring intrusive memories related to their traumas. In fact, recurrent unbidden recollections of a past trauma (along with intense fear and a strong sense of helplessness) are the key symptoms of *posttraumatic stress disorder (PTSD)*, the psychological ailment that some people experience after being exposed to an actual or threatened death or serious injury to the self or a significant other.[33]

Although some World War II combat veterans as well as a number of Jewish survivors of the Holocaust have had these symptoms for 40 years or more, they tend to diminish with time. Several studies have also found that the people most likely to develop PTSD after a grave danger are those who had suffered from earlier traumas. Perhaps because they had several highly threatening experiences, they may have come to believe that a variety of other traumatic events will also happen to them.[34]

What's especially important for us here, though, is that the intrusive recollections are implicit memories that are distinctively different from deliberately retrievable, explicit (or declarative) memories in terms of both how they are brought to mind and their nature. As I've already noted, many trauma victims can recall the disturbing event if they want to do so, whereas the emotional memories often arise involuntarily when they encounter something that reminds them of the threatening episode. The story in Chapter 3 of the Vietnam veteran who panicked when he heard the exploding firecracker is an example. The sound was a cue that automatically reawakened the wartime images and sensations associated with the sound of explosions. These activated implicit memories are typically also qualitatively different from the recollections brought to mind from explicit memory. In their analysis of PTSD memories, psychologists Chris Brewin, Tim Dalgleish, and Stephen Joseph observed that

> [in] many cases the intrusive memories consist of images accompanied by high levels of physiological arousal and are experienced as reenactments of the original trauma ("flashbacks"). Other memories, particularly those associated with traumas in the distant past, may be more fragmentary, consisting of isolated visual, auditory, olfactory, or tactile sensations.[35]

Adding to this picture of the nature of dissociated implicit memories, Schacter reports that the highly emotional images and sensations often have both real and imagined elements.

> In his pioneering study of trauma and World War I veterans, John MacCurdy observed that these overwhelming moments of "reliving" prior experiences often involved veterans' "worst fears" rather than actual combat episodes.[36]

These observations together with other research findings suggest that highly threatening experiences may well be recorded in at least two different memory systems. One is the familiar explicit (or declarative) system composed of what we understand and consciously know about the events. But in addition, there may be an implicit system containing stored images and sensations that can be largely dissociated from, not fully integrated with, the former system. Positing a similar distinction, in their analysis of PTSD, Brewin, Dalgleish, and Joseph hypothesized that traumatic experiences are mentally represented in two different ways. One, that they termed *verbally accessible knowledge*, involves consciously available memories that can be deliberately retrieved. In addition, "extensive nonconscious" information processing gives rise to another kind of mental representation, called *situationally accessible knowledge*, that cannot be accessed deliberately but that can come to mind "automatically when the person is in a context in which the physical features or meaning are similar to those of the traumatic situation."[37]

The psychiatrist Bessel van der Kolk has advanced a neurophysiological theory that attempts to account for this dissociation in terms of the operation of two neural systems deep inside the brain, the amygdala and the hippocampus.[38] You'll recall from Chapter 3 that moderately arousing emotional experiences are typically remembered quite well. To explain this, van der Kolk suggests that moderate activation of the amygdala stimulates the hippocampus to a moderate degree, thereby enhancing explicit memory. However, a very stressful occurrence would presumably produce excessive stimulation of the amygdala that would interfere with the functioning of the hippocampus and thus impede explicit memory. The victim may then be unable to retrieve consciously much of what happened during the incident. Even so, many of the somatic sensations and visual images produced by the traumatic experience are retained because they're stored largely in what van der Kolk calls *sensorimotor modalities* (i.e., in implicit memory). These are the sensations and images that, for Brewin and his colleagues, are represented as situationally accessible knowledge. In this connection, Brewin, Dalgleish, and Joseph note that the victims' attention span may be so narrowed by the extreme stress that their situationally accessible knowledge (implicit memory) has substantial gaps and is thus seriously incomplete.

As you can see, van der Kolk's analysis is compatible with the position taken by several memory researchers, including Schacter, in a number of respects. There is at least one important difference, however. Van der Kolk believes that the images and sensations stored in sensorimotor modalities are "relatively indelible" and unlikely to change with time, whereas, as I pointed out earlier in this chapter, Schacter and other investigators say that these implicit memories are "subject to a degree of distorted recall."[39]

What About Repression?

The reality of psychogenic amnesia and dissociation does not necessarily support the validity of the concept of repression. Highly stressful conditions might impede explicit memory, but this doesn't necessarily mean that the extremely disturbing information has been repressed in the sense of being defensively buried in one's unconscious mind until safety is restored. For some writers this is an extremely important point. Dissociation, they hold, is a passive consequence of the inadequate processing of the information involving traumatic events, whereas repression involves active blocking of the recall of already stored information.[40]

Still, what if repression does occur at times, at least under certain conditions? Let's assume that some of Williams's respondents had indeed repressed memories of the childhood sexual abuse they experienced. This also seems to have happened in the cases of Ross Cheit and the other persons previously mentioned. However, as I've indicated, these (and possibly other) instances of first-repressed-and-then-recovered memories do not seem to be common, and they certainly do not indicate that there is an automatic and prevalent tendency to keep memories of traumatic episodes out of conscious awareness. But they do suggest that a psychological mechanism in the minds of some people may well, under some conditions, defensively prevent them from recalling highly disturbing events.

What could this mechanism be?

Betrayal Trauma?

Psychologist Jennifer Freyd has suggested one possibility. She contends that young children who are abused by a parent or another caretaker are faced with a serious conflict: On the one hand, they sense that they have been betrayed; the caretaker has violated his or her trust. On the other hand, they realize that they depend on this person for their survival. Torn by these opposing cognitions, abused children presumably seek to resolve the conflict by deliberately not recognizing or even forgetting how they have been victimized. According to Freyd:

> Detecting betrayal can be too dangerous when the natural changes in behavior it . . . [would provoke] would threaten primary dependent relationships. In order to suppress the natural reaction to betrayal in such cases, information blockages in mental processing occur.[41]

Freyd suggests that some information regarding the abuse might undergo unconscious processing so that the associated images and sensations are stored in implicit memory. But the information blockage she postulates presumably interferes largely with conscious retrieval of knowledge of the betrayal.

Findings obtained by a number of investigators are consistent with Freyd's betrayal theory, especially her idea that the abuse is more likely to be forgotten the closer is the relationship between abuser and victim. A good example is provided by Linda Meyer Williams's study mentioned earlier. Williams found, you'll recall, that 38% of the women in her sample who were known to have been sexually abused in childhood were unable or unwilling to report this abuse when they were queried in young adulthood. As I noted before, Williams then looked into the relationship between the perpetrator and the victim and discovered that those who couldn't (or wouldn't) recall the abusive episode in this later interview were the ones who tended to have the closest relationship with the abuser. With Williams's cooperation, Freyd went even further into the data and found that the molestation was least likely to be reported if it was incestuous.[42]

However consistent these results are with betrayal theory, they obviously leave many questions unanswered. For instance, we do not know if the failure to report the earlier abuse was due to repression or to conscious unwillingness to speak of the event – or, as I indicated earlier, if the event somehow had been merely forgotten. Freyd recognizes the need for additional research, and we can hope this will be forthcoming in the not too distant future.

What Now?

Where do we now stand? A compromise position somewhere between the believers' and skeptics' views suggests that some adults cannot consciously remember the sexual abuse they actually suffered as children, whether this failure of recollection is due to active repression or psychogenic amnesia or dissociation (or even ordinary forgetting).[43] However, it should be recognized, this compromise does not necessarily support the validity of the procedures employed by many recovered memory therapists in search of the presumed buried memories.

Despite the protests by many of these therapists, there is good reason to believe that memory for past events is highly malleable and susceptible to distortion by even subtle suggestions in the therapy situation. Practitioners may not tell their clients explicitly that they had been molested in childhood, but they can still provide cues inviting the clients to construct supposed memories of abuse and even incest or rape by the questions they ask and the interpretations they offer. Susceptibility to subtle suggestions is especially great under hypnosis, as noted earlier. However, even nonhypnotized persons can get suggestive ideas about past abuse from the therapist or, if they're participating in group therapy sessions, from other clients in their group.

In this connection, Loftus has pointed out that therapists may unwittingly suggest to their clients that they were sexually molested as children because

> [they] have fallen prey to a bias that affects all of us, known as the "confirmatory bias". . . . People in general, therapists included, have a tendency to search

for evidence that confirms their hunches rather than search for evidence that disconfirms.[44]

Believing that certain symptoms – bulimia, low self-esteem, sexual dysfunctions, and so on – are indicative of childhood abuse, they may then question their clients as to whether they have even faint memories of past molestation, and thereby suggest that repressed memories must exist.

Aware of how easy it is for therapists to influence their clients, a number of clinicians have urged their fellow practitioners to be cautious in pursuing recovered memories. In the words of a statement published by the American Psychological Association, "A competent psychotherapist will attempt to stick to the facts [as these are reported by the client]. He or she will be careful to let the information evolve . . . and not steer [the client] toward a particular conclusion or interpretation."[45] Related to this is the issue of how quickly therapists should accept the client's report of a recovered memory of earlier sexual molestation. For many, the psychotherapeutic relationship requires the client to have a sense of safety and complete trust in the therapist, and this means the therapist has to accept what the client says unhesitatingly. It's also quite common for clinicians to maintain that the client's beliefs and perceptions are all that matters, and that it's not their responsibility to determine the validity of the client's recollection. Others take a similar stance because of their sympathy with the past victims of real sexual abuse and their belief that society must become more aware of this horrible crime. "Advocates for those who are sexually abused have spent 15 to 20 years trying to remove the need for corroboration of such crimes and will oppose any move to require independent support for abuse charges."[46]

The California case summarized earlier (as well as the many other cases discussed in the Loftus–Ketcham and Ofshe–Watters books) shows, however, that reality is not quite as simple as these last statements would have us believe: People other than the client are involved, and some of them may suffer severe psychological or even material injury because of the accusations made against them – even though they are innocent of the charges. Are therapists responsible only to their client? Clearly, there are no simple answers to the problem of the apparent recovery of memories of earlier sexual abuse.

I'll conclude with some advice that the American Psychological

Association has offered to people concerned about their childhood memories:

> *First, know that there is no single set of symptoms which automatically indicates that a person was a victim of childhood abuse. . . .*
>
> *Second, all questions concerning possible recovered memories of childhood abuse should be considered from an unbiased position. A therapist should not approach recovered memories with the preconceived notion that abuse must have happened or that abuse could not possibly have happened.*
>
> *Third, when considering current problems, be wary of those therapists who offer an instant childhood abuse explanation, and those who dismiss claims or reports of sexual abuse without any exploration.*[47]

PART III

Affective Influences on Cognitive Processes

The next two chapters should be read as a unit. Although each one covers somewhat different topics, both are greatly concerned with how people's feelings influence the way in which they process the information they glean from their immediate situation. Thus, in focusing on how mood influences judgments and decision making, Chapter 5 will introduce the major theoretical analyses of how these effects come about. These formulations, as you will see, are couched largely in information processing terms. Chapter 6, dealing with affective influences on persuasion, will extend, and sometimes even modify, several of these analyses, as well as present some new theoretical conceptions.

5. The Influence of Feelings on Judgments and Decision Making

The advantage of the emotions is that they lead us astray.
Oscar Wilde, *Picture of Dorian Gray*

We all know, as did Oscar Wilde, the 19-century English playwright and wit, that our feelings can influence our judgments and the decisions we reach. If we're happy at the moment, aren't we likely to think that "God's in His heaven / All's right with the world" and that many of those around us are good and trustworthy people? Our everyday experiences also tell us that negative feelings often have just the opposite effect. For one thing, we're frequently too apt to be harsh in our evaluations of others when we're in a bad mood. But how often does this mood congruency occur? When do our feelings affect our assessments of others, and in what ways does this influence come about? Can we rise above our feelings and reach accurate and impartial judgments despite our emotions, and if so, under what conditions? Then too, how might our affective state influence our decision making? Do negative feelings have only negative effects? Isn't it possible that we become complacent and even mentally lazy when we're in a good mood, so that we actually think more carefully about what is happening when we're somewhat unhappy? The present chapter will review some of the best social psychological studies bearing on these questions. It will start with an examination of mood effects on judgments, and then will consider how feelings can affect decision making and information processing.

Social Judgments

How General Is Mood Congruency in Judgments?

How often can people's feelings sway their judgments? We've all seen this happen at times: how a happy person can view others in the best possible light or how someone in a temporary fit of depression may expect the worst to occur. But how regular is this mood congruency effect? And more particularly, do both pleasant and unpleasant feelings have this influence?

Psychological research hasn't always yielded the same answers to these questions. In a number of studies, mood congruence was found only under limited conditions, such as when the judgments had to do with oneself but not with other persons. In some investigations there was also an asymmetry in the outcome: Positive feelings influenced the assessments but negative feelings did not.[1]

To give you an example of this latter type of limited effect, consider the experiment by Forgas and Bower mentioned in Chapter 3. In that study, you'll recall, after the participants were made to feel either good or bad, they were asked to judge a stranger on the basis of information given them about this person. When the subjects examined this material, they paid most attention to the information having the same valence as their mood. Nonetheless, what's important right now is that their judgments weren't affected equally by both pleasant and unpleasant feelings. The people who were in a good mood had significantly more positive than negative views of the stranger, but in those who were in a bad mood, their feelings evidently had little if any influence on their evaluations.[2]

However, on the other side, some published studies reported that both unpleasant and pleasant moods can influence one's evaluations. For example, two researchers showed that people's estimates of the risk that certain bad events would occur were significantly affected by how they felt on that occasion, and this influence arose in a negative as well as in a positive mood. Persons made to feel bad typically exaggerated how often such undesirable events as street crime or heart attacks or divorce took place, whereas those led to be happy generally underestimated the frequency of these events.[3]

Despite this seeming inconsistency, however, it's now clear that we ordinarily can expect people's judgments to be somewhat in accord with their mood – whether their affect is positive or negative in nature, whether their opinions concern themselves or others, and in everyday life as well as in a research laboratory. Mayer and his colleagues have given us good evidence of the pervasiveness of this mood congruence. Using a random sample of New Hampshire adults, as well as groups of college students from all over the United States, they found that the persons who were feeling good at the time were generally more positive in their views than were their counterparts who were in a bad mood. Moreover, as Mayer and his colleagues saw it, a mood regulation process probably operated in those studies in which negative feelings had no effect on opinions. The unhappy participants had presumably sought to alleviate their bad mood by thinking positively about the people and events around them. (You'll remember from Chapter 3 that this notion of bad mood regulation has also been used to explain why unpleasant feelings occasionally do not affect memory.[4])

> *The Mayer research also tells us more. There are, of course, different kinds of judgments, and some types may be especially susceptible to influence by feelings. Recognizing this, the Mayer team obtained a variety of assessments: Some had to do with the impressions of strangers, as in the Forgas and Bower experiment cited earlier; others involved the favorability of ideas regarding categories of objects; and still others dealt with the estimated likelihood of good and bad events occurring, much as in the risk estimate study mentioned before. Mood affected all of these judgments. Furthermore, it turned out that these different measures tended to cluster together; the people expressing either a positive or a negative view on one of these matters were apt to give the same hedonically toned opinion in the other areas. And so, as would be expected, when the investigators formed a general index combining these different kinds of evaluations, they found that, here too, the participants in a particular affective state typically held congruent opinions. If they felt good, for example, they thought a person described to them was likely to have favorable qualities and also believed there was a good chance that a married couple would be happy together for a long time, whereas people in a bad mood typically expressed negative views on these matters.*

Explaining Mood Congruence in Judgments

Gordon Bower's associative network theory, described in Chapter 3, is often used to account for this mood congruence.[5] According to this network (or, as it is often called, priming) formulation, you'll remember, feelings can be regarded as nodes in a network of associations within memory. When a particular feeling is aroused, the relevant affect-memory node is activated; this activation then spreads to the past experiences, concepts, ways of thinking, and physiological and bodily reactions that are linked in memory to this affective state. If we have to evaluate someone or estimate the likelihood that a particular kind of event will occur, our prevailing mood will prime, or bring to mind, feeling-congruent relevant memories, ideas, concepts, and modes of information processing. Suppose we're asked to say what we think of the statement "A little rebellion, now and then, is a good thing" and didn't know its author was Thomas Jefferson. Feeling good, we're apt to recall instances in which rebellions had (for us) desirable outcomes and to interpret the notion of rebellion in a positive light. Similarly, if we're in a bad mood and have to guess how many marriages will end in divorce, we're likely to think of the divorces we know of and perhaps even exaggerate the prevalence of broken marriages. Then too, as noted in Chapter 3 and as the Forgas–Bower experiment shows, when we're in a complex situation, there's a good chance that we'll pay particular attention to external information that is consistent with our feelings. We'll also think more about this congruent information than about other matters that don't match our mood.[6]

Adding to observations such as these that support the priming/associative network interpretation, we have even better evidence in several experiments that timed how long the participants took to form their judgments. In at least two of Forgas's studies, his subjects were quicker to make judgments that were congruent with their feelings than to make affectively incongruent judgments. It's as if the participants' mood had primed ideas in accord with their feelings, so that these thoughts were rapidly employed in forming the evaluations.[7]

Although the priming/associative network conception of mood congruency has considerable support, a number of social psychologists are troubled by this formulation, primarily for two reasons: First, in their view, the network model gives too much weight to relatively passive associative processes and minimizes the role of cognition, whereas they favor an analysis emphasizing more active, cognitive processing of information. Second, they have misgivings about the network model's concept of affect nodes. Seeing these problems, and perhaps others as well, some psychologists have offered other explanations for the mood congruency in judgments.

The best known of these alternatives does not assume quite as much passivity as is envisioned in the priming/associative network model, but it still postulates some thinking (unconscious as well as conscious) in accounting for mood–judgment consistency. Here I am referring to the *mood-as-information (MAI)* analysis initially advanced by Norbert Schwarz and Gerald Clore.

In Chapter 1, I referred to Daryl Bem's self-perception notion: that when people are uncertain of how they feel about a given object or issue, they may infer what their attitude is by seeing how they have acted in regard to this object or issue. The Schwarz and Clore formulation is a variation on this theme, basically holding that we often evaluate other persons or issues on the basis of our self-perception – more particularly, by noting how we feel at the time when we think of these persons (or issues). As Schwarz and Clore put it, we take our mood as information about our assessment of the judged object or issue.[8]

To spell out this conception in more detail, the theory combines attribution ideas with other cognitive concepts. Dealing with those occasions in which people are emotionally aroused but are unclear as to what had caused this arousal, MAI assumes that their emotional state is apt to be attributed to a salient feature of the surrounding situation. If these persons are evaluating someone at the time, that judgmental target will be very noticeable and could well be seen as the cause of the person's ambiguous feelings. MAI then makes an assumption about the nature of the judges' thinking as they make their assessments: They presumably engage in heuristic information processing, that is, they use only a very small part of the available information because of low motivation and/or little capacity to think actively about what is happening. As a consequence, they follow a heuristic, or rule of thumb, in judging the target.[9] Attributing their mood to the target, the judges in a good mood believe their pleasant feeling means they have a favorable attitude toward the object or issue; if they're in a bad mood, their unpleasant feeling shows that they have an unfavorable view of the target.

One of the central features of this MAI analysis, of course, is the emphasis on mood attribution. One's feelings theoretically will not influence the judgment of a target unless this object or issue is seen as the source of the feelings. A study Schwarz and Clore reported in their original paper on this topic is frequently cited as evidence for their thesis. Consistent with the findings in other investigations, the authors showed that rainy weather tended to lessen people's general satisfaction with their lives. However, this gloomy day–induced depressing effect did not occur when the participants' attention was drawn to the weather conditions before they rated their life satisfaction. According to Schwarz and Clore, if the persons were not conscious of the bad weather, they attributed their bad feelings to their more salient thoughts about their life circumstances. Knowing they were somewhat depressed, they therefore believed their lives were not too good. By contrast, the people made aware of the unpleasant weather presumably blamed the rain for their bad feelings, and their judgments of their life circumstances were not affected.[10]

> An experiment carried out by Shin-Ho Ahn in Korea attests to the widespread applicability of MAI theorizing and shows how cognitive processes can intervene to influence the effect of mood on one's judgments. Adapting a procedure employed earlier by Schwarz, Strack, and their colleagues, Ahn manipulated his subjects' mood by placing them in either a pleasant- or an unpleasant-looking room. In one condition, no mention was made of the room's appearance. In another condition, the experimenter pointedly suggested that the room could be affecting their feelings, so that the participants obviously would be likely to attribute their mood to the room. In yet another condition, the experimenter not only suggested that the room's appearance could influence the participants' feelings but also asked them not to let the room's influence affect their answers to the questions that soon would be presented to them. Soon afterward, the participants rated how happy they were about various aspects of their lives, particularly their general life satisfaction.
>
> Figure 5.1 shows the average level of life satisfaction in each of the conditions. As you can see, in accord with MAI, the people placed in the pleasant room were more satisfied with their life circumstances than were their counterparts in the unpleasant room. This mood congruence was eliminated when the participants were made aware that the room could be affecting their feelings. There was even a trend in the opposite direction in this condition. Interestingly, the people asked to avoid letting the room affect their judgments (those in the "room mention + correct" condition) seemed to bend over backward in correcting for the room's possible influence; those persons in the unpleasant room in this condition were actually significantly happier about their lives than were the "no room mention" people also seated in the bad-looking room. I'll say more about this apparent correction effect later in the chapter.[11]

Although Schwarz and Clore do not say this, it's possible that the priming conception and the mood-as-information model are both valid – but under different conditions. The priming formulation assumes that one's feelings will automatically activate memories, concepts, bodily reactions, and ways of thinking, but it's now clear that cognitions can intervene to suppress – or, for that matter, intensify – these reactions. On the other hand, as I've already noted, and also said in Chapter 2, attribution analyses of affective states, such as MAI,

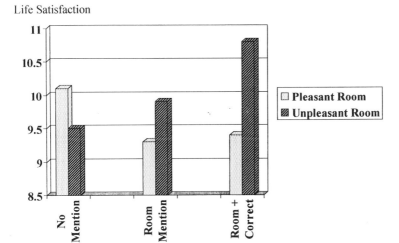

Life Satisfaction

Figure 5.1 Effect of mood cause awareness on life satisfaction (data from Ahn, 1997).

work best when the persons involved are somewhat uncertain as to what had aroused them. Also, given this model's emphasis on heuristic processing, MAI might also be especially pertinent when people are somewhat but not actively and carefully thoughtful about the situation they are in.[12]

In saying that the priming/associative network and MAI analyses hold under different conditions, I am basically taking a multiple-process view of how feelings influence judgments. This brings us to the best-known version of a multiple-process analysis, the *affect infusion model (AIM)* proposed by Joseph Forgas. In his initial AIM papers Forgas gave little explicit attention to the relatively automatic, association-based priming effect discussed earlier and emphasized the role of different kinds of cognitive processes. He argued that any one of four different information-processing strategies can intervene to determine what judgments people reach when they are in a particular affective state.

1. Direct access strategy: the simplest method of reaching a judgment, which involves direct retrieval of preexisting evaluations.
2. Motivated processing, in which "there are strong and specific motivational pressures for a particular judgmental outcome."
3. Heuristic processing, in which "when the target is simple or highly

typical, the personal relevance of the judgment is low, there are no specific motivational objectives . . . and the situation does not demand accuracy or detailed consideration."

4. Substantive processing, which involves fairly active thought and is especially likely to arise when the situation is problematic, such as "when the target is complex or atypical and the judge has no specific motivation to pursue [and] has adequate cognitive capacity. . . ."[13]

Feelings obviously have little if any influence on judgments when the first two strategies are pursued. The third strategy, heuristic processing, is the type of information processing assumed by the mood-as-information analysis and, as I said before, involves only a low level of thought rather than more extensive, more elaborate thinking. The fourth strategy, substantive processing, entails more active thinking. According to AIM, this is the kind of information processing in which "affect infusion" – and the resulting mood congruence – will be most pronounced.

Guided by his analysis, Forgas has carried out a number of experiments demonstrating that active thinking about the given issue (substantive processing) can promote affective congruence in judgments – when these evaluations aren't contrary to one's goals and prior commitments. In these interesting studies, after the experimenter placed his subjects in a good or bad mood, he exposed some of them to other persons who were fairly unusual in some way so that this novelty would excite the subjects' thinking about these individuals.

For example, in one investigation, after the mood was aroused, the participants looked at pictures of couples (each a young man and woman) and rated each pair on a series of evaluative scales. The couples were either matched in their physical attractiveness (both individuals good-looking or both unattractive) or were mismatched (one person attractive, the other not). On the basis of other research showing that many of us believe that the members of heterosexual couples are usually fairly similar (i.e., matched) in physical attractiveness, Forgas hypothesized that the subjects' feelings would have a greater influence on their assessments of the relatively atypical, mismatched couples than on their judgments of the more typical, matched ones.

Figure 5.2 summarizes the findings on the participants' ratings of how good the couples' relationships were. As you can see, the results are much as the investigator had predicted. In this case, as in Forgas's other studies along comparable lines, those people who were shown the atypical couples, and who therefore had presumably done the most thinking about these target persons (i.e., who had engaged in substantive processing), displayed the greatest level of mood congruency. Because they were very active mentally and had no prior opposing opinions of the target persons, the subjects' feelings could bring affectively consistent ideas into their consciousness relatively easily.[14]

Forgas has also conducted other experiments demonstrating how active, substantive information processing is promoted by problematic situations so that mood effects are enhanced. In these studies, Forgas reasonably assumed that serious interpersonal conflict is much more likely to prompt active thinking than is a less serious, emotionally neutral incident. Following his AIM analysis, he therefore expected feelings to have a greater impact on the assessments of serious compared with more trivial disputes. In one investigation, when students having a relationship with another person were asked how they would prefer to resolve a conflict with their partner, their desire to resolve the dispute cooperatively was affected by their mood primarily when the conflict was serious (e.g., a case of jealousy) rather than minor (e.g., a difference of opinion as to which TV program to watch). The participants' feelings had little impact on this preference for cooperation when the case was simple, but they made much more of a difference in the serious conflicts. In these more problematic cases, the happy persons had the greatest preference for cooperation, whereas the sad persons were least likely to want cooperative solutions. Whatever conflict solution the participants preferred, the happy persons formed their judgments fairly quickly, especially when the conflict

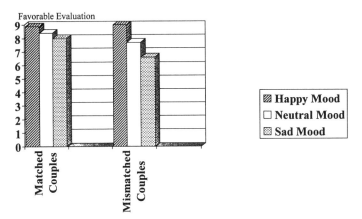

Figure 5.2 Evaluation of couples as a function of participants' mood and the couples' match in attractiveness (data from Forgas, 1993, Experiment 1). Scores are sums of two indices showing mood-match interaction.

was simple, whereas the sad persons facing a serious dispute were slower in making up their minds.[15]

Interestingly, even though Forgas is by no means an opponent of the mood-as-information analysis of affective congruence, he pointed out that some of his research findings are troublesome for MAI. According to the Schwarz–Clore formulation, he noted, "it is truncated, heuristic processing that is the major vehicle for mood congruence. . . . [However,] the present evidence for greater mood effects as a result of longer, more extensive processing is clearly inconsistent with the kind of fast, simple . . . judgmental processes implied by" [MAI].[16]

Don't take this statement to mean that mood congruency in judgments necessarily requires active, substantive processing of judgment-relevant information. In my view, basically in accord with Forgas's insistence on a multiprocess formulation, a number of psychological processes can lead to this effect, and each of the analyses summarized here is valid for some conditions. I believe that substantive information processing facilitates (or enhances) the feeling's influence on an evaluation in a congruent direction when opposing information isn't salient at the time and/or the judge isn't motivated to make an accurate assessment of the target and has no reason to believe that his or her affect-congruent inclination might be wrong.

Regulating the Influence of One's Mood in Order to Be Accurate

This research review shouldn't give you the impression that moods virtually always influence judgments in a congruent manner. Forgas's AIM theory says that affect won't "infuse" judgments when people are motivated to arrive at a particular kind of evaluation. Their wish to assess the target in a particular way will overcome whatever influence their mood might otherwise have. More generally, if people put their minds to it, they can regulate, even limit, the impact of their feelings on their evaluations. You saw earlier that negative affect sometimes has little if any effect, perhaps because of a desire to alleviate the unpleasant mood. What's more surprising, though, is that some studies have even seen results in the opposite direction – where those in a bad mood were actually more favorable to the individual they were evaluating than were their happy counterparts. Their assessments apparently were distorted, but in the direction away from their feelings' hedonic nature. Paradoxically, this seems most likely to happen when the judges are not only highly aware of their affective state but also want to be objective and accurate in their evaluations.

Several investigations in which the participants were primed to have either positive or negative ideas can help us account for these seemingly anomalous findings. In these experiments, persons exposed to a negative priming experience were actually more favorable to the individual being judged than were those given positive priming. For our purposes, these mood-incongruent results can be labeled a *contrast effect* in that they involve an apparent shift away from the priming experience. What's important for us here is that this incongruence/contrast was especially likely to arise when the research participants were highly aware of the particular condition that, they believed, could be influencing their judgments.[17]

A number of theorists have emphasized the role of this awareness in their explanations of the judgmental movement away from the influence source. All of them basically propose that the shift occurs when people realize that their feelings might bias their assessment of the target and that, in attempting to counter this possible distortion, they overcorrect.[18] Most of these schemes also assume, along with the priming/associative network formulation, that the feeling's influence is ordinarily toward affective congruence and that mental effort is required for correction to occur.

Another feature of these accounts is especially pertinent. Implicitly or explicitly, they generally contend that people's beliefs about how feelings bend judgments govern the bias-correction process. The theoretical model offered by Wegener and Petty emphasizes this point. Applied to the specific problem of mood effects, this model says that the individuals in an affective state correct for the way they think their feelings might bias their evaluations of some target when they (1) are aware of their feelings and (2) are motivated to arrive at an accurate assessment. The overcorrection presumably arises because most people's ideas about how feelings affect judgments exaggerate the degree of this influence.[19]

A series of experiments carried out in my laboratory attest to the importance of people's awareness of their feelings in the correction process. Consider, for example, an early study reported by me and Bartholomeu Troccoli:

Half of the female participants kept their nondominant arm extended for 6 minutes so that they experienced strong muscular discomfort, whereas the others rested their arm more comfortably on a nearby table. As they did this, they listened to a tape-recorded autobiographical statement supposedly made by a job applicant. At the end of this statement, half of the persons in each condition were led to be highly aware of their feelings by being asked to rate their mood at that time (Feelings Attention condition). The remaining women were distracted by being given an equally long innocuous word association task (Distracted condition). Then, immediately afterward, each participant responded to a questionnaire in which she rated how unpleasant her outstretched arm had felt and also indicated her impressions of the job applicant's personality on an adjective checklist.

A statistical analysis of the women's impressions of the applicant revealed that their prior degree of attention to their feelings interacted with the level of their felt displeasure to influence their judgments. As can be seen in Figure 5.3, those people whose attention had been diverted from their feelings displayed the usual affective congruence: The worse they felt, the more bad qualities they attributed to the job applicant. More important to us here, the figure also shows there was an affective incongruence when the participants had been made highly aware of their feelings (in the Feelings Attention condition). In this case, the greater their discomfort, the fewer the bad traits they said the job applicant possessed.[20]

This finding was fairly general. To give another example, when Jo and Berkowitz used the unobtrusive Strack, Martin, and Stepper facial expression procedure (mentioned before) to induce anger, we found that those people whose attention was diverted from their unpleasant feelings displayed the customary affective congruence in their judg-

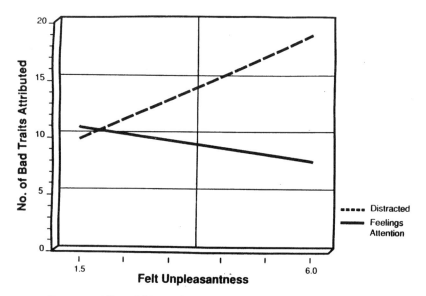

Figure 5.3 Effect of felt unpleasantness on the impression of a target person as affected by the direction of attention (based on regression analysis of data from Berkowitz & Troccoli, 1990).

ment of the target person. But by contrast, and as in the experiment just summarized, the participants made aware of their anger exhibited the incongruent contrast effect; aware of their feelings, the angrier they were, the fewer the undesirable traits they attributed to the target.[21]

It's important to recognize that the contrast effect obtained under attention to feelings is an overcorrection. In trying to eliminate the possible judgment-distorting influence of their negative feelings, the people in these experiments went too far. The Berkowitz and Troccoli study I summarized suggests just such a process. Recall that the participants in this investigation were judging a job applicant. However, before they gave their impressions of this person, the subjects in one condition were told that an expert selection committee had evaluated the applicant and had unanimously approved her for the job, whereas subjects in the other condition were told that the committee had unanimously rejected her. Assuming that the participants' negative feelings had primed negative thoughts in them, this means that the experts' judgment of the job applicant was inconsistent with the participants' negative inclinations if the experts had approved the applicant but was consistent with the experts' negative views if these people had rejected the applicant. If there was any overcorrection effect, it should have been displayed by those in the former, Inconsistent condition; aware of their unpleasant feelings, they should also have been highly conscious that their negative attitude toward the applicant was at variance with the experts' judgment and probably was wrong.

In order to test this reasoning, I first established baseline-level judgment scores: the mean judgment made under low physical discomfort by those attending to their feelings and by those whose attention was distracted. This was the judgment level to be expected in that group when its members had no marked negative inclination toward the applicant. I then determined what effect high physical discomfort had on the judgments of (1) those paying attention to their feelings and (2) those who were distracted by calculating each of these uncomfortable group's difference from their particular low-discomfort–baseline group score. In this case, scores above the baseline level were more hostile to the target, whereas scores below the baseline were more favorable. Figure 5.4 reports the mean difference-from-baseline score for the people experiencing severe physical discomfort under attention to feelings or when their attention had been diverted away from themselves. As you can see, the people who were highly conscious of their unpleasant feelings had evidently bent over backward not to be unfavorable to the target. Aware of the possible biasing influence of their negative feelings, they had evidently overcorrected for this bias, but primarily when their negative attitude was inconsistent with the experts' views, so that their inclination might well be wrong.

Keep in mind, though, that this exaggerated compensation for possible bias came about because of a desire to make accurate judgments. There were indications of this attitude in Ahn's Korean experiment summarized earlier. If you look at Figure 5.1 again, you'll see that when the people in the unpleasant room were told that the room's appearance might affect their opinions and that they should not let this happen, they seemed to overcorrect for the possible distorting influence – to such an extent that they reported the highest level of life satisfaction. Another study from my laboratory provides even better evidence of the role of accuracy motivation, but it also shows that this exaggerated correction requires a high level of mental activity. If there was nothing unusual about the judgmental task, so that the assessments could be made fairly easily, the participants' mood affected their evaluations in an affectively congruent manner; the happy persons regarded the target individuals more favorably than did their sad counterparts. However, we found a contrast effect when the judgmental task was relatively unusual, so that the participants had to think more

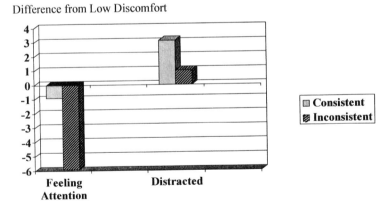

Difference from Low Discomfort

Figure 5.4 Evaluation of a job applicant under high discomfort affected by attention direction and consistency with expert judgments (data from Berkowitz & Troccoli, 1990). Scores are differences from the same condition under low discomfort.

about their assessments. But this apparent overcorrection was greatest when the participants were asked to be careful and accurate in their evaluations. Prompted to think about the relatively unusual task they were given and wanting to be right in their judgments, the people in this condition evidently bent over backward in compensating for the possible biasing influence of their existing mood.[22]

An obvious question here has to do with the hedonic nature of the judgment-biasing mood. Most of the findings just reported occurred under negative affect. Would positive feelings give rise to the same effects? The Wegener and Petty analysis suggests that the answer is "yes." Theoretically, as long as we think that our affective state can distort our judgment, whether this experience is pleasant or unpleasant, and want to be accurate in our assessment, we should attempt to correct for this possible bias. This is just what was found in the last experiment I mentioned, in which we varied the participants' desire to be accurate. When these people had been asked to make accurate judgments and saw the unusual, problematic targets, they overcorrected for the possible distorting influence of their mood whether they had been made happy or sad.

Nevertheless, negative affect might be especially likely to produce this overcorrection effect, particularly if it is not too intense. Several studies indicate that unpleasant feelings often lead to inward-directed attention.[23] As a consequence, there could be greater awareness of the negative affect and, thus, a relatively stronger activation of the "supervisory" psychological system that produces the judgmental overcorrection. Again, however, it's important to note that the research we examined involved only weak or moderately intense affect. Exceedingly strong feelings may have such a powerful influence on one's thoughts and inclinations that they overcome whatever ideals one holds regarding the necessity of fair and objective assessments. Indeed, in the absence of a desire to be accurate, attention to these intense feelings might even lead to greater affective congruence in judgments.

Mood Influences on Information Processing and Decision Making

Suppose that you're the head of a consulting firm seeking to provide clients with innovative solutions to their problems. Wanting to foster your employees' creativity and hoping to get the best work possible from them, you go out of your way to make the employees happy and occasionally even use humor to put them in a positive mood. Is this really a good policy? Does happiness indeed promote creativity and improve problem solving? Are people likely to make better decisions when they're feeling good than when they're in a negative mood?

I'm afraid there are no easy answers to these questions. As is true of so much of psychology – and of life – we have to say "It depends."

Good Thinking in Good Moods

Alice Isen and a number of other investigators have tended to emphasize the benefits of positive feelings, although they also point to the complexities and limiting conditions. Highlighting the desirable consequences, Isen has observed:

> *All else being equal, positive affect tends to promote exploration and enjoyment of new ideas and possibilities, as well as new ways of looking at things. Therefore, people who are feeling good may be alert to possibilities and may solve problems both more efficiently and more thoroughly than [nonhappy] controls.*[24]

Isen based this summary on the results of a large number of experiments, many conducted by herself and her collaborators and some carried out by others, showing that good moods often broaden people's thinking. In several of her studies, for example, happiness widened the range of stimuli that were grouped together in the same conceptual category, whereas sadness had little if any effect. However, this enlarged conception occurred only when the matters being considered were positive or at least neutral in nature, but not when they were hedonically negative. And so, in comparison to the people in a bad mood, those who were feeling good were more apt to conceive of "bartenders" as examples of the positively toned category "nurturant people," but they were not more likely than their bad-mood counterparts to believe that a "genius" belonged in the negative category "unstable people." Their pleasant feelings evidently led to wider interpretations of the neutral and positive ideas they were considering (e.g., "bartenders" and "nurturant people"), but they did not broaden the interpretations of negative concepts (such as "unstable people").

Other experiments testify to the way positive feelings promote creativity. To give you an example, in one of Isen's studies the participants were asked to solve a problem frequently used in psychological investigations of problem solving: They were given a candle, a box of tacks, and a book of matches, and were told to attach the candle to the wall in such a way that it would burn without dripping wax on the floor. The solution requires thinking of one of the items, the box, in a new and different way: Empty the box of its tacks; use one of the tacks to attach the open box to the wall; and then stand the candle on one of the box's sides so that it could be lit without dripping wax onto the floor. The people made to feel good in this study did much better on this problem than did those who were left in a neutral mood. In another investigation, the happy participants in a study of complicated face-to-face bargaining achieved better outcomes than did their neutral-mood controls; they not only were more likely to come to an agreement with the other party in the negotiations, but also were more apt to achieve the optimal agreement possible in that situation, presumably because their pleasant affect facilitated new ideas, promoted the ability to integrate these ideas in novel ways, and increased innovative problem solving.[25]

For Isen, pleasant feelings lead to these and other benefits mainly because positive affect brings to mind (i.e., primes) a wider and more diverse range of ideas and recollections than does negative affect or a neutral mood. Happy persons therefore tend to see more aspects of the matters they are considering and have a broader range of associations to this material. As a consequence, Isen said, they may be cognitively more flexible, and also more interested in novelty and variety, than persons not in a good mood.

All this is not to say that positive affect will always have these positive outcomes. Whether these beneficial results are realized or not depends to a great extent on the nature of the task and the situation one is in. How interesting and/or enjoyable the task seems to be is particularly important. According to Isen, as well as several other psychologists, people who are feeling good are often motivated to maintain their pleasant feelings.[26] They might therefore ignore assignments that threaten to reduce their good mood. I've already noted that positive affect often fails to promote extensive and varied thoughts about negatively toned matters, much as if there is a mental avoidance of the hedonically negative stimuli. Somewhat similarly, when we're happy we might also be especially inclined to turn away mentally from tasks that appear to be unpleasant, boring, or very difficult because this kind of activity could lessen our pleasant mood –

unless we know full well that it's to our direct benefit to succeed on these jobs. Furthermore, if we're feeling good, we're also likely to avoid taking risks that seem to have only a small chance of success, again because the failure could eradicate our happy mood.

Does Happiness Promote Mental Laziness?

Even though Isen has spelled out the factors limiting the benefits of positive affect, she believes that good feelings, by and large, have good effects on creativity, problem solving, and decision making. However, to complicate the picture even further, social psychologists have obtained research findings that seem to contradict Isen's general argument. I'll introduce these findings by summarizing an intriguing experiment by Bodenhausen, Kramer, and Susser.

> *In the first of a series of studies they reported, the undergraduate participants were first placed in either a positive or neutral mood and then were read a case description of how a student on another campus was suspected of having misbehaved. Their task was to judge this person's guilt. For half of the participants the supposed offender was charged with beating up a roommate; for the others, the alleged misbehavior was cheating on a classroom examination. But the identity of the accused was varied. In some instances (in both offenses) he was said to be an Hispanic; in the others, he was an athlete on the university's track and field team. What's important about these descriptions is that the students at this university held stereotypes about these two groups, maintaining that Hispanics were easily aroused to aggression and that athletes were likely to cheat on difficult exams. The identifications were also so arranged that the misbehavior was sometimes in accord with the stereotype (the aggressive offense was committed by the Hispanic student or the athlete was accused of cheating), but at other times it was not (the Hispanic was charged with cheating or the athlete was accused of the aggression).*
>
> *Figure 5.5 shows the mean judgment of the accused individual's guilt under each of the experimental conditions. You can see that the stereotypes had no influence on the guilt ratings when the participants were in a neutral mood. However, their judgment of the individual's likely guilt was more strongly affected by their stereotype of the group to which he belonged if they were happy at the time. They were harsher toward the suspect if the stereotype accounted for the offense than if it did not. Rather than producing careful thought, their positive mood evidently influenced them to follow the simplified conception of the individual's group somewhat automatically.*[27]

Other research results also point to the possible negative consequences of positive feelings, this time in problem solving. For example, when the people in one study were given a series of syllogism

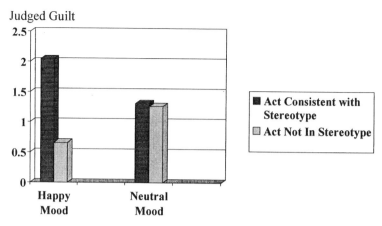

Figure 5.5 Influence of a stereotype on the judged likelihood of the accused's guilt as affected by mood (from Bodenhausen, Kramer & Susser, 1994, Experiment 1; adapted from Figure 1).

problems to solve, those who had been put in a good mood (through the use of humor) did significantly worse than their neutral-mood counterparts. The researcher believed his findings qualified but didn't really contradict the notion that good mood improves performance. Positive affect leads to better outcomes, he held, on tasks requiring the generation of new ideas but to poorer performance when the tasks necessitate careful analysis of several possible solutions. Of course, someone who wanted to extend Isen's thesis broadly could say that the syllogism puzzles might not have been interesting or important enough to engage those who were feeling good. However, the investigator emphasized the possible downside of positive affect: Because of their pleasant feelings, the study participants were unwilling to expend much effort, even mental effort, on their assignment. Rather than think deeply and carefully about the matter at hand, they had presumably engaged in relatively superficial heuristic information processing. Consistent with this argument, the happy persons in this experiment typically were more likely than their neutral-mood counterparts to choose unqualified, very general solutions to their problems rather than qualified and less sweeping, more detailed answers, and also tended to spend less time on this assignment. Other investigators have also reported that positive affect often leads to relatively fast decision making, perhaps because of a fairly casual attitude toward the task.[28]

Several researchers have now accepted the idea that positive moods foster cursory heuristic processing. Norbert Schwarz and Herbert Bless helped popularize this conception of the effect of positive moods in an intriguing paper entitled "Happy and Mindless, But Sad and Smart?"[29]

You'll recall that the mood-as-information formulation advanced by Schwarz and Clore contends that people often consult their feelings in deciding how to evaluate a given object or issue. Theoretically, because they misattribute their affect to the judgmental target, they believe that, say, a positive feeling means that they have a positive attitude toward the target, and they judge it accordingly. Schwarz and Bless extended this line of thought, stating that we use our feelings to decide whether the situation confronting us is safe or not. A pleasant mood presumably indicates that the situation is safe, whereas negative feelings are taken as a sign that the situation is problematic.

Schwarz and Bless then went on to argue that if persons think their personal world is okay, they tend to prefer simple heuristics over more effortful, detail-oriented, and analytic modes of information processing. On the other hand, if they feel bad and think they are threatened by negative outcomes, they will be motivated to alter the situation. Accomplishing a change requires a careful analysis of the situation and an examination of the possible alternatives before them. Unpleasant affect thus triggers modes of thought that are likely to solve the problem successfully. But although they engage in detailed analytic processing of information, they may also seek to avoid risks and novel ideas because the situation is already problematic enough.[30] (As you can see, in this last-mentioned point, Schwarz and Bless basically agree with Isen that positive affect is more likely than negative affect to foster innovative thinking and creativity.)

Some interesting studies of intergroup relations illustrate how this extension of the mood-as-information formulation can be applied. For example, in one experiment reported by Forgas and Fiedler, happy people were far more likely than their sad counterparts to discriminate between ingroup and outgroup members in allocating rewards. The happy persons favored others in their own group over outsiders even though group membership was established on the basis of a very trivial criterion (estimates of an object's size) and the ingroup people were no better known than the outsiders. Feeling good, they evidently relied greatly on the simple heuristic cue of group membership in dispensing rewards. The Bodenhausen team interpreted the stereotype results I summarized earlier by referring to positive mood-engendered heuristic processing. In agreement with Schwarz and Bless, they said that happy people are not motivated to engage in cognitive effort unless the tasks have direct bearing on their own well-being or enjoyment. Not wanting to analyze their problem carefully, they therefore are apt to rely on their stereotypes (or other simple heuristic principles) in making their judgments.[31]

Although this is a digression, I will also make another point here about the influence of feelings on stereotype usage. I have noted on several occasions throughout this book that it's sometimes advisable to differentiate among types of positive or negative affect. Research by Bodenhausen, Sheppard, and Kramer supports this observation by indicating that sadness may well promote the analytic processing postulated by the mood-as-information model, but that angry people are more likely to engage in heuristic processing even though sadness and anger are both negative states. Using the experimental procedure employed in the other Bodenhausen stereotype research described earlier, the investigators found that their angry participants tended to apply their stereotypes of a person's group in judging his likely guilt, whereas the sad participants tended to avoid applying the stereotype.[32] All unpleasant feelings apparently aren't alike in fostering relatively detailed analytic thinking.

Anyway, theoretical formulations frequently change in science, even in regard to affective influences. Bless recently modified the mood-as-information analysis of how positive feelings affect information processing. He now maintains, as before, that people take their pleasant feelings to be a signal that the situation they are in is safe. However, instead of holding that the good mood creates mental laziness, he now proposes that positive affect, as a safety signal, tends to activate "general knowledge structures"; that is, happy persons will employ their general conceptions of the situation before them in thinking about what is happening. These general mental representations usually served them well in the past and are relied on to be appropriate at present. On the other side, negative affect is again said to be an indication that the situation is problematic, but therefore, Bless now contends, the unpleasant feeling lessens reliance on general conceptions. People in a bad mood presumably will think that their usual routines and ways of thinking may be inadequate under the present uncertain circumstances and instead, will focus on the specific details of the situation.[33]

Bless, Clore, Schwarz, and their associates provided support for this knowledge structure interpretation in a series of experiments. One of these is especially informative.

> *After either a happy, sad, or neutral mood was induced in the student partici- pants, they listened to two tape-recorded stories while working on a secondary but distracting task. The stories were about two familiar activities (riding on a tramway and making a telephone call from a public phone booth). Some of the details mentioned in the stories were typical of these familiar activities (in that they usually existed when people rode a tram or phoned from a public telephone booth), but others were atypical. When the tape recording ended, the students were given a brief assignment to dissipate the happy or sad mood that had been induced earlier, and then were asked to say whether each of the details in a list presented to them had actually been mentioned in the stories they heard.*
>
> *The participants' answers were in keeping with Bless's theorizing. The happy persons were more likely than any of the others to say that they had heard typical details, whether these details had actually appeared in the pre- sented story or not. Their reception of the information had been greatly influ- enced by their conception of the kind of situation involved in the stories – to such an extent that they believed they had heard information that actually had not been presented. The sad participants, on the other hand, were least likely to report hearing both the presented and nonpresented typical details, as if their encoding of the stories was least affected by their general knowledge of the given situations. The sad people had a very different pattern when asked about the atypical details. In this case, their reports of having heard the actually presented unusual details were the most accurate of the three mood groups. Because they weren't greatly influenced by their general mental representation of the situations, they were fairly good at detecting the information that was outside this conception.*
>
> *Other findings in this experiment contradict the notion of a happiness- engendered reduction in information processing. When the researchers scored the participants' performance on the secondary distracting task they worked on while the stories were presented, they found that the happy persons had done significantly better than either the sad or neutral groups. As the investigators concluded, "By relying on a script [their conception of the situations], happy participants freed up [cognitive] resources that could be applied to the second- ary task, which resulted in improved performance.*[34]

The study authors do not regard their current formulation as very different from the idea that positive affect fosters simplified heuristic processing. Indeed, to a considerable extent the positions are identical – with one important exception. Heuristics, after all, are highly gener- alized and relatively simple rules of thumb concerning what is likely to be an appropriate or effective way of thinking and acting under particular circumstances, and this is just what Bless and his colleagues mean by the concept of general knowledge structure. When the happy persons employed group stereotypes in Bodenhausen's experiments, they used a general way of thinking – a heuristic/general knowledge – about the group.

But there is an important difference between the present formulation and the earlier analysis offered by Schwarz and Bless. Whereas the original MAI thesis proposed that positive affect leads to a reduction in cognitive effort, the newer general-knowledge notion doesn't necessarily make such an assumption. In fact, Bless's discussions suggest that happiness does not lessen one's motivation to process available information. Further investigation is clearly advisable here.

Finally, it's important to note, Bless, Schwarz, and their associates do not challenge Isen's demonstrations that positive affect can promote creativity. However, whereas Isen held that pleasant feelings foster innovative thinking because they activate a broad range of ideas, Bless and colleagues attribute this benefit largely to the positive mood-induced activation of general knowledge structures.

> *In addition to allowing more efficient processing, general knowledge structures serve . . . to enrich the stimulus information at hand and to provide a basis for making inferences that go beyond the information given. . . . Thus, in dealing with a specific task, individuals may draw inferences and generate new concepts based on their prior general knowledge.*[35]

I do not question this possibility. My guess, however, is that both views are right. People's general knowledge about certain situations undoubtedly serves as a basis for inferences about new forms of these situations. But there is also ample reason to say that positive affect primes a wide variety of positive ideas that can help deal with these occurrences.

6. Feelings, Persuasion, and Motivation

This chapter will deal largely with persuasion: how people's feelings influence their acceptance of the proposals communicated to them. You will see that this matter is more complicated, and perhaps more surprising, than many readers expect. Because the audience members' response to the message depends to a great extent on their thoughts about the information they receive, this survey will extend the examination of the impact of mood on information processing that was introduced in Chapter 3 and continued in Chapter 5.

The first section of this review will be concerned mainly with the role of positive affect. Contrary to the widespread belief that most persons "lead a life of quiet desperation" or are, at best, grudgingly resigned to the ill fortune fate has dealt them, research has consistently demonstrated that the overwhelming majority of people in most societies are actually fairly happy.[1] This being the case, we should ask whether this general happiness can have less than optimal consequences. And so, in considering how feelings can affect persuasibility, we will be especially interested in the notion, introduced earlier, that positive affect often promotes a cursory, somewhat simplified style of thinking. In this connection, we will continue our examination, begun in the previous chapter, of why pleasant feelings frequently have this effect. Chapter 5 discussed the MAI explanation. Here we will take up two other accounts, one emphasizing motivation and the other focusing on limitations on cognitive capacity.

The chapter will conclude with a brief examination of the role of negative affect. We will look at such matters as how the message recipients' unpleasant feelings may mediate their reactions to proposals and also how convincing are communications that frighten the audience.

Good Feelings and Persuasion

To start our discussion of how people's positive mood can influence their acceptance of proposals, imagine the following situation:

> *The coming dinner meeting was very important to the political candidate. Her efforts to win her party's nomination in the approaching election had not been proceeding as well as she had anticipated, and she was now short of the funds she needed for television advertising and the other substantial expenses modern political campaigns inevitably incur. This evening's session with the city's most prominent businesspeople could be her salvation. If she could convince them to provide the financial support she required, her cause might yet be saved. The candidate had gone all out in preparing for the meeting. Wanting to put her guests in the best possible mood, she had ordered the fanciest dinner and the most expensive wines the hotel could provide. She had also worked hard on the speech she would deliver. The talk would begin informally, with some of her best jokes, but then would become more serious, first demonstrating her patriotism and great concern for the nation and then explaining what she would do to solve many of the country's most pressing domestic problems. She had thought of everything, she believed. The evening had to be successful.*

Had the political candidate indeed thought of everything? She clearly believed it was vital to put her guests in a pleasant mood before she made her speech. If her guests felt good, she was convinced, they would think highly of her and be susceptible to her arguments. The politician certainly wasn't alone in making this supposition. Countless advertisers and public speakers have long assumed that their audiences would be more easily persuaded if they were feeling happy at the time, and there undoubtedly is some merit to this widely held belief. But does a good mood always smooth the way to persuasion?

Direct Influence of Feelings on Susceptibility to Persuasion

A generation or so ago, most social psychologists would have said that our politician was correct in trying to put her wealthy guests in a good mood. Studies dating back a half century or more typically reported that happy persons were more susceptible to persuasion than were their less happy counterparts. Whether the positive feelings were induced by free food, enjoyable music, pleasant odors, or signs of anothers' approval, the research participants who were led to feel good at the time were especially likely to accept the views advocated by a message sent to them.[2,3]

Razran's classic demonstrations of this effect suggest that our hypothetical politician was right in treating her guests to a delicious meal. He first had his students evaluate a variety of political slogans (such as "America for Americans"). Later, over a series of sessions, he presented the slogans again, along with a number of new statements to confuse the participants' memories. Some statements were shown while the students were eating a free lunch the researcher provided, whereas others were presented with no accompanying food. When Razran then looked at the students' current opinions, he found that the slogans that had been presented while the participants were eating had, on the whole, gained more approval than the statements not linked with food. In another part of his research, Razran piped foul odors into the room as the slogans were encountered. This time there was a drop in the students' liking for the statements.[4]

Razran and other psychologists of this period interpreted these observations in terms of classical conditioning: Over the repeated sessions, the feeling aroused in the situation (for example, in the first case, the pleasure produced by eating the lunch) had become associated with the particular slogans that were salient at that time. As a consequence, these statements themselves tended to activate this feeling and thus met with greater approval. My discussion of classical conditioning in Chapter 1 pointed out that this kind of learning can affect how people feel about a wide variety of situations, objects, and issues. (Keep in mind, though, that the conditioning can be overridden by already established and strongly held attitudes.[5] The pleasant food and humorous jokes our hypothetical politician lavished on her guests wouldn't improve their approval of her if their existing opinions were already clear and definite.)

Still, even though classical conditioning is a well-documented phenomenon, I noted in Chapter 5 that many social psychologists prefer to use cognitive rather than associationistic terms in talking about findings such as those reported by Razran. The MAI analysis introduced by Schwarz and Clore is a favorite alternative. As you'll remember from my discussion of this formulation in Chapter 5, MAI holds that people are very likely to employ their present affective experience as information regarding how they feel about salient features of the situation before them.[6] However, as you'll also recall, the theory maintains that this inference will be drawn only when the persons believe that these particular situational features had caused their feelings (that is, when they attribute their current mood to this particular individual or issue). And so, according to MAI, if our political candidate's guests were in a good mood because of the delicious meal they had eaten, they would regard the candidate favorably only if they attributed their pleasant feelings to her rather than to the food and wine; they presumably had to think, at some low level of consciousness, that it was the politician who had made them feel good.

Why Does Positive Affect Often Foster Heuristic Processing?

As you know from the previous chapter, Schwarz and Bless, and later Bless, Clore, Schwarz, and their associates, extended the MAI analysis to suggest how information processing can be affected by one's mood. The formulation basically maintains that when people consult their feelings, they regard their pleasant feelings as a signal that all is right, but they take unpleasant affect to mean that the situation confronting them is problematic. In the latter case, the threat of possible negative outcomes presumably motivates a fairly careful consideration of the situation so that relatively detailed, analytic (or substantive or systematic) information processing is promoted. On the other hand, if their world is okay, they theoretically will engage in relatively simplified information processing. Whether this latter processing mode is termed *heuristic processing* (as in the 1991 model) or a reliance on *general knowledge structures* (as in the later version by Bless and his colleagues), the people doing it use only a small part of the available information.[7]

All this has clear implications for those who seek to persuade others. Consider, for example, how diligent the politician had been in preparing the speech she delivered. She had tried hard to marshall the best possible arguments supporting her solutions to the nation's problems. Well, we're told by MAI, and a number of supporting experiments, that the quality of the communicator's message may not matter very much when the recipients are in a good mood. The political candidate's happy guests might have accepted weaker arguments just as well as strong ones.

> A study conducted by Bless, Bohner, Schwarz, and Strack suggests just such an effect.[8] The female university students in this investigation were first placed in either a positive or a negative mood. After this, and supposedly as part of a second study investigating a totally different matter, they heard a tape-recorded

message offering either strong or weak arguments for a proposal to increase student fees at the university. (I should point out here that the participants were asked to focus on the language used in the proposal, so they weren't attending fully to the quality of the arguments. I'll soon indicate why this is important.) At the end of the message, the women expressed their opinions on this issue.

When Bless and his colleagues later examined the subjects' reported opinions, they found, as shown in Figure 6.1, that the women had been influenced by the communication they heard – but not in the simple way our political candidate would have expected. In line with MAI and the results obtained by other researchers, the quality of the message's arguments didn't matter to those who were in a happy mood. You can see in the figure that regardless of whether the fee proposal was well or poorly supported, they now favored an increase in student fees to a greater degree than the neutral-mood people in a control group who hadn't received the communication.

Interestingly, as Figure 6.1 also indicates, it was only those who were led to be somewhat unhappy at the time who were affected by the arguments' quality. Apparently because these negative-mood persons had engaged in analytic processing and had given relatively careful consideration to the strength of the supporting arguments, they were now especially likely to favor the proposal when the arguments had been good, but they accepted the proposal less than did the happy subjects when the arguments were only weak.

Our main question here is why the happy persons in this study failed to give much weight to the merits of the arguments. More generally, why is it that a good mood often leads to truncated, simplified information processing? I'll briefly outline three answers that

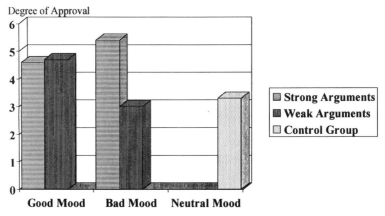

Figure 6.1 Approval of a proposal as a function of mood and argument strength for those not paying special attention to the arguments (data from Bless et al., 1990, Experiment 1).

have been offered. But keep in mind throughout this discussion that we're not dealing with the case in which there are pressures to think deeply about the issue at hand.

We're already familiar with the explanation provided by MAI theory. It holds, you'll recall, that people who are feeling good don't carefully consider the information available to them because they are content with the surrounding situation. A second account traces the superficial information processing to an overloaded mind. Diane Mackie and Leila Worth proposed this alternative by generalizing from the notion of affect priming. Along with Isen (who was discussed in Chapter 5) and associative network theory, they suggested that positive affect tends to prime positive material stored in memory. Because most people have many more positively tinged memories and ideas than negatively linked ones, their good mood presumably will bring more thoughts and recollections to mind than will sadness or even a neutral mood. Those who are feeling good, then, theoretically will have much of their attention and thought taken up by the ideas and memories flooding into their consciousness, and they will therefore have less cognitive capacity available for other information processing tasks.

In the Mackie and Worth experiment, the persons who were feeling good at the time accepted a persuasive message primarily because of the communicator's expertise rather than because of the quality of his arguments, but only when they had to read and consider the message rather quickly. As the investigators saw it, the time pressure restricted the participants' ability to bring all their relevant cognitions to bear on the issue at hand. Their happy mood theoretically reduced their attentional/cognitive capacity even further so that they relied more on the salient heuristic cue, the communicator's expertise, than did their neutral-mood counterparts. By contrast, if the participants had as much time as they wanted to read and think about the communication, the happy persons presumably were better able to process the available information adequately, and therefore used information other than the communicator's expertise in judging the merits of his proposal.[9]

However plausible this cognitive-capacity interpretation might be, the revised version of MAI proposed by Bless, Clore, Schwarz, and their associates questions the Mackie–Worth thesis. These investigators showed that happy people's attentional capacity is not necessarily restricted. Even when they use their somewhat simplified general beliefs in interpreting the situation, they are able to register other, more peripheral information as well.[10]

Preserving One's Pleasant Mood

The last explanation for the good mood–induced cursory, heuristic processing rests on the idea that people are motivated to preserve whatever pleasant feelings they are experiencing at the time. As Isen and Simmonds (mentioned in the last chapter) put it, people don't want to incur any costs, even psychological ones, that might lessen their good mood. Thinking requires some energy expenditure, and, as such, could conceivably dampen whatever pleasant affect they are experiencing.[11]

Wegener and Petty are now the best-known exponents of this line of thought, especially in regard to the effectiveness of persuasive communications. They noted that many of the studies revealing happiness-engendered cursory information processing had exposed their subjects to messages that were basically negative in tone: The communications advocated, for example, such things as an increase in student fees or the establishment of additional comprehensive exams, or they talked about damage done by acid rain. Might it not be, Wegener and Petty asked, that the happy persons in these investigations had refrained from thinking a great deal about these unpleasant matters because they wanted to preserve their existing good mood? Maybe these people hadn't really thought casually about the information before them but had only been trying to keep from feeling bad.[12]

Referring to their conception as a *hedonic contingency analysis,* Wegener and Petty then went further and raised a possibility contrary to MAI. If there is indeed a widespread proclivity to protect one's positive mood, there could also be a readiness to scrutinize the hedonic contingencies in the immediate situation, that is, to examine what implications the available information and possible actions have for one's affective state. Furthermore, they proposed, this kind of readiness could even prompt careful analytic processing of the relevant information. What we have here, then, is a different view of the cognitive consequences of positive affect: Rather than promoting the truncated heuristic processing postulated by MAI, under some conditions pleasant feelings might give rise to relatively active and careful analyses.

For Wegener and Petty, "positive-mood enhancement of [information] processing should be most likely when message recipients expect the content of the message to be uplifting [i.e., positive in nature], whereas positive-mood processing reduction would be most likely when the content of the message is expected to be depressing." To test this reasoning, the theorists carried out a clever experiment designed to demonstrate that people's moods interact with their expectation of the communication's content to determine how carefully they attend to the message's proposals.[13]

Supposedly because they had to evaluate some articles that were given to them, the participants read two articles, the first one intended to place them in either a happy or a sad mood and the second being a persuasive communication saying that students should work for the university in exchange for tuition credits. For some of the students the arguments supporting the proposal were strong and highly credible, whereas for the others the arguments were weak. More important for us here, for half of the subjects the title of the second article framed the communication in a positive manner so that, as they began reading, they expected a positive message content. (The article title was "Students Pleased with Tuition Plan That Gives Them a Break.") In the remaining cases the title's framing was negative and led to a negative expectation ("Students Upset with Tuition Plan That Places New Burdens on Them"). However, within each argument-strength condition, the arguments used in behalf of the proposal were the same, regardless of the introductory framing.

The research question, of course, was whether there would be differences among the mood groups in how much they accepted the proposed work-exchange-for-tuition plan. Figure 6.2 indicates that differences occurred and that they were in accord with the researchers' predictions. By and large, the happy students did take cognizance of the arguments' quality, but primarily when the communication was framed positively so that they expected positive content. In this case, they evidently thought deeply and carefully enough to consider how good the arguments were. On the other hand, the quality of these arguments didn't matter very much when the communication was framed negatively. Expecting a negative message, these happy persons might have processed the communicated information only superficially in order to protect their pleasant mood.

Finally, the figure shows that the sad students were more persuaded by strong rather than weak arguments when they expected an unhappy message. This finding seems consistent with Bower's associative network conception discussed in earlier chapters. Being in an unhappy mood, they could have given particular attention to material they believed would be affectively congruent with their feelings.

Mood as Information About One's Performance at Work

An intriguing line of research initiated by Leonard Martin and his associates suggests that there may indeed be frequent attempts to

Message Acceptance

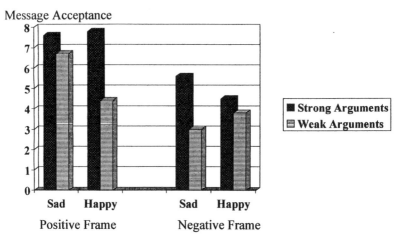

Figure 6.2 Attitude affected by message framing, mood, and arguments quality (data from Wegener et al., 1995, Experiment 2).

maintain one's positive mood – and also provides additional support for the self-perception theorizing in the mood-as-information formulation. Building on MAI, Martin's conception, which he terms a *mood-as-input* analysis, holds that people can use their feelings to decide what their attitude is toward the work they are doing at the time, even when the affective state existed before the work began.[14]

Here's one of his experiments. After the research participants were placed in either a happy or a sad mood, they were given a job (to list all the names of birds they could think of). The second experimental variation had to do with the participants' "stop rules." In one case, they were told to end the list whenever they felt like stopping. In the other condition, they were told to continue with the task as long as they enjoyed it; if they didn't like it, they should stop.

How long the participants worked on their assignment was a function both of their mood and of their stop rule. If they had been told to quit when they felt like stopping, the happy persons halted sooner and listed fewer birds than did those who were sad. Although this wasn't the researchers' interpretation, it seems to me that the former might have believed they could better preserve their good mood by not working too hard on the boring task. However, under the Enjoyment stop rule, those who were feeling good worked longer and came up with more names than did their counterparts. The experimenter's reference to work enjoyment in this condition evidently had made pleasure a highly salient goal. In thinking of their degree of liking for the task, the happy participants evidently inferred that their positive mood was a sign that they liked the work, and they then acted in accord with this inference.

Other research by other investigators corroborates the findings of Martin and colleagues. Given a somewhat different task, when the participants in this study were told only that they could stop at any time, those induced to be happy stopped working sooner than either their sad or neutral mood counterparts. Again, this pattern was reversed when their attention was focused on whether they enjoyed the job; those experiencing good feelings spent much more time on the assignment and did more work than those in the sad and neutral mood groups.[15]

In both studies, then, the happy participants might have tried to maintain their positive mood, but they did this in different ways. If these people had no reason to believe they were enjoying their work, they evidently tried to preserve their good feelings by escaping from the onerous situation as best they could – in this case, by not working hard and stopping soon. However, if they thought the work was fairly pleasant (theoretically because, in being highly conscious of the goal of task enjoyment, they attributed their good mood to the task), they may have attempted to enhance this positive feeling by sticking to the job and working hard.

Happiness Doesn't Always Foster Casual Heuristic Processing

All in all, then, happy persons apparently are often motivated to maintain their good mood. Seeking to preserve their positive affect, they may at times engage in relatively simplified, casual thinking, as we've seen, because they believe it's too much bother to carry out careful, analytic information processing (and perhaps also, as MAI suggests, because they're complacent about the situation they're in). However, this doesn't mean that they will always be mentally lazy, so to speak. Happy people can pay attention to the details of what is happening and think analytically about these details when they believe it is advisable to do so.

There are indications of this in the research by Bless, Bohner, and their colleagues cited earlier in this section about positive affect and heuristic processing.[16] You'll remember that this previous discussion focused on what happened when the participants were somewhat distracted, so that they didn't pay much attention to the caliber of the arguments in the proposal. (As Figure 6.1 shows, those in a good mood apparently paid less attention to argument quality than did their sad counterparts.) However, in another condition of this experiment (not reported in Figure 6.1), the subjects were explicitly instructed to pay attention to the proposal, and they then thought more about the message they were hearing. In this case, the strong arguments were more convincing than the weak ones, and this was true for those in a good as well as a bad mood. The happy persons apparently took the quality of the communication's arguments into account when the situation encouraged them to do so. Indeed, a positive mood may even facilitate the active consideration of a communication's ideas when situational conditions seem to call for active thinking.[17] Putting this another way, it's evidently helpful to differentiate between the default and higher-order modes of information processing. Good moods may automatically and naturally promote simplified and fairly general heuristic processing, but situational demands can bring higher cognitive functions into operation so that thoughtful analytic processing is carried out.

Effects of the Level of Thinking on Persuasion

A major difference between heuristic and analytic information processing, of course, has to do with the amount of thinking that is involved. People may use their general knowledge of the immediate situation when they're engaged in heuristic processing, as I've been suggesting, but they're also not thinking actively about the information they're receiving. Conversely, when they consider the details of a problematic occurrence as they engage in analytic processing, they're actively thinking a great deal about what is happening and the situation they're in. This level of thought, and especially the motivation to think actively about the available information, can greatly affect reactions to persuasive communications. Let me put this in a broader context.

Contemporary theories of persuasion, such as, notably, the Elaboration Likelihood Model (ELM) proposed by Richard Petty and John Cacioppo and Shelly Chaiken's Heuristic-Systematic Processing Model,[18] now agree that attitudes can be formed or modified in a variety of ways. Both conceptions also maintain that people's level of mental activity at the time they receive a persuasive communication determines how they will respond to this message. ELM refers to occasions in which there is little thought as instances of *low elaboration likelihood*, that is, as cases in which the message recipients do not or cannot elaborate further on the communication's arguments in their minds. This analysis holds that the attitudes developed or altered under low elaboration likelihood (i.e., when there is little thought) are not only less stable than the attitude alterations resulting from a good deal of thought, but also are produced by different, and largely more automatic, psychological mechanisms. In general, ELM would say that the attitude change shown by the happy persons in the study by Bless, Bohner, and their colleagues summarized in Figure 6.1 had been produced by automatic psychological processes under little conscious control.

ELM is fairly eclectic in its account of how the message recipients' feelings might operate when they do relatively little thinking, that is, when they engage in little elaboration. The mood-as-information theory may be right, at least at times; the recipients might use their present mood as an indicator of how they feel about the communication and employ only heuristic processing in responding to the message. But the leading proponents of ELM also recognize the possibility of a more passive associative process of the type postulated by Razran in his political slogan experiments; the recipients' feelings might generalize automatically to the communication (and perhaps to the communicator as well) merely because this message was present when they became happy.[19]

Petty, Schumann, Richman, and Strathman have reported experimental findings supporting such an interpretation.[20] After the undergraduates in their study were induced to be in either a good or a neutral mood, they were led to be interested in pens or were kept relatively indifferent to these objects, and then watched a TV advertisement for a particular brand of pen. At the conclusion of the ad, the participants rated their opinion of the advertised pen and also listed what thoughts had occurred to them as they watched the commercial. As you can see in Figure 6.3, regardless of the level of the subjects' interest in this topic, those who were feeling good at the time were more favorably disposed to the advertised product than were those in a neutral mood.

More important for us now, however, a statistical analysis of the data showed that the way in which the participants' feelings had influenced their opinion of the product depended on how involved they were in the issue (and thus on how ready they were to elaborate further on the message's arguments in their thinking). Unlike those who were in the high elaboration likelihood condition because of their interest in the pens, the mood of the less involved subjects evidently had influenced their opinion fairly directly and independently of whatever favorable ideas they had expressed about the advertised pen.

> *Their feelings in this situation apparently had generalized fairly automatically to the salient object (the pen) that happened to be associated with the situation.*

This is not to say, of course, that the associative perspective is superior to the MAI formulation in explaining how happy but unconcerned persons are susceptible to persuasion. Each analysis may well be right, under some conditions but not others. They are complementary rather than rival accounts of mood effects.

Let's say more about the effects of a high level of cognitive activity by returning to the Petty et al. pen advertisement experiment. Recall that the participants in the high involvement condition were ready to think about the topic (pens) because of their interest in this matter. Unlike their uninvolved counterparts, these persons' thoughts about the topic were affected by their mood; the happy subjects had more positive ideas about the advertised pen than did the neutral participants.

In Chapter 5, you'll remember, I referred to Forgas's proposition, in his affect infusion model, that problematic situations tend to prompt active, substantive (or analytic) processing leading to affective congruence.[21] The findings just mentioned add to Forgas's observations. High involvement in the issue at hand apparently can also promote substantive processing and thereby facilitate affectively congruent effects. Putting this another way, we can say that because of

Attitude Favorableness

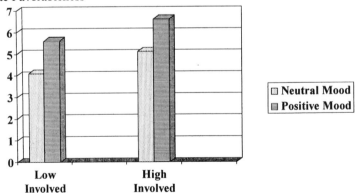

Figure 6.3 Favorableness of attitude toward an advertised pen as a function of mood and involvement (data from Petty et al., 1993, Experiment 2).

their interest in the topic, the participants' positive feelings evidently primed a number of thoughts favorable to the position advocated by the communication. Statistical analyses then revealed that these positive ideas exerted a stronger influence on the participants' resulting opinions than did their mood alone. The outcome, as Figure 6.3 shows, was that these happy and involved persons were the ones who were most strongly persuaded by the communication.

Some Suggestions About Positive Affect and Persuasion

Taking these findings at face value, it would appear that our hypothetical political candidate was probably right in trying to put her audience in a good mood. Her guests' pleasant feelings might have had a direct, unthinking positive effect on their attitudes toward her if they didn't care much about politics and could have promoted ideas favorable to her if they were set to think about this topic. But we also should be aware of some possible limiting conditions: In the laboratory situations we've considered, there was no motivation either to favor a particular point of view or even to be very accurate in one's judgments. The Petty et al. subjects undoubtedly had no established preference for one brand of pen over another and may not have been trying to make the best possible decision. What if the people in the politician's audience had an existing bias or were strongly motivated to be accurate in their judgments? As Forgas has pointed out, preexisting goals could greatly affect the nature and strength of the influence that feelings have on judgments. The happy listeners' judgments conceivably might not have been influenced in a mood-congruent manner if they had a well-established negative opinion of the politician and didn't want to view her positively and/or if they were motivated to be very careful and make an accurate assessment of her qualifications.

Effects of Unpleasant Feelings

Let's now turn to the ways in which unpleasant feelings might affect the audience's reactions to a persuasion attempt. The general position taken here is that these reactions depend largely on the degree to which the audience members think about what is happening.

The MAI theory makes this assumption. As you know, MAI holds that people in a bad mood are apt to take their unpleasant feelings as a signal that something is amiss in the situation confronting them. As a result, they tend to think more about what is occurring and analyze the available information more carefully. I've already mentioned some of the evidence consistent with this formulation. In the research conducted by Bless, Bohner, Schwarz, and Strack that we've been discussing, as you'll recall (and as can be seen in Figure 6.1), the subjects who had been put in a bad mood, unlike their happy counterparts, were evidently more attentive to the quality of the communication's arguments.

A second experiment in the Bless et al. series adds support to this analysis.[22] The researchers reasoned that if the unhappy subjects in their first study had considered the quality of the arguments they heard because they were thinking fairly carefully about the communication, a distraction preventing these persons from giving the message much attention might lessen the difference between the strong and weak argument conditions. To test this possibility, in their second experiment, after the participants were placed in either a good or a bad mood, half of them were distracted by being given another task to work on as they listened to a tape-recorded message presenting either strong or weak arguments for an increase in student fees. The nondistracted subjects showed the same results that had been obtained before: Only the unhappy persons were convinced more by the better-quality arguments than by the poorer ones. However, the outcome was different, as predicted, if the participants' attention had been diverted by their irrelevant task as the communication was delivered. In this case, whether they were in a bad or a good mood, message quality didn't matter much at all. With their attention and thought taken up by the extra job they were given, they no longer had the advantage of the negative affect-engendered heightened information processing.[23]

Negative Feelings Don't Always Promote Careful Consideration of Message Content

However consistent the findings just reviewed are with the MAI view of the effects of unpleasant feelings, many readers probably have a number of questions about the results obtained in these investigations. One of these uncertainties may have to do with the apparent absence of negative mood congruency in the unhappy people's response to the communicated proposals. If they experienced unpleasant feelings, why didn't they judge the message unfavorably? Although this is only conjecture, it seems to me that the answer must lie, at least partly, in the relatively weak affect that was generated in these studies. The methods used to induce the moods, such as getting the participants to recall earlier emotional episodes, probably didn't arouse strong feelings. Then too, ethical considerations didn't permit the researchers to make their subjects feel very bad.

The relatively weak feelings created in most of the studies I've been discussing up to now can be significant. As you'll recall, the MAI-supporting investigations typically showed that people experiencing unpleasant feelings are likely to think carefully about the matters before them. Contrast these experimental findings with other findings. In one study, the participants were made highly anxious by either being embarrassed or threatened with electric shock. More than their nondistressed peers, they subsequently failed to distinguish adequately among the members of a group of strangers they had watched. Similarly, in other research, highly frightened dental patients, in comparison to their less fearful counterparts, were more influenced by superficial aspects of a communication (audience applause) than by the message content. In both cases, the strongly aroused people in these studies apparently had not adequately processed the information available to them.[24]

Why this apparent difference? One plausible reason, it seems to me, is that the persons in these studies experienced much more intense affect than did the people serving in the usual social psychological experiments.

Think back to the discussion of eyewitness memory in Chapter 3. You saw there that a high level of internal excitation tends to diminish the range of cue utilization, that is, the range of informative details in the surrounding situation that is given considerable attention. Highly aroused persons tend to focus on the central aspects of what is happening, think less about the peripheral details, and generally engage in less careful information processing.[25] This suggests that the people who took part in the MAI-supporting experiments engaged in thoughtful, analytic processing because they were only weakly to moderately rather than intensely aroused. In addition, in having no strong affect, they didn't experience the flood of diverse, irrelevant ideas that intense feelings can activate, thoughts that could have interfered with a careful consideration of the communicated proposals. Indeed, some theorists have suggested that negative mood-generated thoughts, especially those produced by depressive feelings, can seriously limit the information processing capacity.[26] Also, because many of these affect-primed thoughts would have been negative, they could have cast the proposals in a negative light.

As it was, though, in experiencing only relatively weak negative feelings, the persons in the standard social psychological experiments were able to think broadly about the wide range of available information. They could keep in mind the desirability of being fair and objective in their examination of the message, and they could attend to the different aspects of what the communicator had to say. They could take the highly salient matter of the communicator's expertise into account, but they could also consider the more peripheral details involved in the proposals.

Going beyond the absence of negative mood congruency, one might also wonder if the nature of the unpleasant feeling limits the extent to which it will foster careful thought. You'll remember from Chapter 5 that even though sadness and anger are both negative, they don't have the same influence on the way information is processed. Whereas the sad participants in the experiment by Bodenhausen, Sheppard, and Kramer cited in that chapter were relatively careful in judging a person's likely guilt, those who were angry were much more apt to engage in simplified, stereotypic thinking in making their assessment. It may be that it is moderate sadness, rather than negative affect in general, that triggers detail-oriented, analytic information processing. Anger is much more likely to prompt impulsive, poorly thought-out judgments. Two of the Bodenhausen et al. studies dealing with persuasion show this. The angry people in these experiments tended to use superficial cues, such as the communicator's trustworthiness or expertise, in judging the merits of his proposal to a much greater extent than did their sad or neutral-mood counterparts. They evidently didn't take the time to consider the quality of the arguments presented to them and reacted only to superficial, easily grasped information.[27]

The anger generated in the Bodenhausen research probably was only fairly mild (because it was aroused by asking the subjects to recall a past event in which they had been provoked). Much stronger anger might have caused the subjects to reject the proposal presented to them altogether, even when the message came from a recognized expert. Angry feelings are usually accompanied by hostile thoughts, so there's a good chance that very angry persons will think ill of communications pressing a particular point of view on them, especially if the messages call on them to do things they're not at all disposed to do. On the other hand, to complicate matters even further, the angry persons' hostile ideas and aggressive inclinations might make it easy to convince them to accept proposals favoring aggressive actions.

Threatening/Fear-Arousing Communications

Up to now, I've been concerned mainly with how people's mood might influence their acceptance of communicated proposals. However, at times we encounter messages that deliberately seek to arouse feelings, and it's worth taking a brief look at the effectiveness of some of these affect-generating communications. What I have in mind here are messages that threaten the audience, such as by warning of the dangers of illegal drugs or of the potentially harmful effects of smoking. Today these communications are often sophisticated and subtle in their attempt to persuade. Years ago, however, they frequently were designed to be exceedingly frightening on the assumption that the fear produced would motivate people to refrain from the possibly dangerous behavior. A safe-driving campaign of more than a generation ago urging people to use automobile seat belts was fairly typical. It employed magazine ads portraying horrendous automobile accidents and containing statements, in boldface letters, such as this:

In a 45 mph crash, the average head hits the average windshield with a force of over a ton.[28]

If contemporary health and safety campaigns are not as blatantly threatening as this, it's probably because research has questioned the general effectiveness of highly frightening messages. Fear-arousing communications can be persuasive at times.[29] But there also are many occasions in which there is a boomerang effect; the scarier the communication, the less willing the recipients are to follow the recommendations.

A classic demonstration of this surprising outcome was published soon after World War II. In that pioneering experiment, high school students were more resistant to the practices advocated by the communication the more frightening the message became. The strongly threatened teenagers apparently had sought to lessen their fear by telling themselves that the depicted threat wasn't personally relevant.

A more recent investigation using adults found somewhat comparable results. In this case, California homeowners were given a written statement urging them to make preparations for possible earthquakes that might hit their area. They were asked, for example, to establish a 4-day emergency food supply. The message was so constructed that it made an earthquake seem more or less probable, and also, if one did occur, more or less severe. Interestingly, when the researchers interviewed the homeowners 5 weeks later, they found that the people given the most threatening communication were not the ones who were most successfully influenced. The persons told that an earthquake was both very probable and also apt to be severe were less likely to have made the recommended preparations than were the homeowners who had also been informed that an earthquake was highly probable but that the damage wouldn't be too bad. A somewhat less threatening communication evidently was more persuasive than a very strong threat.[30]

Two different theoretical schemes have been advanced to explain why fear-arousing communications can be ineffective – or why they might at times be persuasive. The more recent of these accounts is Rogers's protection motivation model.[31] Simply put, this highly rationalistic formulation says that a frightening communication will be persuasive to the extent that the audience is convinced that (1) the negative event is likely, (2) the undesirable consequences will be great if the danger materializes, (3) following the recommended action will minimize these negative consequences, and (4) the message recipients are capable of performing the advocated behaviors. However, although Rogers's model has some support, it does have problems. Most notably, it doesn't satisfactorily account for those instances, such as the two cases I cited before, in which the frightening message seems to result in a defensive avoidance of the recommendation.

I favor the earlier, parallel response model of Leventhal.[32] This model holds that fear-arousing communications evoke two kinds of reactions at the same time: emotional reactions (largely fear-expressive) and those that focus on the communicated threat. According to Leventhal, the action the message recipients undertake depends on which of these two reactions they most want to control, their fear or the perceived danger. If they're more concerned with fear control, they attend mostly to their bodily reactions indicative of fear and try to lessen these reactions. On the other hand, if they focus on danger control, they try to solve the problem, using whatever information they have about the likelihood of the danger, its severity, and their coping ability. We can say that a skilled race car driver suddenly confronted by an emergency on the track might have the same fear-linked bodily reactions we all would have, but would still concentrate on coping with the danger rather than attending to personal bodily sensations.

Leventhal then proposed that people's sense of vulnerability to danger is a primary determinant of whether they focus on their inner fear or on the external threat. Presumably they will be oriented mainly to the danger if they believe they can successfully overcome it or aren't likely to suffer much harm. The race car driver believes she or he can cope with the emergency. However, those who think they are highly vulnerable, who doubt that they can master the threat, may focus on their fear and attempt to lessen its disturbing sensations. People with characteristically low self-esteem are especially likely to have these doubts.

> *One of the studies Leventhal cited in support of his analysis, carried out in the mid-1960s and using people attending a state fair, assessed whether the research participants smoked cigarettes. After this, they saw a film dealing with smoking and lung cancer that was either highly frightening (showing, among other things, the details of a lung cancer operation), moderately disturbing, or, in the third group, innocuous. The communications recommended that the viewers not only stop smoking but also take a chest X-ray at a mobile X-ray unit only a few yards from the movie theater.*
>
> *The participants who smoked, and thus who were most susceptible to lung cancer, were the ones who were most likely to display a defensive-avoidance response to the recommendation; fewer of them took the advocated X-rays after the highly fear-arousing communication than after the less threatening films. The threatening nature of the movie did not affect the nonsmokers' willingness to comply with the recommendation.*
>
> *Interestingly, when all of the participants were queried 5 months later, it was found that a higher proportion of the smokers in the high-fear group reported having tried to cut down on their smoking than did their counterparts in the moderate- or low-fear conditions. Leventhal argued that this finding is consistent with his theory. Defensive avoidance is most likely to be seen, he said, when the fear experience is most intense. Once these bodily sensations diminish, as can happen with the passage of time, they are no longer the focus of attention and there is a greater likelihood that the audience will attempt to cope with the perceived danger.[33]*

There are grounds for hope. People can react rationally and effectively to news of an imminent danger. This may not happen right away. Their fear may be too great when they first learn of the threat, and they may initially engage in defensive avoidance. But their fear can subside with time. As this happens, reason can prevail, and they can become open to recommendations about how best to deal with the potentially harmful occurrence. They will be most likely to accept the advocated proposal, of course, to the extent that it is clearly a good (and perhaps easy) way to avoid the danger they otherwise would face.[34]

PART IV

Influencing Action

7. Feeling Effects on Aggression and Helpfulness

In one way or another, the previous chapters dealt with the influence of feelings on thought processes. We will now take up the effects of mood on two kinds of social behavior. The chapter will first consider the role of unpleasant affect in generating aggressive inclinations, and then, to end on a more positive note, we will look at the ways in which good moods facilitate good behavior.

Hostility and Aggression

The Influence of Negative Feelings on Anger and Aggression

Before we get underway, however, let's look back at what's been said about the psychological consequences of negative feelings. First, in introducing you to Bower's associative network model of affective influences, I cited the evidence demonstrating a frequent mood congruence: People who are feeling bad often have bad memories and negative ideas and are also apt to judge things unfavorably. On the other hand, my discussion of the MAI formulation also noted that negative affect can lead to careful, analytic thinking, so that the evaluations made are relatively free of stereotypes and preconceived notions.

These observations aren't necessarily incompatible. In Chapter 5, I suggested that the influence unpleasant feelings have on judgments depends largely on the intensity of this affect, as well as persons' level of mental activity and the strength of their disposition to make accurate assessments. Simply put, people who are in a negative mood are most likely to engage in analytic information processing, and not express opinions consistent with their bad mood, when this feeling isn't too intense, they're mentally active, and they're motivated to make an accurate (or fair) evaluation of the given target. Otherwise, people are very likely to offer negative judgments congruent with their negative affect.[1]

The MAI investigations typically employed only weak to moderate affective states – states produced, for example, by asking people to recall an earlier emotional event or by placing them in an attractive or unattractive room.[2] Because the induced feelings weren't especially intense, their influence could easily be countered by cognitive controls such as those produced by a desire to be socially appropriate and/or objective in what was said. If I'm right, then, we're much more likely to see people express negative opinions in line with their negative mood when their feelings are quite strong.

Effects of Decidedly Unpleasant Temperatures

My guess is that relatively intense negative feelings occur in the experiments investigating the effects of unpleasantly high temperatures. One of the first of these studies was carried out by William Griffitt more than a generation ago. His male and female university students, seated individually in a room that was either very warm (about 91°F) or comfortable (about 68°F), were asked to give their impressions of a stranger after knowing only that person's opinions on a variety of issues. The worse they felt (according to their self-ratings), the less favorable was their judgment of the stranger. The researcher's conclusion highlighted this mood congruence: "It appears then that when one is feeling good his [or her] response to others will be more positive than when he [or she] is feeling bad."[3]

We can go even further. Decidedly unpleasant temperatures can give rise to angry feelings and aggressive urges as well as negative judgments. William Shakespeare apparently thought this could happen. In the third act of *Romeo and Juliet*, one of the characters admonishes Mercutio to be careful if they encounter the Capulets:

> I pray thee, good Mercutio, let's retire:
> The day is hot, the Capulets abroad,
> And, if we meet, we shall not 'scape a brawl;
> For now these hot days is the mad blood stirring.

Do hot days indeed stir the "mad blood," inflaming passions and promoting violence? Experimental evidence provided by both Robert

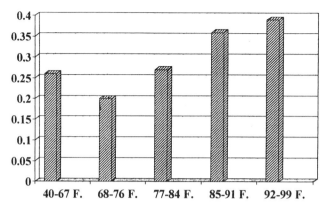

Figure 7.1 Ratio of violent crimes (murder plus rape) to nonviolent crimes (robbery plus arson) as a function of average temperature (data estimated from Anderson & Anderson, 1984, Figure 2). There are approximately the same number of days in each of the temperature categories.

Baron and Craig Anderson indicates that this can happen. A study by Baron and Bell, for instance, found that nonangered subjects attacked a fellow student more strongly (with electric shocks) when they were in a hot room than when they were in more comfortable surroundings.[4] Anderson has now carried the research on the aggressive effects of unpleasant temperatures much further. After first reporting (in a paper with Merrill Carlsmith) that unusually hot weather had probably contributed to the urban riots of the mid-1960s, Anderson looked at the relationship between the daily temperature in Houston, Texas, and the number of violent and nonviolent crimes committed in that city over the more than 300 days for which data were available. This study showed that the number of violent crimes (murder plus rape) reported to the police mounted as the weather became unpleasantly hot. The rate of nonviolent crimes (robbery plus arson) apparently did not fluctuate with temperature.

Figure 7.1 shows that the uncomfortable heat largely affected aggressive behavior. When temperatures were in the pleasant 68°–76°F range, the number of violent crimes was only about one-fifth the number of nonviolent crimes. However, when temperatures were in the much less comfortable 92°–99°F range, the ratio doubled; the number of violent crimes was about 40% of the number of nonviolent offenses.[5]

This aggression-producing effect isn't limited to a brief period of time and to one city. In another paper, Anderson reported that, over a decade, the number of very hot days each year was more closely correlated with the rate of violent crimes, such as murder and aggravated assault than with the rate of nonaggressive offenses such as burglary and theft. Yet another study focusing on crime rates in over 200 U.S. cities indicated that the number of hot days in these communities was related to their violent crime rates even when such social characteristics as unemployment, income, and education were taken into account.[6]

The leading investigators in this area disagree as to whether violent inclinations are linearly or curvilinearly related to temperature. Baron and his associates agree with Anderson (and others such as myself) that it is the negative affect experienced in hot weather that generates the aggressive urge. However, unlike Anderson, Baron and Bell argue that the negative affect–aggression relationship is curvilinear. They hold that the instigation to aggression increases as the temperature rises, but only up to a point. People feeling very strong negative affect, as on very hot days, may well be less aggressive than they would have been on somewhat cooler days because they are more intent on escaping from the heat than on assaulting an available target. Anderson disputes this curvilinear hypothesis. Although he obviously recognizes that the desire to escape from the aversive situation can sometimes be stronger than the heat-induced aggressive urge, he contends that the inclination to escape doesn't necessarily grow stronger than the aggressive tendency as the temperature rises. More recently, Cohn and Rotton have published findings supporting the Baron and Bell curvilinear relationship. In their data, the number of reported violent offenses rose as the weather got hotter – but only up to about 85°F. Above this temperature, violent crimes decreased in number as the temperature rose. Their explanation of the results helps us reconcile the Baron–Bell and Anderson views. They propose that people are apt to restrict their interactions with others when the weather is very uncomfortable. In so doing, of course, they are less likely to have a violence-generating encounter with someone else. Simply put, the impulse to aggression may well become stronger as temperatures rise, but this urge will not result in an open assault unless another person is present and is thought to have misbehaved.[7]

At any rate, whatever the exact nature of the relationship between temperature and number of violent offenses, these (and other similar) findings shouldn't be dismissed as artifactual – as only the result of other influences, such as the greater number of people on the streets on hot days. The laboratory experiments, including the Baron and Bell study cited before, tend to rule out these other possible causes; for example, the experimental participants typically encountered only one person other than the experimenter. Equally important, Anderson's more recent experiments on the effects of unpleasantly high temperatures have demonstrated that aversive heat frequently gives rise to angry feelings and hostile ideas, and often (but not always) to increased aggression, even when the persons affected had not been provoked beforehand.[8]

It's also important to recognize, as Anderson and Baron (and also I and others) have emphasized, that it's not heat per se but the unpleasant feelings aroused by the heat that lead to aggressive inclinations. This being the case, we're not surprised to find that cold temperatures can also increase the likelihood of aggressive reactions. In two experiments cited by Anderson, university students exposed to either hot or cold conditions were more punitive to a peer whom they were judging than were people in a normal-temperature situation. This happened, furthermore, even when the subjects had not previously been provoked by the person they were evaluating.[9]

Heat and cold aren't the only physically uncomfortable stimulants to aggression. James Rotton and his associates have demonstrated, both in their field research and in laboratory experiments, that air pollution can also increase the chance of aggressive encounters. In one of their experiments, undergraduate men exposed to a moderately unpleasant odor punished a fellow student more severely for his supposed mistakes on a learning task than did their counterparts working in a normal atmosphere. These people couldn't blame the student for the foul smell but, being very bothered by the odor, they still were aggressively inclined and showed this in their treatment of him.[10]

Physical pain, of course, is particularly likely to generate bad feelings and therefore frequently arouses the urge to attack someone. A substantial body of research dating back more than 50 years and employing both animal and human subjects has shown that, in many species, individuals exposed to physically painful conditions are often apt to assault an available target, particularly if their pain isn't extremely severe. Thus, when two animals were cooped up together and afflicted by noxious stimuli (such as physical blows, electric shocks, loud noises, or intense heat), they frequently began to fight. A number of investigators have argued that the aggression revealed in these experiments was not merely an intensification of whatever action tendency was ongoing at the time, and further, wasn't only a defensive reaction to the aversive stimuli or an attempt to eliminate these stimuli. Pained animals will strike at a target even when this action cannot possibly lessen their suffering and, according to some research, may even expend effort to obtain a target they can attack.

Many of these findings apparently can be generalized to humans. Observations of human infants indicate that pain may well be an inborn stimulus to anger even in our species. In his review of emotion research, Izard maintains that "pain is a direct and immediate cause of anger. Even in very young infants, we see anger expression to inoculation long before they can appraise or understand what has happened to them."[11]

Berkowitz has added to these observations by noting that several patients suffering from very painful ailments are often angry and aggressive. Reports from the medical literature tell us that many people tormented by severe episodic headaches and women experiencing intense birth pangs engage in angry outbursts at times.[12]

More than producing angry feelings, hostile ideas, and assaultive outbursts, the strong negative affect apparently also generates an aggressive urge, a desire to hurt others. Suggestive evidence for this can be found in two experiments reported by Berkowitz, Cochran, and Embree.

> *Supposedly because they were in an investigation of how supervision was affected by harsh conditions, the women in these studies kept one hand in water as they evaluated the adequacy of a peer's solutions to several business problems. The water was either unpleasantly cold or at a comfortable room temperature. In judging each of their peer's supposed ideas, the participants were to give her anywhere from five rewards (in the form of money) to five punishments (blasts of noise). Half of the women were also told that whatever punishment they delivered would hurt the idea giver (by interfering with her problem solving), whereas the others were informed that the punishments would be helpful by motivating the idea giver to do better.*
>
> *The participants in every condition much preferred to reward rather than punish their peer, but the conditions altered the relative strength of their desire to reward and punish. Therefore, our principal measure here is the preponderance of rewards over punishments they administered. Figure 7.2 summarizes the findings on this measure over the two experiments in this series. As the figure shows, the women whose hand was in the relatively comfortable water apparently had a fairly strong desire not to hurt the idea giver when they had been told that punishments would be hurtful, and they gave many more re-*

wards than punishments. This wish to avoid doing harm seemed to be much weaker in the Very Cold Water condition. In this case, the opportunity to hurt the other led to the fewest rewards and the most punishments, and consequently, to the smallest difference between the number of rewards and punishments. The painfully cold condition evidently had activated a desire to injure someone – even when the target hadn't mistreated the participants.[13]

Social and Psychological Stressors

Let me now add to the evidence supporting my basic argument by leaving the laboratory and turning to real-world observations. Here too we can see that intense negative affect heightens the likelihood of anger and emotional aggression. The research also indicates that many different kinds of unpleasant conditions, social and psychological as well as physical, can generate the decidedly negative feelings that can activate the anger/aggression syndrome.

Some of the relevant evidence comes from studies of the effects of social stress on rates of violent crime. According to several investigators, in many societies, various indicators of unsettled social and economic conditions, such as high unemployment, hyperinflation, or rapid modernization, are associated with increased numbers of illegal aggressive actions.

Landau extended these findings further in his analysis of data from

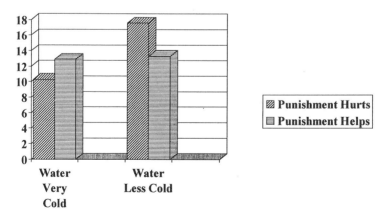

Figure 7.2 Preponderance of rewards over punishments as affected by water unpleasantness and effect of punishment (data from both experiments in Berkowitz et al., 1981). Scores are the difference between the number of rewards and punishments in each condition. The lower the score, the harsher the evaluation.

Israel for the years from 1967 to 1979. High levels of economic, political, and governmental worries in that country during this period, as measured by public opinion surveys, were significantly related to homicide rates. Results such as these have led several criminologists and sociologists to contend that social stresses of many different kinds are important contributors to crime.[14] The unpleasant conditions make many people feel bad, and those persons experiencing strong negative affect who also have antisocial predispositions might well translate their violent inclinations into criminal offenses when an appropriate situation arises.

Other kinds of strong unpleasant feelings can also activate the anger/aggression syndrome. Many readers will be surprised to learn, as a case in point, that several highly depressed persons are unusually assaultive in their dealings with others. Mental health specialists have repeatedly observed that both child and adult depressives are apt to be hostile and susceptible to strong outbursts of temper. One investigation of seriously depressed children found that these youngsters were so aggressive and destructive that their parents and teachers were more concerned about this behavior than about the children's depression.[15]

It's common to explain cases such as these by holding that depression is aggression turned inward; the youngsters in this last-mentioned study might have been depressed because they were hostile toward themselves as well as others. Whatever the validity of this interpretation, however, there's good reason to believe that the depressed affective state could also generate aggressive inclinations fairly automatically. Depression presumably doesn't lead to a prolonged and planned aggressive campaign, but it can produce short-lived, impulsive assaults. In one of the Berkowitz and Troccoli experiments, when subjects were distracted so that they didn't fully monitor their actions, those who were made depressed were highly punitive to a fellow student.[16]

Perhaps even more surprising is the apparent connection between intense sadness and aggression. Various writers, both within and outside the mental health fields, have noted that it's not unusual for people mourning the death of loved ones to display anger and even occasional outbursts of aggression. This point was made by P. D. James, the popular English author of detective novels, who had her chief character once say, "You can feel anger and grief together. That's the commonest reaction to bereavement." The eminent emotion theorist Carroll Izard agrees with James. He tells us that many persons who are grieving because of the loss of a loved one describe themselves as angry as well as sad and distressed.[17]

As you know, the most frequent interpretation of such instances assumes that blame is involved; the mourners presumably are angry because they hold someone, or some entity, responsible for their loss. However, it's possible that the loss and the resulting intense sadness led to the anger without the intervention of any blame. Termine and Izard have argued that conditions eliciting sadness frequently elicit anger as well. They demonstrated that infants often react to their mothers' apparent sadness with facial expressions indicating that they themselves are not only sad but angry as well.[18]

Are Appraisals and Attributions Necessary?

Yet, even with all of these findings, many contemporary theories of emotion cannot easily explain why anger and aggression occur at all. Most contemporary emotion theorists hold that the meaning given to an event is the principal determinant of what emotion it will produce. For them, an unpleasant incident won't infuriate us unless we make an angering appraisal – attribute the occurrence to someone's (or something's) deliberate malevolence. Ortony, Clore, and Collins contend, for example, that a bad occurrence makes us angry only when we think a particular agent was responsible for what had happened and believe that this agent acted in a blameworthy manner. Averill takes essentially the same position. He says that anger "for the person in the street, is an accusation" that "accepted social norms" have been violated. Lazarus, another appraisal theorist, has a very similar view. As he sees it, for anger to arise, the negative occurrence must be regarded as personally significant and as having been caused by an external agent who had control over it and thus could be blamed for the event.[19]

This traditional conception of how anger is produced undoubtedly applies to most anger-arousing incidents in everyday life. When ordinary people are queried about the events that provoked their anger, they typically say they were bothered either by someone's deliberate misdeed or by an incident that could have been avoided if another person had acted properly. Illustrating this, when Averill asked community residents and students about "the most intense episode of anger" they had experienced during the preceding week, he found that

> [the] vast majority of subjects indicated that the incident was either voluntary and unjustified (51%) or a potentially avoidable accident or event (31%). Relatively few persons became angry [about] events which they considered voluntary but justified (11%) or unavoidable (7%).[20]

Still, if we look at Averill's findings more closely, we can see that people are sometimes infuriated by events that aren't attributable to a misdeed. Close to 40% of the respondents in his survey said they had been angered by another person's action even though they had not regarded that behavior as socially improper. Twelve percent even thought the eliciting action had been justified. In addition, people sometimes are provoked by occurrences that couldn't have been controlled; 7% of Averill's respondents reported having become extremely angry when something unavoidable had happened.

The field studies and laboratory experiments I reviewed earlier also point to the shortcomings in the appraisal accounts of anger. The people suffering from the hot weather in Anderson's naturalistic investigations couldn't have blamed anyone for their discomfort, and it is highly unlikely that the experimental participants exposed to the unpleasant room temperature, or foul odors, or cold water attributed their negative feelings to the individual they were judging.

When there's no good reason to assume that blame appraisals led to the anger/hostility in these particular studies, several laboratory findings pose even more difficulties for the appraisal-is-necessary school of thought. In one experiment studying reactions to an aversive situation, the investigators assessed their subjects' attributions and found that these people did not believe the target of their hostile ratings was responsible for their unpleasant state. On top of this, there's the question of whether the blame appraisal is always the cause of the reported anger; sometimes blaming grows out of the unpleasant feeling. Keltner and his associates showed this. When they induced anger or sadness in their participants (for example, by manipulating the subjects' physical pose), they found that the angered individuals were more apt to blame others for mishaps.[21]

Clearly, anger and even aggression can arise at times without the appraisals stipulated by traditional emotion theorizing.[22] Furthermore, given this evidence, shouldn't a truly comprehensive analysis of anger also be able to explain these relatively unusual occurrences as well as the more usual incidents?

Theorizing About the Effects of Negative Affect on Anger and Aggression

Two somewhat different theoretical models have been developed to account for the effects of unpleasant feelings on aggression. One of these, advanced by Craig Anderson and his associates and explicitly concerned with affective aggression, is only a mild departure from conventional appraisal thinking. They hold that the anger, hostile thoughts, and physiological reactions produced by negative affect lead to appraisals, and that these, in turn, shape the afflicted persons' decisions. The uncomfortable persons presumably interpret other people's behavior as hostile to them and then decide to respond in an unfriendly or even aggressive manner.

The second model, termed the *cognitive-neoassociationistic analysis* (CNA), is my own and places much less emphasis on the role of appraisals and attributions. Here I will speak only of this latter formulation because I have been saying that appraisals aren't necessary for anger and aggression to occur.[23]

One way to begin is by recognizing that negative affect doesn't always lead to open aggression. We've all seen suffering persons who don't show overt anger or hostility at all. In fact, a number of investigations have found (as Baron and his colleagues have implied in their negative affect–escape analysis) that many animals and humans would rather escape from the source of their displeasure than attack and destroy it. But this doesn't necessarily mean that intense negative affect doesn't activate any anger and aggressive inclinations. The CNA model suggests that decidedly unpleasant conditions can evoke, among other reactions, *both* flight *and* fight tendencies, not one or the other, and that various influences in the individual's genetic heritage and past learning, as well as in the immediate surroundings, can determine which of these opposing tendencies is dominant on any given occasion. Generally speaking, even though both of these inclinations might be operative at the same time, which course we take openly, whether to escape or attack or engage in constructive problem solving, depends at least partly on our perception of what action will be most effective at the lowest possible cost to us. If one action doesn't succeed, though, the other actions might be tried. The so-called cornered rat might prefer to escape but will strike out at the threatening agent if escape is impossible.

Cognitions other than the person's beliefs about the possible consequences of aggression could also intervene to influence the reactions to negative affect. You've seen throughout this book that the effects of feelings on perceptions, judgments, and actions depend largely on the level of thought that the person is engaged in at the time. In keeping with these observations, the CNA conception of anger and emotional aggression also proposes that the individual's thinking can influence what happens when strong negative affect is experienced. This theory is summarized in Figure 7.3.

The formulation maintains that we typically go through a sequence of psychological processes when something very bad occurs. Initially, the decidedly unpleasant feeling usually activates at least two emotional syndromes, one having to do with the inclination to flee from the perceived source of the affect (the fear/flight syndrome) and the other involving the urge to attack this source (the anger/aggression syndrome). Using the associative network conception of emotions discussed in Chapter 3, I envision each of these syndromes as a network of particular feelings, ideas, memories, physiological response patterns, and motor programs. Thus, according to the CNA model, whatever other reactions we might have when we're feeling bad, theoretically we will also have aggression-related thoughts and memories, as well as the motor reactions that are frequently associated with aggression. We often experience this pattern of responses as anger, although we might also interpret the sensations as irritation or annoyance if they are relatively weak.

CNA regards this initial process as being primitive because these effects supposedly occur automatically and with little if any thought merely because of the associative connections between the various components of the anger/aggression syndrome. However, it's also proposed that many of these first reactions can then be suppressed, intensified, or substantially altered if we engage in higher-order cognitive processing, that is, if we think actively and extensively about the immediate situation we're in and the long-term possibilities. Of course, we might not think very much at all if we are intensely agitated; our feelings might be so strong and the surrounding situation so compelling that our thoughts are only superficial and focus primarily on our suffering. Automatic psychological processes are then dominant. But if we do think deeply and broadly enough, more cognitively

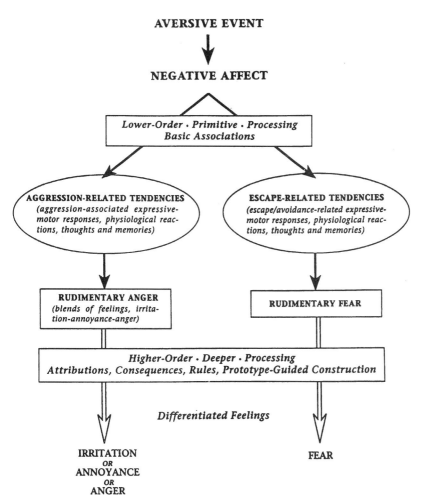

Figure 7.3 A CNA conception of anger.

controlled psychological processes will go into operation. We then engage in the appraisals and attributions emphasized by traditional emotion theorists; we consider how important the emotion-arousing event is to us, try to determine what had caused the incident, and decide what might be an appropriate way of responding in the particular situation. As a consequence of this higher-order processing, our initial emotional state could be modified or even altered substantially. We may then consciously believe we're not angry, just a little annoyed, or maybe disgusted with someone. Or we may even think we're afraid and don't experience any anger at all.

Regulating Feelings-Induced Hostility/Aggression

At this point, I want to say more about the self-regulation that I had mentioned earlier in this chapter and discussed more fully in Chapter 5. I've repeatedly acknowledged that people who are feeling bad don't always express hostile judgments or assault an available target. Sometimes they may restrain themselves out of fear of disapproval or other forms of punishment. But in addition, as I showed in Chapter 5, they may also attempt to regulate, or even correct for, the hostile/aggresive inclinations activated in them by their negative affect. I noted that this is particularly likely to occur when the unhappy persons pay attention to their feelings, when this affect isn't very strong, and when they want their response to others around them to be accurate and/or socially proper. Trying to correct for what they believe is the inappropriate influence of their negative affect, they may even overcompensate by being exaggeratedly positive to the people nearby.

Adding to my discussion in Chapter 5, we have evidence of such a process in an experiment not mentioned before. In this study, university women who had been made sad bent over backwards to avoid rating a photographed man unfavorably, but primarily when they had been made mentally active earlier (by being shown an unusual situation) and had been asked to be accurate in their evaluation. Their high level of thinking apparently had facilitated the overcompensation induced by their desire to be accurate in what they said.[24]

Some Final Comments

Obviously, much still has to be learned about how our feelings influence our behavior toward others. The effects of negative feelings are especially puzzling – and intriguing. Although it may be advisable at times to differentiate among the various negative affective states (as I've noted throughout this book), it still appears that a wide variety of unpleasant feelings can have some common effects. And so, using only a brief sampling of the research literature, I've shown that a remarkably broad range of aversive conditions can activate angry feelings, hostile thoughts, and even aggressive inclinations.

If these findings are supported by further research, we would have to conclude that aggression will always be with us. There's no way to prevent people from having any bad feelings. However, there also are grounds for optimism. People can also learn to react to their negative feelings with the cognitions and actions that will weaken or suppress their initial rudimentary anger/aggression so that more constructive forms of thought and behavior become dominant.

Helpfulness

Surely no one will be surprised to hear that people's moods can affect their willingness to help others in need. You may not realize, however, how subtle and pervasive these mood influences can be or what psychological processes govern their effects. This section will look at a number of social psychological studies that demonstrate the impact of feelings on helpfulness. Let's begin with an examination of the effects of a positive mood and then turn to the consequences of unpleasant feelings.

The Influence of Positive Feelings

A study published almost two decades ago by Michael Cunningham serves as a good starting point for this discussion.

> With the cooperation of the wait staff at a moderately expensive climate-controlled restaurant in one of Chicago's suburbs, the investigator recorded the size of the tips left by customers during several spring weeks, as well as the customers' apparent age, their gender, and the weather conditions at the time of each meal. The researcher found that the customers' generosity was significantly affected by the outside weather even though the inside temperature was always pleasant. They left more money for the servers (relative to the size of their bill) when the sun outside the restaurant's big windows was shining brightly than when the day was overcast. This relationship held, furthermore, even when the age and gender of the customers, as well as the servers' mood, were held constant statistically. Because the data indicated that the servers typically felt better on bright, sunny days (independently of the gratuities they had received), Cunningham concluded that the pleasant weather had also made the customers feel good, so that they then were more generous to the persons waiting on them.[25]

These findings can be extended in a wide variety of ways. An impressive number of experiments have shown that people who are in a good mood are especially apt to be benevolent (in a situationally appropriate manner, of course). Whether their positive feelings stem from their success on an assigned task or from the happy thoughts they have, or even if their pleasure is due to chance occurrences such as the unexpected receipt of a free gift or exposure to pleasant-sounding music, pleasant fragrances, or some other positive experience, they're more likely to be magnanimous to other people nearby than they would have been when in a neutral mood.

Moreover, experiments have demonstrated that the good deeds can vary greatly in nature. The assistance can be in the form of compliance with another's request (such as by agreeing to work for a longer period for someone in need) or it can be voluntarily initiated (such as by freely helping someone pick up papers that apparently had been dropped accidentally). Or the prosocial acts might consist of increased cooperation in a negotiation. In all of these cases, however, the aid given isn't especially costly to the help giver and, more important, doesn't harm someone else. With these possible limitations, happiness seems to increase the chances of goodness.[26]

Why Do Good Moods Promote Helpfulness? Researchers have proposed a number of reasons for these positive effects of positive affect. Many of these explanations probably are right – but each may hold only under restricted conditions. We can't review all of the possibilities that have been raised or describe all of the intricacies that investigators have uncovered. Instead, we'll consider a few of the major theoretical accounts that have been offered for the effects of feeling.

To approach these theoretical interpretations, let's look at an idea suggested by MAI theory. Maybe happy people simply are impulsively helpful because, in feeling good, they're engaged in heuristic processing and don't think very much about the effort or the psychological costs they might incur by rendering aid. However, although there is some empirical support for this possibility,[27] this mood-induced "mental laziness" probably contributes to relatively few instances of benevolence toward others. In many other cases, happy people apparently do more thinking than this MAI interpretation supposes. They seem especially likely to consider whether they will feel good in providing assistance.

We've now returned to the positive mood-maintenance idea I discussed in earlier chapters. You'll recall Isen's suggestion, cited in Chapter 5, that happy persons are often reluctant to think much about difficult or boring tasks because they believe this mental effort might spoil their good mood. Isen and her associates extended this notion in several studies of helpfulness. The earliest of these investigations documents a point I made before: Pleasant feelings increase the willingness to render some kinds of aid, but they don't increase compliance with any kind of request. In this particular experiment, the participants placed in a positive mood were relatively unwilling to assist a stranger when this help would annoy a third party, although they readily agreed to the stranger's request if their activity would help the beneficiary. Feeling good, they apparently were only inclined to do those things that could maintain their pleasant feelings. Another study by Isen adds further support. The happy subjects in this experiment typically agreed to aid someone by carrying out a task they were assured would be pleasant, but they were reluctant to perform an activity that (they were told) they might find depressing.[28]

Other investigations of how positive moods influence helpfulness have obtained similar findings, as Carlson, Charlin, and Miller noted in their survey of the relevant research. In line with the Wegener and Petty hedonic contingency conception discussed in Chapter 6, Carlson and his colleagues suggested that happy persons, in contrast to those in a neutral mood, are apt to be relatively sensitive to the hedonic consequences of the actions they could undertake on behalf of others. They presumably realize that helping others would preserve their positive feelings and that a failure to give assistance would decrease their pleasant mood.[29]

Another psychological process I discussed earlier can also contribute to the positive effects of positive feelings. After Isen's initial, and often ingenious, studies of the impact of mood on helpfulness, she proposed that good feelings could also promote socially good behavior through their influence on thoughts and memories.[30] As was the case in Isen's analysis of why positive affect improves creativity (summarized in Chapter 5), her reasoning here was based on Bower's associative network conception of mood influences (introduced in Chapter 3). Because feelings tend to prime thoughts and memories having an affectively similar meaning, she argued, happy persons are likely to have positive thoughts, and thus think relatively favorably of others around them, including those who require assistance. They are also inclined to believe that their actions (such as the aid they could give) will have desirable consequences, and they may even tend to recall their social ideals calling for help to those who are dependent on them. Clark and Waddell, among others, have provided evidence consistent with all this: Their subjects who were in a good mood typically voiced more positive ideas (in their free associations) when imagining a situation in which it was possible to help someone than did their counterparts in the neutral and negative mood conditions.[31]

In addition to promoting positive ideas about others, pleasant feelings can activate good thoughts about oneself. This is especially likely to occur if those having the pleasant experience happen to be very self-conscious at the time, maybe because they've been thinking about themselves or because they believe they're being compared with others or even because they see their reflection in a mirror.[32] However their self-attention arises, their positive mood could increase their favorable conception of themselves, and this improved self-image might then prompt them to behave in a socially desirable fashion. Essentially they are now more highly motivated to do good things in order to live up to their more positive view of themselves.

> *Berkowitz has reported findings that point to this kind of process in operation. In his second experiment along these lines, individual female subjects were first made to be either highly aware or less aware of themselves as they were placed in a positive, neutral, or negative mood. Afterward, the undergraduate experimenter asked each participant for a favor: Would the participant help her by scoring the data she (the experimenter) had collected in another, entirely unrelated study? The subject could do as little or as much as she wanted.*
>
> *Both the participants' pleasant feelings and their heightened self-awareness contributed to the amount of work they did for the person asking for help (the experimenter in this case), as you can see in Figure 7.4. And as had also been anticipated, a statistical analysis of the data indicated that the good feelings had increased the participants' number of positive self-related ideas and that this heightened self-concept had then led to the greater level of help.[33]*

This research demonstrates once again that mood can influence behavior in a variety of ways. But however this increased benevolence occurs, the research also shows more specifically that happy people are apt to be good people in a number of ways.

Effects of Negative Feelings

What about the other side of the proverbial coin? Common sense and everyday experience tell us that unhappy persons are not likely to be especially helpful to others. Think of people sweltering in a hot, humid room. Few of us would expect them to go out of their way to help a stranger (although perhaps they would do so if there was a clear-cut emergency). And yet, couldn't a case be made for the prop-

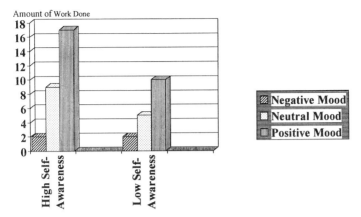

Figure 7.4 Influence of mood and self-awareness on help given to a requestor (data from Berkowitz, 1987, Experiment 2).

osition that negative feelings can motivate positive behavior, at least under certain conditions? If happy persons are sometimes helpful because they want to maintain their good mood, isn't it conceivable that unhappy persons would seek to render aid in order to lessen their negative mood?

For many psychodynamically oriented theorists, at least one type of unpleasant feeling could impel helpfulness and other kinds of socially desirable conduct as well: guilt. Freud thought that unconscious guilt was at the root of virtually all morality and motivated much of the best behavior that people display. Robert Cialdini has gone further in proposing that altruism is often prompted by a very general hedonistic concern not restricted to guilt. His Negative-State Relief model of helpfulness maintains that people experiencing negative affect – especially sadness – are sometimes spurred to aid others because they think this good deed will improve their mood.[34]

Why (Some Kinds of) Negative Feelings Can Promote Helping. Social psychologists have now carried out many studies on the effects of unpleasant feelings on the willingness to assist others. Fortunately, Michael Carlson and Norman Miller have reviewed this extensive literature for us and have provided a careful analysis of the overall findings.[35]

One of their main conclusions argues against the general Negative

State-Relief model. People who feel bad evidently are sometimes in-clined to be helpful, but, Carlson and Miller tell us, this doesn't hap-pen as generally as the Negative State-Relief model implies. More particularly, they say, there is little evidence that sadness, the negative affect emphasized by Cialdini and his colleagues, is especially apt to promote good deeds.

Rather than make a very general statement about the positive ef-fects of negative feelings, we apparently have to limit the beneficial consequences to certain kinds of conditions and perhaps even to cer-tain types of negative affect. Let's start with the relatively specific conditions under which a bad mood might lead to a good outcome. According to Carlson and Miller, one of these conditions is the object of one's concern when something bad takes place. Suppose you were living in Los Angeles when the severe 1993 earthquake occurred. You might have focused your attention on yourself – your own suffering and unhappiness – or you might have thought primarily of the other people who were hit hard by the catastrophe. Generally speaking, the studies suggest, you were more likely to try to help the quake victims if your attention was focused on them rather on than yourself. Being preoccupied with one's own troubles is not conducive to effort on behalf of others. Maybe in focusing on the other persons' problems you empathized with these victims, perceived their needs, and then were motivated to aid them.[36]

Another condition identified by Carlson and Miller has to do with the perceived cause of negative occurrence. We're apparently inclined to aid others after something bad happens if (1) we blame ourselves for the unhappy event and (2) focus our attention on other people rather than ourselves, especially those clearly in need of assistance.

This consideration obviously brings us to the matter of guilt: We're likely to feel guilty, of course, if we believe that we ourselves are responsible for the bad event. If we then see that another person requires help, we might want to aid her (or him) in order to make amends and reduce our guilt feelings. What about this possibility? Is there any evidence that guilt can motivate benevolence?

A line of research initiated more than three decades ago suggests that this can indeed be so. In these experiments, many subjects were led to transgress against traditional rules of conduct. Subsequently they were especially helpful to a person in need, presumably because of the guilt resulting from their transgression.

> *In one of the earliest of these investigations, Freedman, Wallington, and Bless induced male high school students to lie. While each student individually awaited his turn in the experiment, the experimenter's accomplice entered the room, saying he had just finished serving in the study. In half of the cases, the accomplice told the waiting participant about a test the participant soon would take; in the remaining cases, nothing was said about this task. Shortly after the accomplice left, the experimenter came into the room and asked the participant if he had heard about the test to come. All but one of the persons who had been given the information by the accomplice lied, denying knowledge of the test.*
>
> *Each participant was then put to work on his assignment. When this task was completed the session supposedly was over, but the experimenter entered to request help. He told the subject that someone else in the department was looking for students to serve in another investigation but didn't have any money to pay them. Would the subject, the experimenter asked, be willing to take part in that other person's study? About two-thirds of the lying teenagers complied with the request compared with only about one-third of the participants in the control group.[37]*

Although there have been some exceptions, other studies have obtained comparable results. One interesting finding in this research is that the transgressors are often motivated to aid people they hadn't wronged. For instance, they can become more willing to donate their blood to a blood bank. They may even give help voluntarily without being asked.[38]

Another aspect of this research also deserves comment. In a number of studies, the misdeed prompting the helpfulness was inadvertent rather than deliberate. To cite just two examples, in another experiment by Freedman and his colleagues, and also in the Cialdini investigation mentioned before, the transgression committed was the accidental disruption of someone else's work. Here too, those who thought they had misbehaved, even though inadvertently, were especially willing to aid another person (someone other than the one they had wronged).[39]

However, a question now comes to mind. Should we regard the misdeeds involved in these last-mentioned experiments as transgressions producing guilt? We usually think that people will feel guilty, if they do at all, when they have intentionally carried out a socially undesirable action. This is what was involved in the first experiment by the Freedman group; the misbehaving participants had lied. In feeling guilty, these persons basically were chastising themselves; they knew they had deliberately done something bad. In the latter two studies I've just cited, however, the clumsy persons had not wanted to harm anyone or otherwise to misbehave. It might be better to say that the supposed wrongdoers had suffered a loss of self-esteem. If so, the transgression-induced helpfulness could be an attempt to repair a damaged self-concept.

We have some indirect evidence supporting this possibility. In one set of studies, many of the participants agreed to make a speech that opposed one of their strongly held attitudes. However, they apparently quickly realized that they were about to contradict their actual views publicly (and weren't fully aware of how they had gotten into this predicament); as a consequence, their image of themselves was presumably shaken. The research showed that they were then especially likely to assist another person in need of help, even though this other individual hadn't solicited their aid. In an investigation by another researcher, the participants in the crucial condition were deliberately embarrassed: They were informed that they would soon have to do such things as sing the national anthem and imitate a 5-year-old having a temper tantrum. Soon afterward, when they were asked for a favor, these highly embarrassed persons were much more likely to provide the requested assistance than were their nonembarrassed counterparts, and this was so whether the solicitor was the experimenter or someone else.[40] In all of these cases, I think it's fair to say, the participants had become somewhat doubtful about themselves; their self-esteem was disturbed. Their subsequent benevolence could then have been an attempt to regain their favorable view of themselves.

I would go even further. The guilt felt by people who knew they have intentionally acted improperly might also reflect their loss of self-esteem. In fact, there might well be an injured self-concept in guilt, as well as in shame and embarrassment, and there could be much the same felt distress in all of these cases. We give the feelings different labels – guilt or shame or embarrassment – because they arise for different reasons, but the experience in all of these cases is linked to a disturbed self-concept, and all of these disturbances might well prompt socially desirable conduct in an attempt to regain the sense of self-worth and reduce the felt distress.

If this interpretation has any validity, we would expect the transgressors' inclination to be helpful to decline when their self-esteem and/or their mood is restored in some irrelevant way before they have an opportunity to aid someone. This seems to be the case. According to two studies, whether the transgression was an act of clumsiness or a deliberate lie, the wrongdoers were not as helpful as they otherwise would have been if they had received a monetary payment or approval or a flattering report about themselves before the opportunity to help arose. Similarly, there was a reduction in the voluntary assistance provided by persons whose self-concept was shaken by their agreement to speak against their own beliefs if they had heard a humorous tape recording before the sudden emergency arose.[41] The pleasant experience evidently countered the distress stemming from their earlier misdeed, thereby decreasing their motivation to be benevolent.

A Final Thought

Finally, one concluding observation. Whether the feelings involved in guilt, shame, and embarrassment are similar or not, they apparently are somewhat different from those felt in other negative affective states, such as sadness and anger. Throughout this book I've maintained that, for many purposes, it is meaningful to consider only the hedonic value of an experience – whether it is pleasant or unpleasant, positive or negative. However, we've also seen that occasionally it is important to recognize differences among the affective states other than their valence. I've noted in this section that guilt and sadness seem to have different effects on helpfulness, and in earlier chapters I reported that anger and sadness do not have the same influence on the use of stereotypes.

I have little doubt that a truly comprehensive resolution of this problem must be broad and multilevel in scope. Consider the differences between anger and other negative feelings such as fear, sadness, and shame or guilt. All of these affective states are unpleasant and all can prime a range of negative ideas. However, as I noted before, they are also different enough so that they don't always bring to mind exactly the same kinds of cognitions. As just one example, anger is more likely than sadness to prime thoughts about blaming someone else. My guess is that at least part of this difference in what is primed can be traced to the greater level of agitation typically felt when one is angry. This disposition to blame others could also influence angry people's relatively low readiness to be helpful, in comparison to the relatively high willingness to provide help by those feeling shame or guilt. But in addition to making use of cognitive notions, a complete explanation of the differences among the various affective states probably will also have to refer to motivational concepts and/or to the motor-action programs that are characteristically associated with each specific feeling. Thus, whereas fear is typically associated with a relatively predominant avoidance tendency, an urge to get away from the perceived danger, anger is often accompanied by both avoidance and relatively strong approach inclinations, in that the anger experience is usually linked to an urge to approach and strike at some target.

Whatever the exact reasons for the differences among the various affective states, it's an exciting challenge to determine when a feeling's valence is of overriding importance in affecting the psychological and behavioral outcomes and when the specific qualities of the affective experience become more significant.

Notes

Introduction

1. See Oatley and Jenkins (1996, pp. 254–256) for the reference to the Oatley and Duncan study, as well as citations to other research into this phenomenon and a brief discussion of free-floating emotions.
2. From James (1890, Vol. 2, p. 449).
3. Carlson and Hatfield (1992), Izard (1991), and Lazarus (1991).

1. Feelings: Their Nature and Causes

1. See Chapter 4 in Oatley and Jenkins (1996) for an interesting and representative discussion of how many psychological researchers conceive of emotions. As will be pointed out later, I agree with Zajonc's (1980; Winkielman, Zajonc, & Schwarz, 1997) contention that particular stimuli can automatically generate affective reactions even when they are presented below the level of conscious awareness. More pertinent to this difference between moods and emotions, Zajonc's research (e.g., Murphy, Monohan, & Zajonc, 1995) indicates that affective states tend to have a broadly diffuse influence on evaluations of otherwise neutral stimuli when there is little awareness of the source of this affective state (as is often the case with moods) but that this affective influence is more constrained when the source is apparent.
2. See Russell and Feldman Barrett (1999, especially p. 806).
3. Russell and Feldman Barrett (1999). Russell and his colleagues have developed this conceptual model over the past two decades. Russell (1980) was the first to propose that the two affect dimensions define a circumplex in which feelings' descriptors can be located around the perimeter of a circle. Interested readers should also consult Russell and Carroll (1999a, 1999b) for a further discussion of the Russell formulation, especially in regard to differences between this conception and the theoretical scheme advanced by Watson and Tellegen (1985; also see Watson, Wiese, Vaidya, & Tellegen, 1999).
4. See Larsen and Diener (1992, p. 26). In discussing the advantages and

191

shortcomings of circumplex models of emotion, this article reviews the pertinent research literature up to the time of that writing and proposes an integration of the Russell and Watson–Tellegen formulations of the dimensions of affective experience.

5. Russell (1980, pp. 1167–1169). In the first study, Canadian university undergraduates were asked to place each of 28 affect words anywhere along a circle. In other studies, different procedures were employed, such as asking the undergraduates to group the affect words into clusters, depending on their similarity. These procedures all yielded essentially similar results, although there was some variation in the exact placement of a number of affect terms.

6. Watson and Tellegen (1985). The figure presented here, modified from a diagram in that article, is based on a statistical analysis of several studies in which the participants rated their situationally induced moods.

7. See Watson et al. (1999) for an overview of the Watson–Tellegen group's latest research. In this paper the authors summarize a considerable body of evidence, including findings from psychobiological investigations, supporting their thesis. They also point to some problems with details of the earlier Watson–Tellegen formulation.

8. Watson and Tellegen (1985, p. 221).

9. As reported by Reisenzein (1994, p. 537), Lang and his colleagues found that ratings along the pleasure-displeasure dimension varied with muscular activity in the face as well as with heart rate, and that skin conductance varied with arousal ratings.

10. Scherer and Tannenbaum (1986) asked a random sample of telephone subscribers in the San Francisco area about their emotional experiences and found that seemingly incompatible feelings, such as happiness and anxiety, can occur together. But in keeping with both the Russell and Watson–Tellegen models, they also observed that emotional experiences were often a blend of similarly toned feelings. Thus, anger was frequently reported together with fear and sadness. We can speak of generally positive/pleasant and generally negative/unpleasant feelings. The last-mentioned study is Zevon and Tellegen (1982). More recently, Fredrickson (1998) has argued that positive and negative emotions are not only different in feeling tone but also have altogether different psychological functions. Her formulation holds that positive emotions serve to broaden people's "momentary thought-action repertoire."

11. Berenbaum, Fujita, and Pfennig (1995). The findings just mentioned do not mean that the participants did not differentiate at all among the three negative moods. Experiencing any one of the three negative moods in the first 3 weeks was the best predictor that the same kind of mood would be felt in the second 3 weeks. Also, in Study 2 in the Berenbaum et al. (1995) series, the researchers looked at the relationships between the participants' mood trait measures (persistent tendencies to experience a given mood) and the feelings they reported immediately after a midterm examination. They found that the participants' reports of how much they tended to be generally sad or fearful predicted how angry they felt right after the exam,

whereas trait fear and trait anger did not predict feeling sad after the test, and the sadness and anger traits did not forecast feeling afraid.
12. See Davidson (1994, especially p. 240) for citations to the relevant studies.
13. Cacioppo, Gardner, and Berntson (1999). Also see Ito, Cacioppo, and Lang (1998).
14. Larsen and Diener (1992, p. 30). The interested reader would do well to consult these writers' article "Promises and Problems with the Circumplex Model of Emotion." The more recent papers by Barrett and Russell (1998), and Russell and Carroll (1999a) are also pertinent.
15. Watson et al. (1999), especially p. 827). Also see Watson and Tellegen (1999).
16. The first quotation about the bipolar affect dimension is from Watson and Tellegen (1999, p. 609). The following observation is from Russell and Carroll (1999b, p. 614).
17. The new Watson–Tellegen position summarized here is discussed in Watson et al. (1999) and in Watson and Tellegen (1999). The Larsen and Diener (1992) attempted reconciliation is also discussed in Russell and Feldman Barrett (1999). The quoted phrases regarding the new Watson–Tellegen conception are from Russell and Carroll (1999b).
18. Diener and Iran-Nejad (1986), Study 2. Also see Diener (1999).
19. Research by Daly, Lancee, and Polivy (1983) suggests that affective experiences are better described by a three-dimensional conical model than by the more commonly discussed two-dimensional circumplex model. In this revision, affect intensity, ranging from intense to neutral, is the third dimension rising perpendicularly from the two-dimensional base formed by the pleasure-displeasure and arousal-sleep (or active-passive) axes. Analysis of the participants' affect ratings in this study revealed that their happy experiences were typically more intense, and thus closer to the circumplex base, than were any amused feelings they had. The data also indicated that the extent or range of the pleasure-displeasure and active-passive dimensions tends to diminish with height above the plane, that is, as intensity decreases. If distance apart on the pleasure-displeasure axis can then be taken as an index of the degree of incompatibility of the positive affect and negative affect systems, this conical model suggests that they are less and less in opposition to each other as affect intensity declines.

　　A number of studies have now shown that intensity is an important aspect of affective experience, whether one is concerned with this experience at a moment in time (i.e., with affective states) or over a fairly long interval (i.e., with affective traits). Nevertheless, as Frijda, Ortony, Sonnemans, and Clore (1992) have pointed out, emotions researchers by and large have given relatively little attention to affective intensity. Notable exceptions can be found in papers by Diener cited in this section and by Reisenzein (1994). Frijda et al. (1992) have also discussed some of the complexities and problems in the assessment of affective intensity.
20. See Schimmack and Diener (1997).
21. Watson and Tellegen (1999); Russell and Carroll (1999b).

22. Haslam (1995).
23. Niedenthal's research is reported in Niedenthal, Halberstadt, and Setter-
    lund (1997). Among the several other theorists who also posit discretely
    different emotional states are Izard (1991) and Oatley and Johnson-Laird
    (1987).
24. Scherer and Wallbott (1994).
25. Scherer and Wallbott (1994, p. 326). However, see Rimé, Philippot, and
    Cisamolo (1990) for an opposing view.
26. There may also be personality differences in the readiness to regard affec-
    tive experiences as discrete states or as varying along a continuum. Barrett
    (1998) found that people who think of their affective experiences primarily
    in terms of their valence (i.e., how pleasant or unpleasant they are) tend
    to group similarly valenced states together, whereas those who focus
    mainly on their arousal level are much more apt to view these states as
    discretely different.
27. Larsen and Diener (1992, pp. 26–27).
28. For the influence of pleasant sunshine on mood, see Schwarz and Clore
    (1983) and Cunningham (1979). The room-appearance manipulation was
    used in experiments by Schwarz and Clore (1983) and by Schwarz, Strack,
    Kommer, and Wagner (1987). In the latter study, the pleasant room was
    furnished with comfortable armchairs and decorated with flowers and
    posters, whereas the unpleasant room was a small lab room containing
    cleaning and painting tools that was dirty, smelled bad, and was lit only
    by a flickering light bulb. Fried and Berkowitz (1979) employed brief
    music selections to affect their subjects' mood. In their experiment, Men-
    delssohn's "Songs without Words" put the participants in a pleasant
    mood, whereas Coltrane's "Meditations" evoked unpleasant feelings.
    More recent research using this procedure was reported by Eich and
    Metcalfe (1989) and Niedenthal and Setterlund (1994). For an overview of
    the use of music as a mood induction procedure, see Clark (1983).
29. The experiment mentioned here was reported by Gale and Jacobson in
    1970 and is cited in Bandura (1986, p. 185). Psychologists studying condi-
    tioning do not altogether agree on just what is involved in this learning.
    Bandura (1986), among others, prefers Rescorla's argument that the con-
    ditioned stimulus develops its effect primarily through its ability to pre-
    dict or signal the coming of the unconditioned stimulus. However, Bae-
    yens, Eelen, and van den Bergh (1990) hold that there is a difference
    between signal conditioning (emphasized by Rescorla and Bandura) and
    what they termed *evaluative conditioning*. This latter type of learning is
    based on the association of particular feelings with certain environmental
    cues, and this is what is of concern to us here. The Baeyens team, among
    others, presented evidence that this conditioning can occur without con-
    scious awareness of the connection between the previously neutral stimu-
    lus (the conditioned stimulus) and the affect source.
30. Strack, Schwarz, and Gschneidinger (1985) have reported that the recollec-
    tion and reporting of the past incident will elicit an emotional reaction to
    the extent that (a) the event is described vividly and in detail, rather than

being mentioned only briefly, and (b) the occurrence is described concretely from the perspective of an active participant rather than abstractly as an outside, uninvolved observer.

31. Many researchers have employed the imagery procedure to induce particular moods in their subjects, including Bodenhausen, Kramer, and Susser (1994) and Strack et al. (1985). Berkowitz and Troccoli (1986) provide a survey of studies that used the Velten Mood Induction Procedure, and also examine the often repeated criticism that the subjects aren't emotionally aroused but only exhibit demand compliance; they supposedly have only adopted the role they believe the experimenter expects of them. In their survey, Berkowitz and Troccoli note the evidence showing that the procedure does indeed evoke depressed and happy feelings; thus, many of the induced effects are too subtle to be only the result of pretense. I should also note here that movie scenes depicting highly emotional incidents are usually also effective elicitors of particular emotional states (see Philippot, 1993) and that this procedure is conceptually similar to the Velten procedure.

32. The quotations here are adapted from Harrison's (1977) summary of public reactions to the Eiffel Tower, first shortly after it was completed and then over the years. Harrison's review of the studies of the mere exposure effect is an excellent survey of the published research up to the time of that writing.

33. Zajonc's original statement of his mere exposure thesis can be found in Zajonc (1968). As was noted just before, Harrison (1977) provided a later summary of relevant research. The most recent overview of this thesis can be found in Zajonc (1998, pp. 614–616). The mirror-image experiment was published by Mita, Dermer, and Knight and is summarized in Zajonc (1998, p. 614).

34. The claim, made by Smith and Bond in 1993, is quoted in Zajonc (1998, p. 614).

35. Harrison (1977).

36. Murphy et al. (1995). Also see Zajonc (1998). Bornstein, Leone, and Galley (1987) demonstrated that the subliminal mere exposure effect can influence attitudes toward other persons. It should be noted, however, that already established and strongly held attitudes are unlikely to be affected.

37. Titchener's proposal was published in 1910. The quotation is taken from Moreland and Zajonc (1977, p. 191). Zajonc's orienting response explanation is discussed in Zajonc (1998, p. 616).

38. Unpublished study by Monahan, Murphy, and Zajonc (1997), "Subliminal Exposure Effects: Specific, General, or Diffuse?" kindly shown to me by R. B. Zajonc.

39. Zajonc (e.g., 1980, 1998) argues, partly on the basis of his research showing that affective reactions can occur without cognitive input, that affect and cognition are conceptually different processes.

40. There are several different theoretical analyses of how past experience with a range of stimuli of a certain kind (e.g., sounds of various frequencies, lifted weights, or even previously heard opinions on a particular

political issue) influences judgment of a later-encountered stimulus of that kind. Here I've made reference to Helson's (1964) adaptation-level formulation, which basically assumes that the adaptation level is the weighted geometric mean of the previously experienced stimuli of that kind.

41. Diener, Colvin, Pavot, and Allman (1991) have discussed the role of judgmental processes in affective experiences and have reported evidence that "naturally occurring intensely positive experiences are often preceded by negative ones" (p. 492).

42. E.g., see Bandura (1986), especially Chapter 6.

43. This procedure was used, for example, by Isen, Shalker, Clark, and Karp (1978) in an important relatively early social psychological experiment on the effects of mood on memory.

44. Bem (1972, p. 2).

45. See Bandler, Madaras, and Bem (1968) for an analogous study.

46. Duval and Wicklund (1972) originally termed their formulation a *theory of objective self-awareness* because they were interested in the effects of taking oneself as the object of one's own consciousness. The aggression experiment is reported in Carver (1975). Demonstrating heightened self-awareness, in one study mentioned in Scheier and Carver (1977, p. 625), when the participants were asked to finish the thoughts in incomplete sentences, those placed before a mirror used more self-referential ideas than did those in the no-mirror group.

47. The first two self-awareness experiments were reported by Scheier and Carver (1977). Evidence for the prediction about reactions to fear-arousing situations can be found in Scheier, Carver, and Gibbons (1981). Berkowitz (1987) found that mirror-heightened self-awareness increased the positive impact of a happy mood on subjects' helpfulness and tended to decrease the helpfulness of those in a negative mood. Carver and Scheier (1981, p. 107) cite one study, among several, indicating that attention to one's pain tends to intensify it.

48. See Carver and Scheier (1990) for these writers' first statement of their theory regarding the effects of rate of progress toward the goal. A later version of this formulation is presented in Carver, Lawrence, and Scheier (1996). The Hsee and Abelson study, first published in 1991, is summarized on p. 24 of this article by Carver et al. The findings reported here are taken from the Carver et al. summary.

2. More on the Causes of Feelings

1. James (1890, pp. 449–450).

2. Schachter and Singer (1962). Also see Schachter (1964). Agreeing with Schachter that "widely different emotions show relatively little differences in physiological patterns," Mandler (1975) also maintained that a cognitive process was primarily responsible for the differences among the emotional states, not specific reactions in the viscera or other bodily parts.

3. Marshall and Zimbardo (1979, p. 983). Whereas Marshall and Zimbardo, following the Schachter–Singer procedure, had injected epinephrine to induce physiological arousal, Maslach (1979) aroused her participants hypnotically and also failed to confirm the 1962 study's results. On examining the original findings closely, she questioned whether Schachter had drawn the proper conclusions from the results he and Singer had obtained. Plutchik and Ax (1967) published an early critique of the Schachter–Singer methodology.
4. Reisenzein (1983).
5. Ross, Rodin, and Zimbardo (1969). One person in the No Noise Attribution condition spent an equal amount of time on both puzzles.
6. Calvert-Boyanowsky and Leventhal (1975), among others, failed to find misattribution effects and offered a non-Schachterian suggestion about what was involved in these effects. The Nisbett and Schachter experiment was published in 1966.
7. See, e.g., Weiner, Graham, and Chandler (1982).
8. Arnold's reference to William James cited here is from p. 108 in the first volume of her 1960 book, *Emotion and Personality*. Her characterization of appraisals as "direct, immediate, nonreflective . . . [and] automatic" can be found, among other places, on p. 174 of this volume. Although Arnold spurred the use of the appraisal concept, several writers have noted that this idea has a long history and was essentially discussed by a number of philosophers including Aristotle, Descartes, and Spinoza. See, e.g., Scherer (1993).

   Readers interested in the suggested difference between the attribution and appraisal concepts would do well to consult Leon and Hernandez (1998). In their study, the subjects read about an incident while imagining themselves as either a participant in the episode or an outside observer. The presented information was varied to create certain attributions or appraisals. On analyzing the level of anger and guilt the subjects said they would feel as a consequence of the episode, the authors concluded that the appraisal model was superior to the attribution one in predicting the emotional outcome, especially when the subjects' personal involvement in the situation was high.
9. See especially Lazarus (1991) and Smith and Lazarus (1993). In the latter paper, Smith and Lazarus tested their model by asking their university students to imagine themselves in certain described situations and then to report on their appraisals and emotions. The results provided good support for the researchers' conception of the appraisals and core relational themes involved in anger, guilt, and fear/anxiety but much weaker support for their analysis of sadness, apparently because the model did not differentiate sufficiently between sadness and fear.
10. Space doesn't allow a citation of every relevant appraisal model and/or important discussion of these conceptions. Interested readers would do well, however, to consult at least the following papers for an introduction to these theoretical schemes: Ellsworth and Smith (1988); Frijda; Kuipers,

and ter Schure (1989); Lazarus (1991); Mauro, Sato, and Tucker (1992); Roseman (1991); Scherer (1997, 1999); Smith and Ellsworth (1985); Smith and Lazarus (1993); Stein and Levine (1990).

11. Scherer (1997, 1999) has noted that appraisal theories differ in the number of appraisal dimensions they propose. He suggested that in advancing their ideas of what appraisal dimensions are advisable, the theorists in this area have followed either (a) a minimalist approach based on notions of supposedly fundamental motives or themes (as in Lazarus' model), or (b) an eclectic approach that seeks to list as many dimensions as are necessary to maximize the differences among the various emotional states, or (c) a principled approach guided by "psycho-logical" considerations of what dimensions are necessary and sufficient to predict the arousal of the major emotions.

12. Mauro et al. (1992). The quotation regarding cultural differences in perceived control is taken from p. 310, and the quotation having to do with pan-cultural dimensions of appraisal is from p. 315. The appraisal dimensions these researchers identified were close to those listed by Smith and Ellsworth (1985).

    Using data from the study reported by Scherer and Wallbott (1994), Scherer (1997) also investigated cross-national differences employing measures of his "stimulus evaluation checks" (his appraisal dimensions). He also concluded that "a relatively small number of appraisal dimensions may be sufficient to classify the major emotion categories" (p. 113) and that "appraisal theories developed in Western contexts" are relevant to other cultures, although "there may well be culture-specific modulations of appraisal patterns," particularly in regard to "external causation," "immorality," and "unfairness." Testifying to some of these national differences, in another analysis of the same data, Wallbott and Scherer (1988) found that participants from poorer countries were more likely than those from richer countries to believe that fate and other persons were responsible for their emotional experiences. Interested readers should also consult Ellsworth and Smith (1988) and Frijda et al. (1989).

13. See Parkinson and Manstead (1992) and Frijda (1993) for a fairly thorough discussion of the problems facing appraisal theorizing.

14. Scherer (1997, p. 115) lists studies using each of these procedures. In addition to these, Levine (1996) analyzed reactions to Ross Perot's withdrawal from the 1992 presidential race in order to test her appraisal model of sadness, anger, and hope.

15. Parkinson and Manstead (1992, pp. 130–131).

16. Parkinson and Manstead (1992); Frijda (1993). Later chapters in this book, especially Chapters 5 and 6, discuss the effects of positive and negative moods on information processing.

17. Frijda (1993). He suggested that anger "involves the action readiness to remove an obstacle or wrong; attributions can be understood as efforts to identify a responsible agent at which the actual removal efforts may be directed" (p. 371) and that "attributing one's misery to a responsible agent . . . provides an object through which change can be affected and, in addi-

tion, it can produce some appraisal of controllability" (p. 372). The research providing supporting evidence was reported by Keltner, Ellsworth, and Edwards (1993).

18. See Zajonc (1980, 1984, 1998) for more complete elaborations of Zajonc's arguments. For Zajonc there are a number of reasons, in addition to the mere exposure research findings, why we should consider emotions and cognitions as being governed by separate systems, such as these: (a) neuroscience findings show that the hippocampus is the "major site for cognitive participation in the emotions," whereas the amygdala is "responsive to the affective valence of sensory stimulation." These structures "allow [an] affective response to be made before stimulus identification or recognition take place" (1998, p. 598; also see LeDoux, 1989); (b) there is an infinite number of distinct cognitions but only a small number of distinct emotions; (c) the concept of basic emotions is reasonable but not the concept of basic cognitions; (d) cognitions are about something, whereas affect can be free-floating.

19. Lazarus (1984). The quotation is from p. 124 in this article. Zajonc (1984) answered that Lazarus's conception of cognition is overly broad and vague.

20. See Parkinson and Manstead (1992), LeDoux (1989), and Leventhal and Scherer (1987) for various views of this argument.

21. See Leventhal (1980) for an overview of his theory of emotion and Leventhal and Scherer (1987) for their application of Leventhal's approach to the Zajonc–Lazarus controversy.

22. Izard (1993), for one, has theorized that emotional reactions can best be understood in terms of four hierarchically organized but separate systems ranging from a neural system at the lowest level to the cognitive system at the highest.

23. Adelmann and Zajonc (1989) provide a brief but scholarly history of this thesis in which they present information new to most psychologists. The Darwin quotation is from Darwin (1872, p. 22).

24. Cited by Adelmann and Zajonc (1989, p. 252). Adelmann and Zajonc, as well as Izard (1977) and Laird and Bresler (1990), have also pointed out that James's theory recognized the role of muscular reactions in initiating the emotional experience. However, to be completely accurate in this summary of James's theory, we should note that he was most definite about the effects of bodily reactions on the "coarser emotions," those in which there was "a strong organic reverberation": "grief, fear, rage [anger], love" (James, 1890, p. 449). We won't make much of this possible limitation here, however, because some research (e.g., Riskind & Gotay, 1982; Stepper & Strack, 1993) indicates that bodily reactions can affect emotional states other than those listed by James.

25. Tomkins (1962, pp. 205–206). Also see Izard (1977). As Adelmann and Zajonc noted (1989, p. 256), Tomkins downplayed the role of facial muscles somewhat in his later theorizing by holding that the facial skin was more important in the creation of emotional feelings.

26. Izard (1993).

27. Citations for these writers were given earlier. The paper by Adelmann and Zajonc (1989) also offers a convenient list of references. A good overview of Laird's theorizing can be found in the articles by Laird and Bresler (1990, 1992).

28. Lanzetta, Cartwright-Smith, and Kleck (1976). In his 1984 review of experiments testing the facial feedback hypothesis, Laird distinguished between the studies in which "facial expressions are manipulated more or less muscle by muscle" and the investigations in which "subjects are asked to exaggerate or minimize their expressive reactions, usually to deceive a purported observer" (Laird, 1984, pp. 909–910). Although there are experiments of both kinds that are pertinent to the weak version of the facial feedback hypothesis (e.g., Laird, 1974), the present discussion will focus mainly on the second of Laird's categories.

29. The best-known failure to confirm the facial feedback hypothesis was reported by Tourangeau and Ellsworth (1979). Laird (1984), among others, responded to this study, defending the facial feedback thesis. Matsumoto (1987) carried out a meta-analysis of the 18 facial feedback experiments cited by Laird (1984) and indicated that "the effect size of facial behavior on self-reported mood is actually only of small to moderate value" – a mean of .34 across all of the studies. However, Wood and her associates (1991) have pointed out that effect sizes of this magnitude are very common in social psychological experiments and aren't necessarily trivial. At any rate, what's important for us here is that facial expressions have at least some effect on emotional feelings. Adelmann and Zajonc (1989) have added to the list of studies showing this effect (up to 1988). Relevant investigations were also cited by Laird and Bresler (1990).

30. McCanne and Anderson (1987).

31. Buck (1980), for example, mentioned the first of these possibilities in his thoughtful review of the feedback studies prior to the 1980s. He suspected that many of the subjects might have caught on to the experimental hypothesis because, in most of these investigations, the subjects served in all of the experimental conditions and thus could have realized that the researcher was studying the effects of different facial expressions. Along with many other psychologists, Buck assumed that the participants who were aware of the research hypothesis would then be motivated to try to confirm this hypothesis – a somewhat questionable assumption in at least some instances. The second possibility would be favored by writers who like to think that emotional states are the result of mental rather than physical activity.

32. Strack, Martin, and Stepper (1988), Experiment 1. The second study in this paper demonstrated that the people in the pen-in-teeth group felt more amused than those in the pen-in-lips condition while they were looking at the cartoons. Note that the participants in these experiments served only in one condition, unlike the subjects in many of the earlier feedback studies. Conceptually similar results have been reported by Larsen, Kasimatis, and Frey (1992), who manipulated their subjects' facial expressions by taping two golf tees on their foreheads and then asking them either (a)

to contract their forehead muscles so that the tees were brought together or (b) to keep the tees still. The former condition actually activated the muscles ordinarily involved in the facial expression of grief. Again in accord with the facial feedback hypothesis, when the subjects looked at photos of sad scenes, those who had moved the tees together, thereby taking on the "grief" expression, rated themselves as feeling sadder than those in the control condition.

33. As was mentioned before, Tomkins (1962) was the best-known proponent of the facial feedback hypothesis. Also see Adelmann and Zajonc (1989) for a summary of Tomkins's views. The first posture study cited here was carried out by Stepper and Strack (1993) and the second one by Riskind and Gotay (1982). A later experiment by Riskind found that posture influenced people's reactions to success as expected, although nonpredicted results were obtained after failure. This anomaly is discussed by Duclos et al. (1989).

34. Winton (1986).

35. This experiment, carried out by Jo and Berkowitz, is reported in detail in Jo (1993), Experiment 4.

36. Zajonc, Murphy, and Inglehart (1989), Experiment 1.

37. Duclos et al. (1989), Experiment 2. When each participant was queried at the end of the session, only 1 of the 54 guessed the feelings the postures were intended to produce.

   In the first and very similar experiment reported in this paper, the male and female participants rated their feelings after moving particular groups of facial muscles. They reported feeling stronger fear when they activated the "fear" muscles than when they made the other facial expressions; similarly, they felt sadder when they took on the sad expression compared with the other facial actions. In sum, movement of the muscles usually involved in these emotional states tended to activate the feelings also involved in these states.

38. Keltner et al. (1993).

39. James (1890, p. 462).

40. The unpublished experiment just cited was conducted by Jo and Berkowitz in 1992 (see Jo, 1993). A more extensive summary is given in Berkowitz, Jaffee, Jo, and Troccoli (1999). The facial manipulation procedure employed in that study was devised by Martin, Harlow, and Strack (1992). Similar to the Berkowitz et al. experiment, this earlier investigation found that the people holding the "smile" expression had a more favorable reaction to an ambiguous story they read than did those maintaining the "frown" expression. This reaction, it should be noted, was initiated by the facial expressions and wasn't merely an intensification of an existing judgment. The Martin team also reported that engaging in a physically demanding exercise just before the mouth manipulation was carried out eliminated the influence of the facial expressions. For Martin and his colleagues, the subjects in this expression-immediately-after-exercise group had attributed whatever feelings had been generated by their facial expression to the exercise so that their reaction to the story was unaffected.

From the present perspective, however, it's also possible that the subjects in this exercise group were very attentive to their feelings and bodily sensations so that they regulated the effects of their facial expressions.

41. The interested reader would do well to consult other analyses of bodily feedback effects, such as Tomkins's original 1962 formulation, Izard's (1993) most recent discussion, and Zajonc's vascular theory of emotion (e.g., Zajonc et al., 1989).

42. Levenson, Ekman, and Friesen (1990).

43. The first-mentioned research was reported by Keltner et al. (1993). For the arm movement experiments, see Cacioppo, Priester, and Berntson (1993) and Priester, Cacioppo, and Petty (1996).

44. The best introduction to Laird's theorizing can be found in his recent papers with Bresler (Laird & Bresler, 1990, 1992), although he has employed this self-perception approach since the time of his doctoral dissertation (Laird, 1974). The 1992 paper provides citations to the studies mentioned in this section. The interested reader should also consult Martin et al. (1992) for a somewhat similar conception. The latter writers here offered "a theory of private self-perception in which people use their bodily sensations as information when making judgments" (p. 412).

45. Laird, Wagener, Halal, and Szegda (1982). Consistent with Laird's argument here, as well as with the Scheier and Carver self-awareness analysis discussed in Chapter 1, Kleinke, Peterson, and Rutledge (1998) found that the effect of facial expressions on affect is strengthened when people become highly aware of themselves as a result of seeing their reflection in a mirror.

46. Duclos et al. (1989).

3. Influences of Feelings on Memory

1. Bargh and Pietromonaco (1982). Daniel Schacter has summarized several of his pioneering investigations of implicit memory employing priming procedures in his 1996 book *Searching for Memory*.

2. Schacter (1996, p. 210).

3. Singer and Salovey (1988).

4. Snyder and White (1982), Experiment 1. The subjects' mood was established by the Velten procedure, which requires the participant to read a series of emotionally evocative statements, usually termed either "depressive" or "elated" in nature.

5. The best overall summaries of Bower's semantic network theory can be found in Bower (1981, 1991, 1992) and Gilligan and Bower (1984). Singer and Salovey (1988) have provided a useful overview of Bower's formulation up to the time of their review. Other theoretical models of emotion also could have been mentioned here, such as Leventhal's (1984) Perceptual-Motor Theory and especially the Interacting Cognitive Subsystems (ICS) formulation advanced by Barnard and Teasdale (1991). Much more complicated than Bower's theoretical account, ICS "assumes that mental activity reflects the collective action of a substantial number of specific

processes, each of which fulfills a particular function in the manipulation, storage or recovery of mental representation. Processes are organized into distinct subsystems. Processes within each subsystem operate on a particular kind of mental representation" (p. 2). Whereas Bower's analysis talks only of semantically mediated codes in propositional form for the registration of experience (e.g., "The dog bit me"), Barnard and Teasdale postulate an "implicational subsystem" in addition to a "propositional" one. This implicational subsystem presumably codes experience in a more abstract, schematic form than is done by the propositional subsystem. Other psychologists are troubled by the seeming inconsistencies in the research findings, such as the occasional failure to obtain evidence of mood congruency in memory and/or the failure to find state-dependent memory. (Both of these matters are taken up later in the chapter.) Still other critics question the Bower model's conception of an automatic, i.e., passively operating system. Still, with all of these questions, the present discussion is confined to Bower's formulation because this is the best-known and, I believe, the most integrative analysis of how feelings and memory interact, as well as the easiest to summarize here.

6. Bower (1981, pp. 136–138) has made an interesting observation in this connection that, unfortunately, doesn't seem to have been followed up in later years. He proposed that we can tell how similar one emotional state is to any other emotional state by determining the degree to which material learned in one state can be recalled while in the other state. Exploring this notion, a preliminary study employing hypnotically induced moods suggested that anger is more similar to sadness than to fear and that joy may be more similar to anger than to sadness.

7. Mayer, McCormick, and Strong (1995).

8. This 1975 experiment is cited in Baddeley (1990). Baddeley offered a general discussion of context-dependent memory in this book on pp. 268–271. Singer and Salovey (1988) also discussed people's affect as a context in which they learn particular material.

9. This 1978 experiment, by Bower, Monteiro, and Gilligan, and an earlier, conceptually similar one by Weingartner and colleagues in 1977, are cited in Bower (1981, p. 134).

10. Bower's failures to confirm his initial results are reported in Bower and Mayer (1989). Blaney (1986) also suggested that the phenomenon was real but very weak.

11. Eich (1995a) has provided a helpful overview of his research and thinking. The evidence showing that mood-dependent memory is more likely to be found with internally generated information is reported in Eich and Metcalfe (1989) and Beck and McBee (1995). Also, see Ucros (1989) for a meta-analytic review confirming the existence of mood state-dependent memory.

12. This quotation is taken from Eich (1995a, p. 70). Supporting evidence can be found in Eich and Metcalfe (1989), Experiment 1. In his seminal 1981 paper, Bower had explicitly proposed that the mood state-dependent effect would be seen most clearly when there was free recall, i.e., when

there were few if any cues present in the situation facilitating the remembrance of material.

13. Eich (1995b).

14. There are now many other findings consistent with this reasoning. For example, in some experiments, after the participants were affectively primed, they had to say quickly whether each word in a set of words shown to them very rapidly was positive or negative in meaning. In another investigation, they only had to pronounce each of these words. These studies typically showed that the response to a presented word in the list was faster if the word's meaning had the same affective valence as the priming stimulus. Moreover, this effect also occurred when the affective priming occurred below the level of conscious awareness (Hermans, De Houwer, & Eelen, 1994). In lexical decision tasks, participants have to decide whether a string of letters quickly shown to them is a word or a nonword. Here too, participants placed in a particular emotional state usually recognize the words more quickly to the extent that these words have the same meaning as the state they are in Niedenthal et al. (1997). Niedenthal has pointed out that affective congruence is not always obtained in these lexical decision-making tasks. On the basis of her research findings, she argues that the congruence in decision making is most likely to occur when the presented word is in the same specific category as the person's affective state (e.g, when the person is sad and the word has a specifically sad meaning) rather than when the word has only the same general positive or negative valence.

15. Matt, Vazquez, and Campbell (1992).

16. Mayer et al. (1995) account for the relative prevalence of pleasant memories in normal persons by noting that many people in our society regard themselves as more happy than sad. Their pleasant memories are thus congruent with their prevailing mood. When these researchers subdivided their subject samples into those who were relatively happy or relatively sad, they found that the thought associations that came most readily to the subjects' minds tended to be affectively consistent with the subjects' natural moods.

17. The more recent research was reported by Ruiz-Caballero and Gonzalez (1994) in Spain. The explicit memory task required the participants to recall words freely, and the implicit memory task involved completing incomplete words. Another relevant observation was offered by Burt, Zembar, and Niederehe (1995) in their meta-analytic survey of studies investigating memory impairment in clinically depressed persons. They found, as we would expect, that depressed persons' memory was worse for previously presented positive than for negative or neutral stimuli (p. 295). Showing how complicated the effects of clinical depression on memory can be, Burt et al. (1995) also noted that the depressives' free recall memory is more impaired soon after the material is learned rather than after a long delay (p. 296).

18. Bower (1992, p. 20). Bower suggested that as a consequence of the greater attention given to emotionally relevant information, the information pro-

cessing resources available to the person are depleted, so that very little information about emotionally irrelevant events is then stored in memory (1992, p. 17). Niedenthal and her colleagues (e.g., Niedenthal et al., 1997) have also emphasized how affective states influence what information is extracted from the surrounding environment. They suggested that an "emotional state primes . . . information specifically associated with the emotion. A consequence of this priming is that less sensory information is required from . . . [emotion-congruent information] than from emotion-incongruent information . . . for activation of the code to exceed the perceptual threshold" (p. 425).

19. Forgas and Bower (1987). Also see Bower (1992, p. 20). It is interesting to note in this connection that, according to Mineka and Sutton (1992), anxiety produces increased attention to threatening material, whereas depression does not. This difference might occur because information about possible threats isn't especially relevant to depression.

20. See Niedenthal et al. (1997).

21. Bower (1981) discussed in some detail how the better learning of mood-congruent material comes about. He summarized evidence for emotional selectivity in memory, including the better memory of strongly arousing occurrences, in Bower (1992, pp. 15–17).

22. The Bargh and Pietromonaco (1982) experiment cited earlier in the chapter is relevant here. Following the reasoning used in connection with this study, we can say that the person's angry feelings primed hostile ideas (bringing thoughts of this kind out of implicit memory), so that these ideas then shaped the person's impression of the ambiguous stranger.

23. See Blaney (1986) and Singer and Salovey (1988) for discussions of these apparent exceptions.

24. Isen et al. (1978). Mayer et al. (1995) have noted that in many investigations of naturally occurring moods, there was affective congruence in memory for positive moods but not for negative moods. However, one of their studies did reveal significant memory congruence for naturally occurring negative moods.

25. See Isen et al. (1978, p. 10) for Isen's proposal that a mood regulatory process promotes affective asymmetry. Isen (1993) later emphasized the different consequences of positive and negative affect, holding that negative affect is a less effective retrieval cue for negative material than is positive affect.

26. Taylor (1991) has conjectured that there is a widespread automatic tendency to try to minimize an existing negative affect by shifting one's thoughts, memories, and judgments in a positive direction. Available evidence indicates, however, that this tendency is not as automatic and prevalent as Taylor suggested. Highlighting the inconsistency in the findings regarding the effect of bad moods on memory, in the three studies of mood congruency under natural conditions reported by Mayer et al. (1995), two found no congruent effect for people experiencing unpleasant feelings, but the third investigation did find that those who were feeling bad did have a tendency to remember bad events.

206 Notes to pp. 82–89

27. Smith and Petty (1995).
28. Parrott and Sabini (1990). Blaney (1986) had also suggested that mood-congruent recall might result from the subjects' attempt to maintain their existing mood.
29. Parrott (1991).
30. Wilson and Brekke (1994) and Wegener and Petty (1997). Also see Berkowitz and Troccoli (1990).
31. Laird et al. (1982).
32. Riskind (1983).
33. Much of the discussion in this section is guided by Sven-Ake Christianson's (1992a, 1992b) surveys of the research on the effects of stress on memory accuracy. The interested reader would also do well to look at the somewhat different review and conclusions offered by Egeth (1994), as well as Peters's (1997) review of pertinent research. The section also takes up matters not considered in any of these surveys.
34. The survey of psychologists' opinions was conducted by Kassin, Ellsworth, and Smith (1989). Egeth (1994) has emphasized, however, that the research done up to that time actually did not support such a sweeping conclusion. He pointed to a review of 21 separate studies that reported improved memory under stress in about half of the investigations and worse memory under stress in the other cases (see p. 247).
35. Christianson (1992a) has summarized the 1982 Loftus and Burns experiment on p. 290 of his article.
36. The fire alarm experiment is Experiment 1 in Peters's (1997) summary of his research. The 1972 study by Baddeley is mentioned in Christianson (1992a, p. 285).
37. Cited in Christianson, Goodman, and Loftus (1992, p. 220). Loftus has discussed the possible errors in eyewitness testimony in her book *Witness for the Defense* (Loftus & Ketcham, 1992).
38. Egeth (1994) has highlighted this inconsistency. The research review just cited was carried out by Deffenbacher.
39. Yuille, Davies, Gibling, and Marxsen (1994).
40. The results of the interviews with the witnesses to the post office robberies, carried out by Christianson and Hubinette, are summarized in Christianson (1992a, p. 287). The study of the memory of the witnesses to the gun fight is published in Yuille and Cutshall (1986). Christianson (1992a) has also surveyed some of the research on the effects of emotion arousal on eyewitness memory showing an emotion-strengthened effect. Cahill, Prins, Weber, and McGaugh (1994) have added to the evidence regarding the memory-facilitating influence of the beta-adrenergic stress hormone system under emotion arousal.
41. Brown and Kulik published their paper on flashbulb memories in 1977. See Schacter (1996, pp. 195–201) for a summary of the Brown and Kulik research, as well as the results of later investigations.
42. Neisser and Harsch (1992). Larsen's observations, as well as the findings of other investigations of flashbulb memories, are summarized in Schacter (1996).

43. Weaver (1993).
44. According to Christianson (1992a, 1992b) and Christianson et al. (1992), the differences in the research results regarding the effects of stress on eyewitness memory are not due simply to whether the research used real-world events or laboratory simulations. In these articles, Christianson noted that these two kinds of studies often yielded similar results when they asked similar questions.
45. The quotation is from Easterbrook (1959, p. 183). Easterbrook's hypothesis is discussed at some length in Christianson (1992a, 1992b) and Eysenck (1984).
46. Useful discussions of the arousal concept can be found in Christianson (1992a) and Eysenck (1984).
47. See Eysenck (1984), especially pp. 334–335, and Bacon (1974) for summaries of research bearing on Easterbrook's thesis. Some of these studies question the possibility suggested by Christianson (following Bower) that memory will be affected only by arousal states that are attributed to the witnessed occurrence. These investigations found that high arousal levels increased attentional selectivity, much as Easterbrook predicted, even when this excitation was generated before the required task was encountered. If we are already aroused for some reason when we see the critical incident, our existing feelings might facilitate our later recall of a visually prominent feature of the event because our attention is now focused on this particular perceptually central detail.
48. See Christianson (1992a), especially p. 287. The *resource allocation model* offered by Henry Ellis and Patricia Ashbrook suggests another process that might contribute to the witnesses' relatively poor memory for peripheral details, at least when they are greatly upset. This analysis basically maintains that individuals have a limited amount of attention that can be allocated to the tasks before them at any one time. Theoretically, any emotional state they may be experiencing will draw some of their attention and thus will use up at least some of their attentional capacity, so that the attentional "resources" that are then available for other cognitive activities (such as the recall of past events) are lessened. In accord with this possibility, in one of their experiments an induced negative mood lessened the subjects' ability to recall peripheral information given them just before. It's not that emotions will impede recall of all previously encountered information. According to Ellis and Ashbrook, feelings will have the strongest impact on isolated items of information that are not well linked to other items and/or to an overriding idea, and peripheral details are apt to be of this nature.
49. Christianson and Loftus (1991). Although only the data from the third experiment are reported here, the results were quite consistent, generally speaking, over all of the studies. The findings in a more recent experiment by Wessel and Merckelbach (1998) also support the Easterbrook analysis. Young women, some of whom were very fearful of spiders, were required to look at a bulletin board on which were pinned various stimuli: (a) the crucial stimuli – a dead spider and a picture of a spider – and (b) more

emotionally neutral stimuli – pictures of a baby and of a pen. The women who feared spiders (the spider phobics) were the ones who were most emotionally aroused by the sight of the bulletin board. Then, when all of the participants were later asked to recall what they had seen, the highly aroused spider phobics tended to remember best what was for them the central, threat-related stimuli, the spiders, and had the lowest recollection of the more peripheral, emotionally neutral stimuli. Wessel and Merckelbach concluded that the results supported an attention-narrowing interpretation of emotional memory rather than a cognitive-avoidance account.

50. The study of memory for everyday happenings mentioned here was reported by Brewer in 1988 and was cited by Bower (1992, pp. 15–16). The quotation is from Bower (1992, p. 15).

51. The experiments cited here in which time spent viewing the crucial slides was deliberately controlled are by Christianson, Loftus, Hoffman, and Loftus and are reported in Christianson (1992a, pp. 300–301). Christianson (1992b) and Bowers (1992, pp. 15–16) list other research with comparable findings, and both offer a number of reasons why emotional events are often better remembered than neutral occurrences. Several theorists other than Bower, including Nancy Stein and her colleagues (1996), have also proposed that many persons who experience highly emotional events continue to ruminate about these incidents for a considerable time afterward. Whether stress engenders brooding or not, an interesting experiment by Cahill and his associates (1994) indicates that arousal-improved memory can also be due, at least in part, to the neurochemical reactions generated by the disturbing event. All of their participants were asked to recall a variety of scenes they had been shown earlier. Those who had previously been given a drug blocking the activity of stress-related hormones had no better memory of emotionally upsetting pictures than of neutral ones, whereas the participants who had been given a placebo demonstrated the usual better recall of the disturbing scenes than of the neutral scenes.

52. Bargh and Pietromonaco (1982).

53. See Christianson (1992a, p. 301) for a somewhat fuller discussion of this conjectured "preattentive processing" of emotional stimuli. It's worth noting that other psychologists have also theorized about the operation of automatic, preattentive mechanisms in emotional reactions. For example, see Hermans et al. (1994) and Johnson and Multhaup (1992). The latter writers proposed that some emotional events are first apprehended by automatically operating "perceptual memory subsystems" before these stimuli are then processed by "reflective subsystems" that activate more deliberate thinking and planning.

54. See Bower (1992), Eich and Metcalfe (1989), and Eich, Macaulay, and Ryan (1994).

4. Personal Traumas and Memory

1. See Loftus and Ketcham (1994, p. 142), for the references to Herman and Blume. Also see Loftus (1993) for an acknowledgement of the seriousness

of childhood sexual abuse. The estimate of the percentage of all women experiencing sexual abuse in childhood is taken from Williams (1994, p. 1167), and a more detailed review of relevant research is summarized by Pope and Hudson (1992). Especially notable is a national telephone survey cited by the latter authors (p. 460) indicating that between one-quarter and one-third of all women had been sexually abused. Without necessarily questioning this estimate, one should be cautious in accepting the figures that are given in some studies because the definition of sexual abuse and/or incest is at times quite vague and perhaps overly broad. Indicating this, on p. 142 of their book Loftus and Ketcham quoted Blume as contending that incest needn't involve intercourse, genital contact, or even touch, but "can occur through words, sounds, or even exposure of the child to sights or acts that are sexual but do not involve her." It is also worth noting that psychotherapists differ in the extent to which they regard their adult female clients as having been sexually abused as children. According to a survey of U.S. and British doctoral-level psychotherapists conducted by Poole, Lindsay, Memon, and Bull (1995), two-thirds of these practitioners believed that only a very small proportion of their clients had experienced penile penetration when they were children, whereas 10% of the therapists in the sample thought more than half of their clients had had such an experience (Poole, et al., 1995, p. 429).

2. The skeptics who voice serious doubts about the claim that repressed memories are extremely common are well represented by Loftus and Ketcham (1994) and Ofshe and Watters (1994). The quotation from Loftus in this paragraph is from Loftus and Ketcham (1994, p. 32). Loftus (1993) has also given careful consideration to this problem, and the interested reader would do well to examine this paper. She cited Blume's estimate of the frequency of repressed memories on p. 521 of this latter article.

3. This is the *Ramona v. Ramona* case summarized in the article by Loftus and Rosenwald (1993), published before the outcome (given here) was known.

4. In his "Autobiographical Study," written about 1924, Freud indicates that his early conception of repressed memories had to do with a warding off of ideas that were unpleasant to the self (ego). He had believed, he said, that "Everything that had been forgotten had in some way or other been distressing; it had been either alarming or painful or shameful by the standards of the subject's personality" (Strachey, 1953–1974: p. 29). However, many students of Freud's writings agree that as psychoanalytic theory developed, Freud conceived of repression as being motivated by anxiety arising from the unconscious anticipation that disapproved instinctual impulses could come into consciousness. Also see Erdelyi and Goldberg (1979, p. 376), for a discussion of the Freudian concept. From the perspective of this later, somewhat more restrictive conception, then, it might be best not to regard the failure to recall traumatic incidents as cases of repression. However, this term will be used here because so much of the controversy is couched as an argument about repressed memories.

5. Holmes (1990).

6. Pope and Hudson (1992, p. 455). These writers also show how vague the notion of sexual abuse is in many studies. In some cases, the term is quite

broad and involves such actions as "inappropriate touching." Moreover, according to Pope and Hudson, in several investigations it was possible that the reported abuse occurred after the bulimia developed. Contrast this evidence to the idea that bulimia results from sexual abuse with the testimony given by a psychologist to a New York legislative committee that "90 percent of patients hospitalized for eating disorders had been abused as children" (cited in Ofshe & Watters, 1994, p. 71). As Poole and associates have pointed out in another context (1995, p. 435), a number of clinicians may believe that eating disorders are associated with childhood sexual abuse because of their "confirmatory bias," a well-known tendency to remember best those instances that appear to confirm one's expectations; initially believing that a childhood trauma leads to eating problems, they may recall most clearly those cases in which the client has an eating disorder and also seems to have been molested as a child – and don't remember the other instances in which this linkage was not present.

7. Blume's claims are quoted in Loftus and Ketcham (1994, p. 22). Blume is hardly alone in believing that many different symptoms and problems are indicative of childhood sexual abuse. The Poole, et al. (1995) survey of highly trained clinicians in the United States and Great Britain found that many of these practitioners thought that certain client symptoms and/or problems were signs that the client had been abused in childhood. However, there was little agreement among these clinicians as to just what symptoms revealed this early mistreatment. ". . . Only one indicator (sexual dysfunction) was listed by more than 14% of the clinicians" (p. 430). The American Psychological Association's statement was made in its Internet release of October 1997, "Questions and Answers About Memories of Childhood Abuse."

8. Kaplan and Sadock (1991, p. 674), and Rogers and Wettstein (1988), among others, have objected to the idea that sodium amytal can be regarded as a truth serum. The latter writers also voiced concern about the suggestibility that this drug conceivably could establish (p. 197).

9. Baddeley (1993) provides a good introductory survey of what psychologists have learned about memory.

10. This quotation is taken from the report published by the American Medical Association's Council on Scientific Affairs (1985, p. 1919). The characterization of people in a hypnotic state in the preceding paragraph is taken from the same page of this article. The following paragraph summarizes the gist of the Council's conclusions. See the conclusion of the Council's report on pp. 1922–1923.

11. The interested reader might want to consult the two chapters on hypnotically influenced memories in Ofshe and Watters (1994), as well as the article by Lynn, Lock, Myers, and Payne (1997), for additional references to research on this general topic. We have another example of how subtle cues can influence what people report under hypnosis in Spanos's (1994) review of hypnosis effects. In one of Spanos's studies, some subjects were led to believe, before they were hypnotized, that children were frequently abused in past eras, whereas this "information" was not provided to the

other subjects. When all of the participants were then hypnotized and led to think they were returning to a "previous life," those subjects who had received the abuse suggestion were most likely to report, in their hypnotized "prior life" state, that they had been abused (p. 147) in that earlier life. Lynn and colleagues (1997) were also impressed with how readily hypnotized subjects developed false recollections. Although they believed hypnosis could be a valuable psychotherapeutic tool, they concluded that "the answer to the question of whether hypnosis should be used to recover historically accurate memories in psychotherapy is 'no' " (p. 82).

12. Loftus and Ketcham (1994) report letters Professor Loftus has received from parents crying out in anguish at the charges leveled against them by their grown children who, in the course or counseling or psychotherapy, recently "recovered" memories of having been sexually abused by their parents.

13. Terr's report of the children who had been buried underground is cited in Loftus and Ketcham (1994, p. 57) and is also summarized in Schacter (1996, pp. 205–206).

14. Malmquist, cited in Ofshe and Watters (1994, p. 42).

15. See Schacter (1996, pp. 202–203). The quotation is from p. 203.

16. This study, reported by Pynoos and Nader in 1989, is summarized in Ofshe and Watters (1994, pp. 41–42) and in Loftus (1993, p. 532).

17. Schacter's comment is from p. 206 of his 1996 book. The Ceci and Bruck observation is from p. 193 of their 1995 book.

18. See Loftus and Ketcham (1994) and Ceci and Bruck (1995).

19. See Loftus and Ketcham (1994, pp. 76–77). The quoted passage can be found in Baddeley (1993, pp. 192–193) and in Loftus and Ketcham (1992, pp. 17, 19).

20. Loftus and Ketcham (1994, pp. 96–97). Loftus does not claim that the experience of being lost somewhere is necessarily as disturbing as being molested by a parent or relative. She does believe, however, that the creation of "a false memory of being lost and frightened through [suggestion] might involve a psychological mechanism very similar to that involved in the creation of a false memory of abuse" (Loftus & Ketcham, 1994, p. 212). More recently, Loftus (1997) has summarized other studies demonstrating that false memories can be implanted in adults as well as in children. In the studies she reviewed in this paper, 15–25% of the adult participants accepted the suggestion leading to the false recollection. One of the investigations found that the tendency to adopt a false memory was correlated with high scores on the Creative Imagination Scale, a measure of hypnotizability (p. 62).

21. De Rivera (1997) discussed these and other criticisms of the charge that many patients recalling childhood memories of sexual abuse are actually the victims of falsely implanted memories. Pezdek et al. (1997) have shown how suggestions are accepted to the degree that they seem plausible, and Pezdek is the psychologist who questioned whether memories of childhood molestation can be easily implanted in patients. See de Rivera, (1997, p. 272).

22. Ofshe and Watters (1994, pp. 172–173).
23. Loftus and Ketcham (1994, p. 57). Shobe and Kihlstrom (1997) have questioned the validity of Terr's notion that repeatedly experienced traumas are especially likely to be repressed. They cited an investigation of children who had undergone an embarrassing and stressful catheterization of their urinary tract more than once. "Memory for the procedure was unaffected by its repetition. . . ." (p. 71).
24. Holmes (1990).
25. Freyd's discussion of the former Miss America's case can be found on pages 76–77 of her 1996 book. The present summary of the Cheit case is based on the reports in Schacter (1996, p. 249) and in Freyd (1996, pp. 6–9). In her discussion of this case, Freyd also answers a critic who questioned the idea that Cheit had experienced repression (see p. 13). Both Freyd and Schacter also summarize the case of Frank Fitzpatrick, a 38-year-old claims adjuster, who had remembered being molested by a parish priest a quarter of a century earlier. The priest later admitted his guilt (see Freyd, 1996, p. 5, and Schacter, 1996, p. 257). In his commentary on the Fitzpatrick case, Schacter also tells us that other people also came forward to accuse this priest of molesting them once the case had drawn the attention of the media, and he noted that about 20% of these persons said they hadn't thought about the abuse until the news story broke decades later.
26. Williams (1994). Her conclusion is given on p. 1173 of this article. Whereas critics might hold that the apparent failure to recall the molestation by a relative is simply due to a conscious reluctance to report the abuse, Williams answers by noting that "of those who did not recall the index abuse, over one third (35%) told the interviewer about other sexual abuse perpetrated by family members" (p. 1170).
27. Loftus, Garry, and Feldman (1994). Ofshe and Watters (1994) have taken a similar position in their discussion of Williams's results, saying that they show only that traumatic incidents sometimes can be forgotten (p. 306). This latter critique also points out that (a) only 12% of the interviewed sample had no memory of the target abusive incident, as well as no recollection of other abuses, and (b) contrary to Terr's contention that one repression enhances the likelihood of later repressions, those women who did not remember the recorded incident were just as likely as those who did recall their recorded abuse to report a later molestation (p. 306).
28. Schacter (1996, p. 261).
29. See Schacter (1996, pp. 242–247) and Freyd (1996, pp. 99–127) for discussions of how traumatic events can impair memory. It should be noted that these two memory researchers are not in complete agreement. Also see Erdelyi and Goldberg (1979) for reports of psychogenic amnesias.
30. Loftus's argument, as well as the quotations, are from Loftus and Ketcham (1994, p. 216). Schacter's comment is from his 1996 book (p. 256).
31. American Psychiatric Association (1994, p. 477).
32. See Schacter (1996, pp. 231–232).
33. See American Psychiatric Association (1994, pp. 424–425). Schacter de-

votes considerable attention to these unbidden recurrent memories in his discussion of the effects of trauma on memory (see Schacter, 1996, pp. 202–205). His examination of follow-up studies indicates that "the frequency of intrusive recollections tends to diminish but not disappear" with the passage of time (p. 203). Brewin, Dalgleish, and Joseph (1996) have published an especially interesting analysis of posttraumatic stress disorder.

34. See Brewin (1996) for the references to these and other findings.
35. Brewin et al. (1996, pp. 670–671).
36. Schacter (1996, p. 207).
37. Brewin et al. (1996, p. 676).
38. Neuroscientists studying memory now tend to believe that the hippocampus and related cortical areas mediate explicit memory, whereas the amygdala is involved with fear-related implicit memories. Both regions function in traumatic situations. Later, if one encounters a stimulus linked to the trauma, the hippocampal system operates in recalling the "cold facts" about the event, whereas the amygdala is responsible for the emotional/physiological reactions such as the muscle tension and increased heart rate.
39. Van der Kolk's theory is summarized in Freyd (1996, pp. 99–101). The suggestion of Brewin et al. (1996) about attention narrowing under stress, apparently based on Easterbrook's conception of how arousal affects the "range of cue utilization" (discussed in Chapter 2), appears on p. 677 of their article. Schacter's views on the possible distortions of traumatic memories can be found on pp. 205–209 of his 1996 book.
40. See Bowers and Farvolden (1996, pp. 358–359). As these writers pointed out, the psychiatrist Terr has insisted on this distinction between dissociation and repression even though she believes that victims of repeated traumas can repress their memories of these occurrences.
41. Freyd (1996, p. 129).
42. See Freyd (1996, pp. 148–149).
43. In their discussion of Williams's paper, Loftus, Garry, and Feldman (1994) raise a question first asked by psychiatrists Pope and Hudson: If repression occurred in only 10% of the perhaps 10 million cases of childhood trauma, we would have at least 1 million Americans who now possess repressed memories of childhood molestation. Why, then, are there "no published studies of groups of patients exhibiting well-documented cases of total repression and reliable recovery later" (p. 1180)? The American Psychological Association's Working Group on the Investigation of Memories of Childhood Abuse took a more middle-of-the-road position in their Interim Report on this matter and suggested that "it is possible for memories of abuse that have been forgotten for a long time to be remembered." However, they also noted that "The mechanisms by which such delayed recall occurs are not currently well understood."
44. Loftus (1993, p. 530).
45. Taken from the American Psychological Association Internet Website on Oct. 17, 1997.
46. Landers (1994).

47. Taken from the American Psychological Association Internet Website (www.apa.org) dealing with "Questions and Answers About Memories of Childhood Abuse" Oct. 17, 1997.

5. The Influence of Feelings on Judgments and Decision Making

1. See Mayer, Gaschke, Braverman, and Evans (1992) for a list of investigations that found mood congruence only under limited conditions.
2. Forgas and Bower (1987). As I noted in Chapter 3, Isen (1993) suggested that negative feelings are less likely than positive feelings to have affectively congruent effects. This asymmetry in outcome is far from inevitable, however, and several writers have proposed that affective congruence is ordinarily to be expected unless a regulatory process is activated that is aimed at lessening an unpleasant mood.
3. Johnson and Tvershy (1983).
4. Mayer et al. (1992).
5. See Bower (1981) and especially, Bower (1991).
6. Bower (1991) presents a helpful overview of his analysis of mood congruity in judgments. It's worth noting that the network theory's assumption that different emotions are represented as separate nodes in memory is consistent with the idea (discussed in Chapter 1) that we often respond to the specific nature of emotional feelings rather than only to their location along the two dimensions in the circumflex model: their pleasantness-unpleasantness and passivity-activity. The reader should also recall Niedenthal's contention (also mentioned in Chapter 1; see Niedenthal and Setterlund, 1994) that emotionally aroused people generally attend to external stimuli to the degree that these stimuli match their specific emotional state much more than to the degree that the stimuli are consistent with the hedonic value of their feelings.

   At any rate, two experiments conducted by Erber (1991) provide interesting support for the priming interpretation of mood effects on judgment. After establishing either positive, negative, or neutral moods in his participants, Erber showed that the happy persons generally believed there was a good likelihood that people said to have positive traits would behave in a positive, trait-related manner, whereas the negative-mood persons typically believed that people having negative traits were relatively likely to display negative, trait-related actions. The participants' prevailing mood apparently had primed affectively congruent ideas relevant to the mentioned trait, so that affectively congruent trait-related actions seemed more probable.
7. Forgas (1994); Forgas and Bower (1987).
8. See Schwarz and Clore (1983) for the initial statement of this MAI theory and Clore and Parrott (1991) for a later elaboration. In this later paper, Clore and Parrott said that MAI "focused on the implications of Wyer and Carlston's (1979) suggestion that a generally overlooked function of affective states is that they provide information or feedback to the experience that can be used in subsequent information processing" (1991, p. 109).

9. Chaiken (1980) popularized the use of this concept in social psychology. See Schwarz and Bless (1991), Schwarz, Bless, and Bohner (1991), and Forgas (1992a, 1992b) for more detailed discussions of the heuristic processing interpretation of the influence of moods on judgments when there is little thought.

10. This is Experiment 2 in the Schwarz and Clore (1983) paper. A later paper by Schwarz et al. (1987) reported that general, relatively nonspecific judgments are more likely to be affected by one's mood than are judgments of clearer, more specific matters, theoretically because people are often apt to simplify a complex judgmental task by engaging in heuristic processing.

11. Shin-Ho Ahn is Professor of Psychology at Pusan University in Korea. He plans to report this experiment fully in a Korean psychology journal. The original use of room appearance to manipulate mood can be found in Schwarz et al. (1987). Stapel, Martin, and Schwarz (1998) would refer to Ahn's third condition, in which the participants were asked to avoid letting their feelings affect their ratings, as involving a "blatant warning." Stapel and his colleagues found, as did Ahn, that this "warning" led to the greatest judgmental shift away from the influence source.

12. Contrary to the position taken here, Clore and Parrott (1991) seem to regard the priming and MAI conceptions as rival explanations of mood effects on judgments. They believe that priming effects influence "judgment only at the encoding stage of processing" (p. 116). Our examination of mood state-dependent memory in Chapter 3 has demonstrated, however, that there can also be priming effects at retrieval. Nevertheless, it is now clear that the priming account should be supplemented by bringing in cognitive processes.

13. See Forgas (1995a) for the most readily available statement of his affect infusion model. The quotations here are from p. 47 in this article.

14. The experiment described here is the first study described in Forgas (1993). Another paper, Forgas (1992b), reports three experiments showing greater mood congruence in memory and judgments of atypical compared with typical target persons.

15. See Forgas (1994), especially Fig. 5 (p. 65).

16. See Forgas (1995b, p. 762). The same point is made in Forgas (1995a).

17. For example, Martin, Seta, and Crelia (1990), Strack, Schwarz, Bless, Kubler, and Wanke (1993), and Stapel et al. (1998).

18. See Wegener and Petty (1997). These analyses include Martin's set/reset model (Martin et al., 1990), the Schwarz and Bless (1992) inclusion/exclusion analysis, the mental contamination account formulated by Wilson and Brekke (1994), and the flexible correction model advanced by Wegener and Petty (1997). Strack's (1992) account should also be included in this group. Interested readers are advised to consult Stapel et al. (1998) for a more recent and very thoughtful analysis of correction processes in social judgments. Stapel and his colleagues do not talk of an overcorrection effect and discuss only judgmental shifts toward or away from the influence source. In accord with the findings I'm presenting, these

writers argue that "people's ability to identify sources of bias is rather limited" (p. 805) and that corrections for this possible bias "do not come easily" (p. 806).

19. The Wilson and Brekke (1994) conception is very similar to the Wegener and Petty (1997) model. Terming their formulation the *flexible correction model*, Wegener and Petty provide evidence that judgmental corrections are steered by the individual's theory regarding the direction and magnitude of the biasing influence (see Wegener & Petty, 1997, p. 171, and Stapel et al., 1998, for a summary of this evidence). My analysis in this section is guided mainly by this model. It's also worth pointing out that the affect infusion model would say that the participants displaying the contrast effect had engaged in motivated processing because they sought to correct for a possible affect-induced judgmental bias. However, up to the time of his 1995 presentation of this formulation, Forgas's discussion of motivated processing emphasized only that this processing would minimize or even eliminate affective congruence in judgments. Nothing was said about how it could lead to a contrast effect.

20. The findings reported here are from Experiment 2 in Berkowitz and Troccoli (1990). The statistical analysis, a multiple regression analysis of the data, is not reported in this paper.

21. The Jo and Berkowitz experiment is summarized in Berkowitz et al. (1999). A multiple regression analysis of the data showed an interaction between feeling attention and reported anger level in affecting the number of bad traits attributed to the job applicant when the subjects were holding the anger-inducing frown expression: In this facial expression condition, the angrier the participants said they were when they were highly aware of their feelings, the greater the number of negative traits they attributed to the target.

22. This experiment, by Jaffee and Berkowitz, is summarized in Berkowitz et al. (1999).

23. Wood, Saltzberg, and Goldsamt (1990); Sedikides (1992).

24. Isen (1993, p. 274). This article provides a good review of relevant research, as well as her analysis of when and why positive affect promotes creativity and problem solving. Also see Isen (1987) for another survey of her research, as well as an examination of the effects of positive mood on social behavior. Aspinwall (1998) has extended Isen's line of reasoning to the matter of self-regulation.

25. Isen's research on the influence of affect on categorization, problem solving, and risk-taking is summarized and discussed in Isen (1993). The summary given here is taken mostly from this paper. The bargaining study, discussed on pp. 266–267 of that article, involved "integrative bargaining," in which trade-offs had to be made on issues of different value to them.

26. The study reporting a happiness-induced decrement in solving physics problems was carried out by Isen et al. and is cited in Isen (1993). In accord with Isen's argument here, Nygren (1998) has also shown that positive moods generally lead to a fairly strong desire to avoid possible losses when the chance of losing is high, but they promote greater risk-

taking when there is only a low probability of losing. Although Isen had offered such an idea in a 1978 paper with Simmonds, and spelled out this notion in greater detail in the 1993 chapter I'm now summarizing, the most recent and best-known statement of such a motive has been advanced by Wegener and Petty. See Wegener and Petty (1994) and Wegener, Petty, and Smith (1995) for these writers' proposal of a desire to perpetuate one's positive mood and studies supporting this thesis.

27. Bodenhausen, Kramer, and Susser (1994).
28. Melton (1995). Several of Forgas's experiments also found that positive affect often promotes faster decision making, particularly when the matter being considered is personally involving to the participants (e.g., Forgas, 1991, 1995b; Forgas & Fiedler, 1996). Hirt, McDonald, and Melton (1996a) list other studies that found a positive mood-induced decrement in cognitive performance. Adding to the studies they cited, Basso, Scheft, and Hoffmann (1994) reported that people who characteristically had intensely positive feelings when pleasantly aroused did worse on a learning task than did those who typically were low-intensity reactors. The researchers believed that the intensely positive affect was detrimental because it led these persons to divert their attention from the task.
29. Schwarz and Bless (1991).
30. Schwarz and Bless (1991), especially pp. 58–62.
31. Forgas and Fiedler (1996); Bodenhausen, Kramer, and Susser (1994).
32. The previously mentioned study was reported by Bodenhausen, Kramer, and Susser (1994). The experiment just cited was by Bodenhausen, Sheppard, and Kramer (1994).
33. See Bless and Fiedler (1995) and Bless et al. (1996).
34. Bless et al. (1996). The quotation is from p. 673 of this article.
35. The quotation is from Bless et al. (1996), p. 677. The earlier article by Schwarz and Bless (1991) had also accepted Isen's observations regarding improved creativity under positive affect.

6. Feelings, Persuasion, and Motivation

1. See Diener and Diener (1996) for a convenient summary of the evidence.
2. A comprehensive review of early studies on the effects of mood on persuasion can be found in McGuire (1985). Petty and Wegener (1998) provide a much more up-to-date survey of the major research and theories dealing with the factors influencing attitude change.
3. Razran (1940). Razran believed this increased approval had arisen unconsciously because the students, when queried later, were unable to recall which slogans had been present while they were eating and which had not. Janis, Kaye, and Kirschner (1965) reported a better-controlled version of Razran's experiment that supported the original findings. Informal interviews with the subjects at the end of the session indicated that the food had also led to a more favorable attitude toward the experimenter.
4. See, for example, Cacioppo et al., cited in Wegener and Petty (1996, p. 332).

5. Schwarz and Clore (1983); also see Clore and Parrott (1991), Schwarz and Bless (1991), and Schwarz et al. (1991) for later discussions of this theoretical model.

6. See Schwarz and Bless (1991) for the original version and Bless et al. (1996) for the later modification.

7. Bless, Bohner, Schwarz, and Strack (1990), Experiment 1. The findings reported here were replicated in their second study and also by Bless, Mackie, and Schwarz (1992). I should point out that the subjects in this research, as in a number of the other experiments mentioned in this section, were asked to adopt a view counter to their existing opinions. A convenient summary of this experiment can also be found in Schwarz et al. (1991). This article also reports the conceptually similar results obtained by others, including Worth and Mackie (1987).

8. Mackie and Worth (1989). Here, as in the previously mentioned Bless et al. (1990) research, the participants were asked to accept a position contrary to their initial views. Interested readers should know that other writers have also proposed that moods can lessen attentional/cognitive capacity. Most notably, Ellis and Ashbrook (1989) have discussed how this capacity can be limited by a depressive mood.

9. Bless et al. (1996).

10. Isen and Simmonds (1978).

11. See Wegener et al. (1995), Wegener and Petty (1996), and Petty and Wegener (1998). Recent findings reported by Forgas (1998) can be understood in terms of this notion of happy people being unwilling to think much about negative matters. Forgas found that happy people are much more likely than their sad or neutral-mood counterparts to explain other people's behavior by employing an oversimplified and common conception of why people act as they do. However, this simple conception was used primarily when the explained action was undesirable for them. It could be, then, following Wegener and Petty, that Forgas's happy people were reluctant to think deeply about a negative matter that might lessen their positive feelings.

12. The quotation in this paragraph is from Wegener and Petty (1996, p. 348). The experiment to be summarized here is Wegener et al. (1995), Experiment 2.

13. See Martin, Ward, Achee, and Wyer (1993) and Martin and Stoner (1996). Hirt et al. (1996a) summarized the Martin et al. (1993) theory and findings and described their own research with supporting findings.

14. See Hirt et al. (1996a) for a summary of the study and findings. The complete report can be found in Hirt, Melton, McDonald, and Harackiewicz (1996b). Interestingly, in this study, as in Isen's research, the happy people came up with the most creative ideas.

15. Bless et al. (1990).

16. See Petty, Schumann, Richman, and Strathman (1993), Petty, Gleicher, and Baker (1991), Schwarz et al., (1991), and Forgas (1992a, 1995a) for summaries and discussion of relevant research.

17. The Elaboration Likelihood Model is discussed in Petty and Cacioppo

(1986) and Wegener and Petty (1996). Chaiken introduced her Heuristic-Systematic Processing conception in Chaiken (1980).
18. See Wegener and Petty (1996, p. 332).
19. Petty et al. (1993). This study is also summarized in Petty et al. (1991, pp. 191–193).
20. Petty et al. (1993).
21. Forgas (1992a).
22. Bless et al. (1990), Experiment 2. The interaction between mood and argument quality obtained in the two Bless et al. (1990) experiments was also obtained in a later study, using the same procedure, carried out by Bless et al. (1992). Also see Schwarz et al. (1991), especially p. 166, and Schwarz and Bless (1991) for a more complete explication of the reasoning involved in these studies.
23. Other findings obtained in the two Bless et al. (1990) experiments, as well as in later research by Bless et al. (1992) and others (e.g., Mackie & Worth, 1989), are consistent with the notion that people in a moderately bad mood may pay closer attention to the quality of the arguments presented by a communication than people in a good mood. In all of these studies, the thought-listing scores indicated that both the unpleasant feelings and the strong arguments fostered active thinking. Those in a bad mood listed a higher proportion of favorable ideas and a smaller proportion of unfavorable ideas than did the happier subjects when the arguments they encountered were strong rather than weak. In other words, the analytic processing evidently engaged in by those in a bad mood apparently did not necessarily make for a negative or even cautious appraisal of the high-caliber arguments. We'll soon discuss a possible reason for this affective incongruence. Other evidence (e.g., Forgas, 1998) indicates that the moderately negative feelings in experiments such as these did not interfere with the reception of the salient information but instead resulted in inadequate consideration of this information.
24. The first study was Wilder and Shapiro (1989), Experiment 3; the second investigation was Baron, Inman, Kao, and Logan (1992), Study 2.
25. Easterbrook (1959). Also see Eysenck (1984) and Baron, Logan, Lilly, Inman, and Brennan (1994, p. 182).
26. E.g., Ellis and Ashbrook (1989).
27. Bodenhausen, Sheppard, & Kramer (1994), Experiments 2 and 3.
28. An advertisement sponsored by the Mobil Oil Company and shown in Berkowitz (1975), p. 314.
29. Petty and Wegener (1998, p. 354) cited a meta-analysis of the fear-arousing appeals studies indicating that, over all the investigations, increased fear tends to involve increased persuasion.
30. The first experiment was by Janis and Feshbach (1953), and the second one was by Mulilis and Lippa (1990).
31. See Wegener and Petty (1998, p. 354) and Mulilis and Lippa (1990) for overviews of the Rogers model.
32. Leventhal (1970).
33. This latter experiment was by Leventhal and Watts and is discussed in

Leventhal (1970, pp. 140–141). In his 1970 paper Leventhal showed that personality factors, such as the individual's characteristic level of self-esteem, could contribute to the sense of vulnerability. He also presented other evidence indicating that the high fear-produced defensive avoidance often diminishes with time.

34. Experiments by Baron et al. (1992) and Baron et al. (1994) indicate that frightened people can think carefully about proposals made to them when the advocated behavior is seen to be a very effective way of avoiding the imminent danger.

7. Feeling Effects on Aggression and Helpfulness

1. Evidence consistent with this analysis can be found in Berkowitz et al. (1999) and is summarized in Chapter 5. In discussing Forgas's affect infusion model in Chapter 5, I suggested that a relatively high level of cognitive activity (termed the *substantive processing mode* by Forgas) increases the likelihood of affective congruence when there is no strong contrary opinion and no particular desire to be accurate in one's judgments.

2. Schwarz and Clore (1983) and Schwarz et al. (1987).

3. Griffitt (1970). The quotation is from p. 243. It should be noted that the effect of room temperature on the subjects' judgments was independent of the influence of the stranger's supposed opinions; the uncomfortable people in the hot room didn't give more (or less) attention to these views than did their comfortable counterparts.

4. A convenient summary of all of Baron's studies on this topic, as well as of other relevant studies, can be found in Baron and Richardson (1994), especially pp. 166–177.

5. The investigation of the possible effects of temperature on the urban disorders of the 1960s is summarized in Carlsmith and Anderson (1979). The study of temperature effects on crime in Houston is Study 2 in Anderson and Anderson (1984).

6. A detailed, comprehensive review of the many investigations bearing on the temperature–aggression relationship, by Anderson and by others, can be found in Anderson (1989). More recent analyses of the temperature–violent crime relationship, which compare the strength of the heat effect with the influence of the "southern culture of violence," can be found in Anderson and Anderson (1996) and Anderson and Anderson (1998). Baron and Richardson (1994) also summarize several of Anderson's studies.

7. Baron and Bell (1975) introduced their curvilinear hypothesis on the basis of a laboratory experiment. Anderson and Anderson (1984) and Anderson and Anderson (1998) argued against this notion, maintaining that temperature is monotonically related to the incidence of violent crimes. Cohn and Rotton (1997) provided evidence for a curvilinear, nonmonotonic relationship between temperature and number of violent offenses. They also reported other findings consistent with their explanation. It's also noteworthy, according to J. Rotton (personal communication), that the

curvilinear relationship is most pronounced for relatively minor acts of violence, such as disorderly conduct, and seems to become less curvilinear for more serious offenses.

8. See Anderson, Deuser, and DeNeve (1995), Anderson, Anderson, and Deuser (1996), and, most recently, Anderson and Anderson (1998).

9. These experiments, conducted by Ehor Boyanowsky and his associates, are cited in Anderson (1989, p. 91).

10. Rotton, Frey, Barry, Milligan, and Fitzpatrick (1979). Several of Rotton's studies are cited in Berkowitz (1993a). Also pertinent here is the experiment by Zillmann, Baron, and Tamborini (1981), which exposed subjects to irritating cigarette smoke. The participants in one condition could not attribute the irritation to the person they were judging, but they still punished him fairly severely.

11. See Moyer (1976) and Berkowitz (1990, 1993a, 1993b) for citations to relevant animal studies. The quotation from Izard is from Izard (1991, p. 237).

12. Also see Hutchinson (1983) and Fernandez and Turk (1995). The effects of physical pain on aggression are examined at some length in Berkowitz (1993b); this paper also cites some relevant medical observations.

13. The experiments cited by Anderson were conducted by Ehor Boyanowsky and his associates and are mentioned in Anderson (1989, p. 91). The latter studies by the Berkowitz group are described in Berkowitz, Cochran, and Embree (1981) and are also summarized in Berkowitz (1993a, pp. 54–55).

14. Landau's (1988) paper provides many references to studies investigating the relationship between objective and subjective indicators of social and economic stress and crime measures. Also see Berkowitz (1993a) for several references. Mawson (1987) is only one of several theorists who have emphasized the role of social stress in generating inclinations to crime.

15. Berkowitz (1993a, pp. 63–64) cites a number of analyses and investigations bearing on this connection between depression and aggression. The observations of the behavior of depressed children were reported by Poznanski and Zrull (cited in Berkowitz, 1993a, p. 63).

16. Berkowitz and Troccoli (1990), Experiment 1.

17. The James quotation is from p. 381 of her 1989 novel, *Devices and Desires*. Izard's statement regarding the sadness–anger linkage was made in his 1977 book *Human Emotions*. Both citations are given in Berkowitz (1993a, p. 62).

18. Termine and Izard (1988).

19. Ortony, Clore, and Collins (1988), Averill (1982), and Lazarus (1991). Also see Scherer (1993). Other theorists have taken what is essentially the same position, although they talk in terms of attributions. Averill's (1982) monograph provides a useful review of how philosophers and psychologists have analyzed anger-arousing incidents over the ages. See Berkowitz (1993a, 1999) for summaries and discussions of some of the better-known traditional social psychological accounts of how anger arises.

20. Averill (1982, p. 171).

21. Berkowitz (1999) discusses appraisal conceptions of anger at some length, citing other theorists as well as other findings. The experiment assessing

the afflicted participants' attributions for the unpleasant condition they were in was by Riordan and Tedeschi (1983). The research reporting the influence of induced anger and sadness on subsequent appraisals can be found in Keltner et al. (1993). Another study, by Quigley and Tedeschi (1996), also concluded that anger can sometimes cause blame rather than being a consequence of blame.

22. In actuality, many people do recognize that they are apt to become angry and aggressive when bad things happen to them – even when the causal agent had not intended to harm them. When Stein and Levine (1989) asked a sample of persons (young children as well as college students) how they would feel when various events occurred, the respondents were most likely to say that they would become angry if the causal agent had deliberately tried to hurt them. But a number of them indicated that they would feel angry after an unpleasant event even when it occurred accidentally or was caused naturally.

23. See Anderson et al. (1995) and Anderson et al. (1996) for discussions of the Anderson model and supporting evidence. My conception is spelled out in several places including Berkowitz (1990, 1993a).

24. The experiment, by Jaffee and Berkowitz, is summarized in Berkowitz, Jaffee, Jo, and Troccoli (1999).

25. Cunningham (1979), Study 2. Even thinking of a pleasant surrounding can promote helpfulness. Sherrod et al. (1977, Experiment 1) asked their student subjects to describe either the pleasant or unpleasant aspects of their residential environment and then solicited the students' assistance in solving a series of arithmetic problems. Presumably because they were in a better mood, the persons asked to think of the pleasant qualities of their residence worked longer to provide this aid than did those who thought of the negative qualities of their residence.

26. See Carlson, Charlin, and Miller (1988), Dovidio (1984), and Isen (1987) for listings of the many studies showing that a positive mood promotes positive behavior. On the basis of their review of the research literature, Carlson and his colleagues (1988) have noted that a pleasant event is less likely to lead to increased helpfulness when (a) someone else rather than the potential helper is the beneficiary of the positive occurrence and/or (b) the helping action lasts long (presumably so that the good mood diminishes with time and effort). For a later experiment showing that people exposed to pleasant fragrance are especially apt to be helpful, see Baron (1997).

27. Bohner, Crow, Erb, and Schwarz (1992).

28. The first experiment was by Isen and Levin, and the second study was by Forest, Clark, Mills, and Isen. See Isen (1987) for the citations.

29. Wegener and Petty (1996); Carlson et al. (1988).

30. Isen et al. (1978). Also see Isen (1987) for a general discussion of the effects of positive moods.

31. Clark and Waddell (1983).

32. Research growing out of the Duval and Wicklund (1972) self-awareness

theory testifies to the many different kinds of situations that lead people to focus their attention on themselves.

33. Berkowitz (1987), Experiment 2. Following the procedure employed in many studies of self-awareness (cf. Duval & Wicklund, 1972), the high self-awareness was established by stationing a large mirror nearby so that the subjects had to see a reflection of themselves. The moods were manipulated by asking the subjects to write an essay describing in detail a recent happy, emotionally neutral, or negative incident. Mood ratings indicated this procedure had been effective.

34. Cialdini, Darby, and Vincent (1973).

35. Carlson and Miller (1987). The interested reader will find another useful review in Dovidio (1984).

36. See Batson (1987) for an extensive discussion of how empathy can motivate altruism. Batson argues that empathy-motivated altruism is not egocentric in that it is impelled by a genuine sympathy for the victim and does not seek the reduction of one's own vicariously experienced distress.

37. Freedman, Wallington, and Bless (1967), Experiment 1.

38. The transgression-induced willingness to donate blood was shown by Darlington and Macker (1966). Regan, Williams, and Sparling (1972) demonstrated how a transgression can promote voluntary helpfulness.

39. Freedman et al. (1967), Experiment 2, and Cialdini et al. (1973). See Dovidio (1984) for a list and discussion of other experiments showing that transgressions can promote helpfulness.

40. The first set of experiments was by Kidd and Berkowitz (1976). The last-mentioned study was by Apsler (1975).

41. In the McMillen and Austin (1971) experiment the transgressors had lied, and their self-esteem was restored by giving them favorable feedback about their results on a test they had taken before. The clumsy subjects' inclination to be helpful in the Cialdini et al. (1973) experiment was reduced somewhat when they were paid money but was lowered even more when they received the experimenter's approval. The last-mentioned study was Experiment 1 in Kidd and Berkowitz (1976).

References

Adelmann, P. K., & Zajonc, R. B. (1989). Facial efference and the experience of emotion. *Annual Review of Psychology, 40*, 249–280.

American Psychiatric Association. (1994). *Diagnostic and statistical manual of mental disorders* (4th ed.). Washington, DC: Author.

Anderson, C. A. (1989). Temperature and aggression: Ubiquitous effects of heat on occurrence of human violence. *Psychological Bulletin, 106*, 74–96.

Anderson, C. A., & Anderson, D. C. (1984). Ambient temperature and violent crime: Tests of the linear and curvilinear hypotheses. *Journal of Personality and Social Psychology, 46*, 91–97.

Anderson, C. A., & Anderson, K. B. (1996). Violent crime rate studies in philosophical context: A destructive testing approach to heat and southern culture of violence effects. *Journal of Personality and Social Psychology, 70*, 740–756.

Anderson, C. A., & Anderson, K. B. (1998). Temperature and aggression: Paradox, controversy, and a (fairly) clear picture. In R. G. Geen & E. Donnerstein (Eds.), *Human aggression: Theories, research, and implications for social policy* (pp. 248–298). San Diego, CA: Academic Press.

Anderson, C. A., Anderson, K. B., & Deuser, W. E. (1996). Examining an affective aggression framework: Weapon and temperature effects on aggressive thoughts, affect, and attitudes. *Personality and Social Psychology Bulletin, 22*, 366–376.

Anderson, C. A., Deuser, W. E., & DeNeve, K. M. (1995). Hot temperatures, hostile affect, hostile cognition, and arousal: Tests of a general model of affective aggression. *Personality and Social Psychology Bulletin, 21*, 434–448.

Apsler, R. (1975). Effects of embarrassment on behavior towards others. *Journal of Personality and Social Psychology, 32*, 145–153.

Arnold, M. B. (1960). *Emotions and personality* (2 vols.). New York: Columbia University Press.

Aspinwall, L. G. (1998). Rethinking the role of positive affect in self-regulation. *Motivation and Emotion, 22*, 1–32.

Averill, J. R. (1982). *Anger and aggression: An essay on emotion.* New York/Heidelberg: Springer-Verlag.

Bacon, S. J. (1974). Arousal and the range of cue utilization. *Journal of Experimental Psychology, 102*, 81–87.

Baddeley, A. (1990). *Human memory: Theory and practice.* Boston: Allyn & Bacon.

Baddeley, A. (1993). *Your memory: A user's guide.* London/Garden City, NY: Prion.

Baeyens, F., Eelen, P., & van den Bergh, O. (1990). Contingency awareness in evaluative conditioning: A case for unaware affective-evaluative learning. *Cognition and Emotion, 4*, 3–18.

Bandler, R. J., Jr., Madaras, G. R., & Bem, D. J. (1968). Self-observation as a source of pain perception. *Journal of Personality and Social Psychology, 9*, 205–209.

Bandura, A. (1986). *Social foundations of thought and action: A social cognitive theory.* Englewood Cliffs, NJ: Prentice-Hall.

Bargh, J. A., & Pietromonaco, P. (1982). Automatic information processing and social perception: The influence of trait information presented outside of conscious awareness on impression formation. *Journal of Personality and Social Psychology, 43*, 437–449.

Barnard, P. J., & Teasdale, J. D. (1991). Interacting cognitive subsystems: A systemic approach to cognitive–affective interaction and change. *Cognition and Emotion, 5*, 1–39.

Baron, R. A. (1997). The sweet smell of . . . helping: Effects of pleasant ambient fragrance on prosocial behavior in shopping malls. *Personality and Social Psychology Bulletin, 23*, 498–503.

Baron, R. A., & Bell, P. A. (1975). Aggression and heat: Mediating effects of prior provocation and exposure to an aggressive model. *Journal of Personality and Social Psychology, 31*, 825–832.

Baron, R. A., & Richardson, D. R. (1994). *Human aggression.* New York: Plenum Press.

Baron, R. S., Inman, M. L., Kao, C. F., & Logan, H. (1992). Negative emotion and superficial social processing. *Motivation and Emotion, 16*, 323–346.

Baron, R. S., Logan, H., Lilly, J., Inman, M., & Brennan, M. (1994). Negative emotion and information processing. *Journal of Experimental Social Psychology, 30*, 181–201.

Barrett, L. F. (1998). Discrete emotions or dimensions? The role of valence focus and arousal focus. *Cognition and Emotion, 12*, 579–599.

Barrett, L. F., & Russell, J. A. (1998). Independence and bipolarity in the structure of current affect. *Journal of Personality and Social Psychology, 74*, 967–984.

Basso, M. R., Schefft, B. K., & Hoffmann, R. G. (1994). Mood-moderating effects of affect intensity on cognition: Sometimes euphoria is not beneficial and dysphoria is not detrimental. *Journal of Personality and Social Psychology, 66*, 363–368.

Batson, C. D. (1987). Prosocial motivation: Is it ever truly altruistic? In L. Berkowitz (Ed.), *Advances in experimental social psychology* (Vol. 20, pp. 65–122). San Diego, CA: Academic Press.

Beck, R. C., & McBee, W. (1995). Mood-dependent memory for generated and repeated words: Replication and extension. *Cognition and Emotion, 9,* 289–307.

Bem, D. J. (1972). Self-perception theory. In L. Berkowitz (Ed.), *Advances in experimental social psychology* (Vol. 6, pp. 2–62). New York: Academic Press.

Berenbaum, H., Fujita, F., & Pfennig, J. (1995). Consistency, specificity, and correlates of negative emotions. *Journal of Personality and Social Psychology, 68,* 342–352.

Berkowitz, L. (1975). *A survey of social psychology.* Hillsdale, IL: Dryden Press.

Berkowitz, L. (1987). Mood, self-awareness, and willingness to help. *Journal of Personality and Social Psychology, 52,* 721–729.

Berkowitz, L. (1989). The frustration-aggression hypothesis: An examination and reformulation. *Psychological Bulletin, 106,* 59–73.

Berkowitz, L. (1990). On the formation and regulation of anger and aggression: A cognitive-neoassociationistic analysis. *American Psychologist, 45,* 494–503.

Berkowitz, L. (1993a). *Aggression: Its causes, consequences, and control.* New York: McGraw-Hill.

Berkowitz, L. (1993b). Pain and aggression: Some findings and implications. *Motivation and Emotion, 17,* 277–293.

Berkowitz, L. (1999). Anger. In T. Dalgleish & M. Power (Eds.), *Handbook of cognition and emotion* (pp. 411–428). Chichester, UK: Wiley.

Berkowitz, L., Cochran, S., & Embree, M. (1981). Physical pain and the goal of aversively stimulated aggression. *Journal of Personality and Social Psychology, 40,* 687–700.

Berkowitz, L., Jaffee, S., Jo, E., & Troccoli, B. T. (1999). On the correction of feeling-induced judgmental biases. In J. P. Forgas (Ed.), *Feeling and thinking: The role of affect in social cognition and behavior* (pp. 131–152). New York/Cambridge: Cambridge University Press.

Berkowitz, L., & Troccoli, B. T. (1986). An examination of the assumptions in the demand characteristics thesis: With special reference to the Velten mood induction procedure. *Motivation and Emotion, 10,* 339–351.

Berkowitz, L., & Troccoli, B. T. (1990). Feelings, direction of attention, and expressed evaluations of others. *Cognition and Emotion, 4,* 305–325.

Blaney, P. H. (1986). Affect and memory: A review. *Psychological Review, 99,* 229–246.

Bless, H., Bohner, G., Schwarz, N., & Strack, F. (1990). Mood and persuasion: A cognitive response analysis. *Personality and Social Psychology Bulletin, 16,* 331–345.

Bless, H., Clore, G. L., Schwarz, N., Golisano, V., Rabe, C., & Wolk, M. (1996). Mood and the use of scripts: Does a happy mood really lead to mindlessness? *Journal of Personality and Social Psychology, 71,* 665–679.

Bless, H., & Fiedler, K. (1995). Affective states and the influence of activated general knowledge. *Personality and Social Psychology Bulletin, 21,* 766–778.

Bless, H., Mackie, D. M. & Schwarz, N. (1992). Mood effects on attitude judgments: Independent effects of mood before and after message elaboration. *Journal of Personality and Social Psychology, 63,* 585–595.

Bodenhausen, G. V., Kramer, G. P., & Susser, K. (1994). Happiness and stereo-typic thinking in social judgment. *Journal of Personality and Social Psychology, 66*, 621–632.

Bodenhausen, G. V., Sheppard, L. A., & Kramer, G. P. (1994). Negative affect and social judgment: The differential impact of anger and sadness. *European Journal of Social Psychology, 24*, 45–62.

Bohner, G., Crow, K., Erb, H. P., & Schwarz, N. (1992). Affect and persuasion: Mood effects on the processing of message content and context cues and on subsequent behaviour. *European Journal of Social Psychology, 22*, 511–530.

Bornstein, R. F., Leone, D. R., & Galley, D. J. (1987). The generalizability of subliminal mere exposure effects: Influence of stimuli perceived without awareness on social behavior. *Journal of Personality and Social Psychology, 53*, 1070–1079.

Bower, G. H. (1981). Mood and memory. *American Psychologist, 36*, 129–148.

Bower, G. H. (1991). Mood congruity of social judgments. In J. P. Forgas (Ed.), *Emotion and social judgments* (pp. 31–53). Oxford/New York: Pergamon Press.

Bower, G. H. (1992). How might emotions affect learning? In S. A. Christian-son (Ed.), *Handbook of emotion and memory: Research and theory* (pp. 3–33). Hillsdale, NJ: Erlbaum.

Bower, G. H., & Mayer, J. D. (1989). In search of mood-dependent retrieval. *Journal of Social Behavior and Personality, 4*, 121–156.

Bower, K. S., & Farvolden, P. (1996). Revisiting a century-old Freudian slip: From suggestion disavowed to the truth repressed. *Psychological Bulletin, 119*, 355–380.

Brewin, C. R., Dalgleish, T., & Joseph, S. (1996). A dual representation theory of posttraumatic stress disorder. *Psychological Review, 103*, 670–686.

Buck, R. (1980). Nonverbal behavior and the theory of emotion: The facial-feedback hypothesis. *Journal of Personality and Social Psychology, 38*, 811–824.

Burt, D. B., Zembar, M. J., & Niederehe, G. (1995). Depression and memory impairment: A meta-analysis of the association, its pattern, and specificity. *Psychological Bulletin, 117*, 285–305.

Cacioppo, J. T., Gardner, W. L., & Berntson, G. G. (1999). The affect system has parallel and integrative processing components: Form follows function. *Journal of Personality and Social Psychology, 76*, 839–855.

Cacioppo, J. T., Priester, J. R., & Berntson, G. G. (1993). Rudimentary determi-nants of attitudes: II. Arm flexion and extension have differential effects on attitudes. *Journal of Personality and Social Psychology, 65*, 5–17.

Cahill, L., Prins, B., Weber, M., & McGaugh, J. L. (1994). Beta-adrenergic activation and memory for emotional events. *Nature, 371*, 702–704.

Calvert-Boyanowsky, J., & Leventhal, H. (1975). The role of information in attenuating behavioral responses to stress: A reinterpretation of the misat-tribution phenomenon. *Journal of Personality and Social Psychology, 32*, 214–221.

Carlsmith, J. M., & Anderson, C. A. (1979). Ambient temperature and the occurrence of collective violence: A new analysis. *Journal of Personality and Social Psychology, 37*, 337–344.

Carlson, J. G., & Hatfield, E. (1992). *Psychology of emotion*. Orlando, FL: Harcourt Brace Jovanovich.

Carlson, M., Charlin, V., & Miller, N. (1988). Positive mood and helping behavior: A test of six hypotheses. *Journal of Personality and Social Psychology* 55, 211–229.

Carlson, M., & Miller, N. (1987). Explanation of the relation between negative mood and helping. *Psychological Bulletin, 102*, 91–108.

Carver, C. S. (1975). The facilitation of aggression as a function of objective self-awareness and attitudes toward punishment. *Journal of Experimental Social Psychology, 11*, 510–519.

Carver, C. S., Lawrence, J. W., & Scheier, M. F. (1996). A control-process perspective on the origins of affect. In L. Martin & A. Tesser (Eds.), *Striving and feeling: Interactions among goals, affect, and self-regulation* (pp. 11–52). Mahwah, NJ: Erlbaum.

Carver, C. S., & Scheier, M. F. (1981). *Attention and self-regulation*. New York: Springer-Verlag.

Carver, C. S., & Scheier, M. F. (1990). Origins and functions of positive and negative affect: A control process view. *Psychological Review, 97*, 19–35.

Ceci, S. J., & Bruck, M. (1995). *Jeopardy in the courtroom: A scientific analysis of children's testimony*. Washington, DC: American Psychological Association.

Chaiken, S. (1980). Heuristic versus systematic information processing and the use of source versus message cues in persuasion. *Journal of Personality and Social Psychology, 39*, 752–576.

Christianson, S.-A. (1992a). Emotional stress and eyewitness memory: A critical review. *Psychological Bulletin, 112*, 284–309.

Christianson, S.-A. (1992b). Remembering emotional events: Potential mechanisms. In S.-A. Christianson (Ed.), *Handbook of emotion and memory: Research and theory* (pp. 307–340). Hillsdale, NJ: Erlbaum.

Christianson, S.-A., Goodman, J., & Loftus, E. F. (1992). Eyewitness memory for stressful events: Methodological quandries and ethical dilemmas. In S.-A. Christianson (Ed.), *Handbook of emotion and memory: Research and theory* (pp. 217–241). Hillsdale, NJ: Erlbaum.

Christianson, S.-A., & Loftus, E. F. (1991). Remembering emotional events: The fate of detailed information. *Cognition and Emotion, 5*, 81–108.

Cialdini, R. B., Darby, B. L., & Vincent, J. E. (1973). Transgression and altruism: A case for hedonism. *Journal of Experimental Social Psychology, 9*, 502–516.

Clark, D. M. (1983). On the induction of depressed mood in the laboratory: Evaluation and comparison of the Velten and musical procedures. *Advances in Behaviour Research and Therapy, 5*, 27–49.

Clark, M. S., & Waddell, B. A. (1983). Effects of moods on thoughts about helping, attraction, and information acquisition. *Social Psychology Quarterly, 46*, 31–35.

Clore, G. L., & Parrott, G. (1991). Moods and their vicissitudes: Thoughts and feelings as information. In J. P. Forgas (Ed.), *Emotion and social judgments* (pp. 107–124). Oxford/New York: Pergamon Press.

Cohn, E. G., & Rotton, J. (1997). Assault as a function of time and temperature:

A moderator-variable time-series analysis. *Journal of Personality and Social Psychology, 72*, 1322–1334.

Council on Scientific Affairs. (1985). Scientific status of refreshing recollection by the use of hypnosis. *Journal of the American Medical Association, 253*, 1918–1923.

Cunningham, M. R. (1979). Weather, mood, and helping behavior: Quasi-experiments with the sunshine samaritan. *Journal of Personality and Social Psychology, 11*, 1947–1956.

Daly, E. M., Lancee, W. J., & Polivy, J. (1983). A conical model for the taxonomy of emotional experience. *Journal of Personality and Social Psychology, 45*, 443–457.

Darlington, R. B., & Macker, C. F. (1966). Displacement of guilt-produced altruistic behavior. *Journal of Personality and Social Psychology, 4*, 442–443.

Darwin, C. R. (1872). *The expression of emotions in man and animals*. London: John Murray.

Davidson, R. J. (1994). Complexities in the search for emotion-specific physiology. In P. Ekman & R. J. Davidson (Eds.), *The nature of emotion: Fundamental questions* (pp. 237–242). New York/Oxford: Oxford University Press.

de Rivera, J. (1997). The construction of false memory syndrome: The experience of retractors. *Psychological Inquiry, 8*, 271–292.

Diener, E. (1999). Introduction to the special section on the structure of emotion. *Journal of Personality and Social Psychology, 76*, 803–804.

Diener, E., Colvin, C. R., Pavot, W. G., & Allman, A. (1991). The psychic costs of intense positive affect. *Journal of Personality and Social Psychology, 61*, 492–503.

Diener, E., & Diener, C. (1996). Most people are happy. *Psychological Science, 7*, 181–185.

Diener, E., & Iran-Nejad, A. (1986). The relationship in experience between various types of affect. *Journal of Personality and Social Psychology, 50*, 1031–1038.

Dovidio, J. F. (1984). Helping behavior and altruism: An empirical and conceptual overview. In L. Berkowitz (Ed.), *Advances in experimental social psychology* (Vol. 17, pp. 362–427). San Diego, CA: Academic Press.

Duclos, S. E., Laird, J. D., Schneider, E., Sexter, M., Stern, L., & Van Lighten, O. (1989). Emotion-specific effects of facial expressions and postures on emotional experience. *Journal of Personality and Social Psychology, 57*, 100–108.

Duval, S., & Wicklund, R. A. (1972). *A theory of objective self-awareness*. New York: Academic Press.

Easterbrook, J. A. (1959). The effect of emotion on cue utilization and the organization of behavior. *Psychological Review, 66*, 183–201.

Egeth, H. (1994). Emotion and the eyewitness. In P. M. Niedenthal & S. Kitayama (Eds.), *The heart's eye: Emotional influences in perception and attention* (pp. 245–267). San Diego, CA: Academic Press.

Eich, E. (1995a). Mood as a mediator of place dependent memory. *Journal of Experimental Psychology: General, 124*, 293–308.

Eich, E. (1995b). Searching for mood dependent memory. *Psychological Science, 6,* 67–75.

Eich, E., Macaulay, D., & Ryan, L. (1994). Mood dependent memory for events of the personal past. *Journal of Experimental Psychology: General, 123,* 201–215.

Eich, E., & Metcalfe, J. (1989). Mood dependent memory for internal versus external events. *Journal of Experimental Psychology: Learning, Memory, and Cognition, 15,* 443–455.

Ellis, H. C., & Ashbrook, P. W. (1989). The "state" of mood and memory research: A selective review. *Journal of Social Behavior and Personality, 4,* 1–21.

Ellsworth, P. C., & Smith, C. A. (1988). From appraisal to emotion: Differences among unpleasant feelings. *Motivation and Emotion, 12,* 271–392.

Erber, R. (1991). Affective and semantic priming: Effects of mood on category accessibility and inference. *Journal of Experimental Social Psychology, 27,* 480–498.

Erdelyi, M. H., & Goldberg, B. (1979). Let's not sweep repression under the rug: Toward a cognitive psychology of repression. In J. F. Kihlstrom & F. J. Evans (Eds.), *Functional disorders of memory* (pp. 355–402). Hillsdale, NJ: Erlbaum.

Eysenck, M. W. (1984). *A handbook of cognitive psychology.* London/Hillsdale, NJ: Erlbaum.

Fernandez, E., & Turk, D. C. (1995). The scope and significance of anger in the experience of chronic pain. *Pain, 61,* 165–175.

Forgas, J. P. (1991). Affective influences on partner choice: Role of mood in social decisions. *Journal of Personality and Social Psychology, 61,* 708–720.

Forgas, J. P. (1992a). Affect in social judgments and decisions: A multiprocess model. In M. Zanna (Ed.), *Advances in experimental social psychology* (Vol. 25, pp. 227–275). San Diego, CA: Academic Press.

Forgas, J. P. (1992b). Mood and the perception of atypical people: Affect and prototypicality in person memory and impressions. *Journal of Personality and Social Psychology, 62,* 863–875.

Forgas, J. P. (1992c). On mood and peculiar people: Affect and person typicality in impression formation. *Journal of Personality and Social Psychology, 62,* 863–875.

Forgas, J. P. (1993). On making sense of odd couples: Mood effects on the perception of mismatched relationships. *Personality and Social Psychology Bulletin, 19,* 59–70.

Forgas, J. P. (1994). Sad and guilty? Affective influences on the explanation of conflict in close relationships. *Journal of Personality and Social Psychology, 66,* 56–68.

Forgas, J. P. (1995a). Mood and judgment: The affect infusion model (AIM). *Psychological Bulletin, 117,* 39–66.

Forgas, J. P. (1995b). Strange couples: Mood effects on judgments and memory about prototypical and atypical relationships. *Personality and Social Psychology Bulletin, 21,* 747–765.

Forgas, J. P. (1998). On being happy and mistaken: Mood effects on the fundamental attribution error. *Journal of Personality and Social Psychology, 75,* 318–331.

Forgas, J. P., & Bower, G. H. (1987). Mood effects on person-perception judgments. *Journal of Personality and Social Psychology, 53,* 53–60.

Forgas, J. P., & Fiedler, K. (1996). Us and them: Mood effects on intergroup discrimination. *Journal of Personality and Social Psychology, 70,* 28–40.

Forgas, J. P., Levinger, G., & Moylan, S. J. (1994). Feeling good and feeling close: Affective influences on the perception of intimate relationships. *Personal Relationships, 2,* 165–184.

Fredrickson, B. L. (1998). What good are positive emotions? *Review of General Psychology, 2,* 300–319.

Freedman, J. L., Wallington, S. A., & Bless, E. (1967). Compliance without pressure: The effect of guilt. *Journal of Personality and Social Psychology, 7,* 117–124.

Freyd, J. J. (1996). *Betrayal trauma: The logic of forgetting child abuse.* Cambridge, MA: Harvard University Press.

Fried, R., & Berkowitz, L. (1979). Music hath charms . . . and can influence helpfulness. *Journal of Applied Social Psychology, 9,* 199–208.

Frijda, N. H. (1993). The place of appraisal in emotion. *Cognition and Emotion, 7,* 357–387.

Frijda, N. H., Kuipers, P., & ter Schure, E. (1989). Relations among emotion, appraisal, and emotional action readiness. *Journal of Personality and Social Psychology, 57,* 212–228.

Frijda, N. H., Ortony, A., Sonnemans, J., & Clore, G. L. (1992). The complexity of intensity: Issues concerning the structure of emotion intensity. In M. S. Clark (Ed.), *Review of personality and social psychology: Emotion* (Vol. 13, pp. 60–89). Newbury Park, CA: Sage.

Gilligan, S. G., & Bower, G. H. (1984). Cognitive consequences of emotional arousal. In C. E. Izard, J. Kagan, & R. B. Zajonc (Eds.), *Emotions, cognition, and behavior.* (pp. 547–588). Cambridge/New York: Cambridge University Press.

Griffitt, W. (1970). Environmental effects on interpersonal affective behavior: Ambient effective temperature and attraction. *Journal of Personality and Social Psychology, 15,* 240–244.

Harrison, A. A. (1977). Mere exposure. In L. Berkowitz (Ed.), *Advances in experimental social psychology* (Vol. 10, pp. 39–83). New York: Academic Press.

Haslam, N. (1995). The discreteness of emotion concepts: Categorical structure in the affective complex. *Personality and Social Psychology Bulletin, 21,* 1012–1019.

Helson, H. (1964). *Adaptation-level theory.* New York: Harper & Row.

Hermans, D., De Houwer, J., & Eelen, P. (1994). The affective priming effect: Automatic activation of evaluative information in memory. *Cognition and Emotion, 8,* 515–533.

Hirt, E. R., McDonald, H. E., & Melton, R. J. (1996a). Processing goals and the affect–performance link: Mood as main effect or mood as input. In L. L. Martin & A. Tesser (Eds.), *Striving and feeling: Interactions among goals, affect, and self-regulation* (pp. 303–328). Mahwah NJ: Erlbaum.

Hirt, E. R., Melton, R. J., McDonald, H. E., & Harackiewicz, J. M. (1996b). Processing goals, task interest, and the mood–performance relationship: A mediational analysis. *Journal of Personality and Social Psychology, 71,* 245–261.

Holmes, D. S. (1990). The evidence for repression: An examination of sixty years of research. In J. L. Singer (Ed.), *Repression and dissociation: Implications for personality theory, psychopathology, and health* (pp. 85–102). Chicago: University of Chicago Press.

Hutchinson, R. R. (1983). The pain–aggression relationship and its expression in naturalistic settings. *Aggressive Behavior, 9,* 229–242.

Isen, A. M. (1987). Positive affect, cognitive processes, and social behavior. In L. Berkowitz (Ed.), *Advances in experimental social psychology* (Vol. 20, pp. 203–253). San Diego, CA: Academic Press.

Isen, A. M. (1993). Positive affect and decision making. In M. Lewis & J. M. Haviland (Eds.), *Handbook of emotions* (pp. 261–277). New York/London: Guilford Press.

Isen, A. M., Shalker, T. E., Clark, M., & Karp, L. (1978). Affect, accessibility of material in memory, and behavior: A cognitive loop? *Journal of Personality and Social Psychology, 36,* 1–12.

Isen, A. M., & Simmonds, S. (1978). The effect of feeling good on a task that is incompatible with mood. *Social Psychology Quarterly, 41,* 346–349.

Ito, T. A., Cacioppo, J. T., & Lang, P. J. (1998). Eliciting affect through the International Affective Picture System: Trajectories through evaluative space. *Personality and Social Psychology Bulletin, 24,* 855–879.

Izard, C. E. (1977). *Human emotions.* New York/London: Plenum Press.

Izard, C. E. (1991). *The psychology of emotions.* New York: Plenum Press.

Izard, C. E. (1993). Four systems for emotion activation: Cognitive and non-cognitive processes. *Psychological Review, 100,* 68–90.

James, W. (1890). *The principles of psychology.* New York: Henry Holt.

Janis, I. L., & Feshbach, S. (1953). Effects of fear-arousing communications. *Journal of Abnormal and Social Psychology, 48,* 78–92.

Janis, I. L., Kaye, D., & Kirschner, P. (1965). Facilitating effects of "eating-while-reading" on responsiveness to persuasive communications. *Journal of Personality and Social Psychology, 1,* 181–185.

Jo, E. (1993). *Combining physical sensations and ideas in the construction of emotional experiences.* Madison, WI: Unpublished doctoral dissertation, University of Wisconsin.

Johnson, E. J., & Tversky, A. (1983). Affect, generalization, and the perception of risk. *Journal of Personality and Social Psychology, 45,* 20 1.

Johnson, M. K., & Multhaup, K. S. (1992). Emotion and MEM. In S.-A. Christianson (Ed.), *Handbook of emotion and memory: Research and theory* (pp. 33–66). Hillsdale, NJ: Erlbaum.

Kaplan, H. I., & Sadock, B. J. (1991). *Synopsis of psychiatry: Behavioral sciences, clinical psychiatry.* Baltimore: Williams & Wilkins.

Kassin, S. M., Ellsworth, P. C., & Smith, V. L. (1989). The "general acceptance" of psychological research on eyewitness testimony: A survey of the experts. *American Psychologist, 44,* 1089–1098.

Keltner, D., Ellsworth, P. C., & Edwards, K. (1993). Beyond simple pessimism: Effects of sadness and anger on social perception. *Journal of Personality and Social Psychology, 64,* 740–752.

Kidd, R. F., & Berkowitz, L. (1976). Effects of dissonance arousal on helpfulness. *Journal of Personality and Social Psychology, 33,* 613–622.

Kleinke, C. L., Peterson, T. R., & Rutledge, T. R. (1998). Effects of self-generated facial expressions on mood. *Journal of Personality and Social Psychology, 74,* 272–279.

Laird, J. D. (1974). Self-attribution of emotion: The effects of expressive behavior on the quality of emotional experience. *Journal of Personality and Social Psychology, 29,* 475–486.

Laird, J. D. (1984). The real role of facial response in the experience of emotion: A reply to Tourangeau and Ellsworth, and others. *Journal of Personality and Social Psychology, 47,* 909–917.

Laird, J. D., & Bresler, C. (1990). William James and the mechanisms of emotional experience. *Personality and Social Psychology Bulletin, 16,* 636–651.

Laird, J. D., & Bresler, C. (1992). The process of emotional experience: A self-perception theory. In M. S. Clark (Ed.), *Review of personality and social psychology: Emotion* (Vol. 13, pp. 213–234). Newbury Park, CA: Sage.

Laird, J. D., Wagener, J. J., Halal, M., & Szegda, M. (1982). Remembering what you feel: Effects of emotion on memory. *Journal of Personality and Social Psychology, 42,* 646–657.

Landau, S. F. (1988). Violent crime and its relation to subjective social stress indicators: The case of Israel. *Aggressive Behavior, 14,* 337–362.

Landers, S. (1994, January). Walking the fine line of abuse recall. *NASW News,* p. 3.

Lanzetta, J. T., Cartwright-Smith, J., & Kleck, R. E. (1976). Effects of nonverbal dissimulation on emotional experience and autonomic arousal. *Journal of Personality and Social Psychology, 33,* 354–370.

Larsen, R. J., & Diener, E. (1992). Promises and problems with the circumplex model of emotion. In M. S. Clark (Ed.), *Review of personality and social psychology: Emotion* (Vol. 13, pp. 25–59). Newbury Park, CA: Sage.

Larsen, R. J., Kasimatis, M., & Frey, K. (1992). Facilitating the furrowed brow: An unobtrusive test of the facial feedback hypothesis applied to unpleasant affect. *Cognition and Emotion, 6,* 321–338.

Lazarus, R. S. (1984). On the primacy of cognition. *American Psychologist, 39,* 124–129.

Lazarus, R. S. (1991). *Emotion and adaptation.* New York/Oxford: Oxford University Press.

LeDoux, J. E. (1989). Cognitive–emotional interactions in the brain. *Cognition and Emotion, 3,* 267–289.

Leon, I., & Hernandez, J. A. (1998). Testing the role of attributions and appraisals in predicting own and other's emotions. *Cognition and Emotion, 12,* 27–43.

Lerner, J. S., Goldberg, J. H., & Tetlock, P. E. (1998). Sober second thought: The effects of accountability, anger, and authoritarianism on attributions of responsibility. *Personality and Social Psychology Bulletin, 24,* 563–574.

Levenson, R. W., Ekman, P., & Friesen, W. V. (1990). Voluntary facial action generates emotion-specific autonomic nervous system activity. *Psychophysiology, 27,* 363–384.

Leventhal, H. (1970). Findings and theory in the study of fear communications. In L. Berkowitz (Ed.), *Advances in experimental social psychology* (Vol. 5, pp. 120–186). New York: Academic Press.

Leventhal, H. (1980). Toward a comprehensive theory of emotion. In L. Berkowitz (Ed.), *Advances in experimental social psychology* (Vol. 13, pp. 139–207). New York: Academic Press.

Leventhal, H. (1984). A perceptual-motor theory of emotion. In L. Berkowitz (Ed.), *Advances in experimental social psychology* (Vol. 17, pp. 117–182). New York: Academic Press.

Leventhal, H., & Scherer, K. R. (1987). The relationship of emotion to cognition: A functional approach to a semantic controversy. *Cognition and Emotion, 1,* 3–28.

Levine, L. J. (1996). The anatomy of disappointment: A naturalistic test of appraisal models of sadness, anger, and hope. *Cognition and Emotion, 10,* 337–359.

Loftus, E. F. (1993). The reality of repressed memories. *American Psychologist, 48,* 518–537.

Loftus, E. F. (1997). Memory for a past that never was. *Current Directions in Psychological Science, 6,* 60–65.

Loftus, E. F., Garry, M., & Feldman, J. (1994). Forgetting sexual trauma: What does it mean when 38% forget? *Journal of Consulting and Clinical Psychology, 62,* 1177–1181.

Loftus, E. F., & Ketcham, K. (1992). *Witness for the defense: The accused, the eyewitness, and the expert who puts memory on trial.* New York: St. Martin's Press.

Loftus, E. F., & Ketcham, K. (1994). *The myth of repressed memory: False memories and allegations of sexual abuse.* New York: St. Martin's Press.

Loftus, E. F., & Rosenwald, L. A. (1993). Buried memories, shattered lives. *American Bar Association Journal, 79,* 70–73.

Lynn, S. J., Lock, I. G., Myers, B., & Payne, D. G. (1997). Recalling the unrecallable. *Current Directions in Psychological Science, 6,* 79–83.

Mackie, D. M., & Worth, L. T. (1989). Processing deficits and the mediation of positive affect in persuasion. *Journal of Personality and Social Psychology, 57,* 27–40.

Mandler, G. (1975). *Mind and emotion.* New York: Wiley.

Marshall, G. D., & Zimbardo, P. G. (1979). Affective consequences of inadequately explained physiological arousal. *Journal of Personality and Social Psychology, 37,* 970–988.

Martin, L. L., Harlow, T. F., & Strack, F. (1992). The role of bodily sensations in the evaluation of social events. *Personality and Social Psychology Bulletin, 18,* 412–419.

Martin, L. L., Seta, J. J., & Crelia, R. A. (1990). Assimilation and contrast as a function of people's willingness and ability to expend effort in forming an impression. *Journal of Personality and Social Psychology, 59,* 27–37.

Martin, L. L., & Stoner, P. (1996). Mood as input: What we think about how we feel determines how we think. In L. L. Martin & A. Tesser (Eds.), *Striving and feeling* (pp. 279–301). Mahwah, NJ: Erlbaum.

Martin, L. L., Ward, D. W., Achee, J. W., & Wyer, R. S., Jr. (1993). Mood as input: People have to interpret the motivational implications of their moods. *Journal of Personality and Social Psychology, 64,* 317–326.

Maslach, C. (1979). Negative emotional biasing of unexplained arousal. *Journal of Personality and Social Psychology, 37,* 953–969.

Matsumoto, D. (1987). The role of facial response in the experience of emotion: More methodological problems and a meta-analysis. *Journal of Personality and Social Psychology, 52,* 769–774.

Matt, G. E., Vazquez, C., & Campbell, W. K. (1992). Mood-congruent recall of affectively toned stimuli: A meta-analytic review. *Clinical Psychology Review, 12,* 227–255.

Mauro, R., Sato, K., & Tucker, J. (1992). The role of appraisal in human emotions: A cross-cultural study. *Journal of Personality and Social Psychology, 62,* 301–317.

Mawson, A. R. (1987). *Transient criminality: A model of stress-induced crime.* New York: Praeger.

Mayer, J. D., Gaschke, Y. N., Braverman, D. L., & Evans, T. W. (1992). Mood-congruent judgment is a general effect. *Journal of Personality and Social Psychology, 63,* 119–132.

Mayer, J. D., McCormick, L. J., & Strong, S. E. (1995). Mood-congruent memory and natural mood: New evidence. *Personality and Social Psychology Bulletin, 21,* 736–746.

McCanne, T. R., & Anderson, J. A. (1987). Emotional responding following experimental manipulation of facial electromyographic activity. *Journal of Personality and Social Psychology, 52,* 759–768.

McGuire, W. J. (1985). Attitudes and attitude change. In G. Lindzey & E. Aronson (Eds.), *Handbook of social psychology* (3rd ed., Vol. 2, pp. 136–314). New York: Random House.

McMillen, D. L., & Austin, J. B. (1971). Effect of positive feedback on compliance following transgression. *Psychonomic Science, 24,* 176–179.

Melton, R. J. (1995). The role of positive affect in syllogism performance. *Personality and Social Psychology Bulletin, 21,* 788–794.

Mineka, S., & Sutton, S. K. (1992). Cognitive biases and the emotional disorders. *Psychological Science, 3,* 65–69.

Moreland, R. L., & Zajonc, R. B. (1977). Is stimulus recognition a necessary condition for the occurrence of exposure effects? *Journal of Personality and Social Psychology, 35,* 191–199.

Moyer, K. E. (1976). *The psychobiology of aggression.* New York: Harper & Row.

Mulilis, J.-P., & Lippa, R. (1990). Behavioral change in earthquake preparedness due to negative threat appeals: A test of protection motivation. *Journal of Applied Social Psychology, 20,* 619–638.

Murphy, S. T., Monahan, J. L., & Zajonc, R. B. (1995). Additivity of nonconscious affect: Combined effects of priming and exposure. *Journal of Personality and Social Psychology, 69,* 589–602.

Neisser, U., & Harsch, N. (1992). Phantom flashbulbs: False recollections of hearing the news about Challenger. In E. Winograd & U. Neisser (Eds.), *Affect and accuracy in recall: Studies of "flashbulb memories."* (9–31). Cambridge: Cambridge University Press.

Niedenthal, P. M., Halberstadt, J. B., & Setterlund, M. B. (1997). Being happy and seeing "happy": Emotional state mediates visual word recognition. *Cognition and Emotion, 11,* 403–442.

Niedenthal, P. M., & Setterlund, M. B. (1994). Emotion congruence in perception. *Personality and Social Psychology Bulletin, 20,* 401–411.

Nisbett, R. E., & Schachter, S. (1966). Cognitive manipulations of pain. *Journal of Experimental Social Psychology, 2,* 227–236.

Nygren, T. E. (1998). Reacting to perceived high- and low-risk win–lose opportunities in a risky decision-making task: Is it framing or affect or both? *Motivation and Emotion, 22,* 73–98.

Oatley, K., & Johnson-Laird, P. N. (1987). Toward a cognitive theory of emotions. *Cognition and Emotion, 1,* 29–50.

Oatley, K., & Johnson-Laird, P. N. (1996). The communicative theory of emotions: Empirical tests, mental models, and implications for social interaction. In L. L. Martin & A. Tesser (Eds.), *Striving and feeling* (pp. 363–393). Mahwah, NJ: Erlbaum.

Ofshe, R., & Watters, E. (1994). *Making monsters: False memories, psychotherapy, and sexual hysteria.* New York: Scribner's.

Ortony, A., Clore, G. L., & Collins, A. (1988). *The cognitive structure of emotions.* Cambridge/New York: Cambridge University Press.

Parkinson, B., & Manstead, A. S. R. (1992). Appraisal as a cause of emotion. In M. S. Clark (Ed.), *Review of personality and social psychology: Emotion* (Vol. 13, pp. 122–149). Newbury Park, CA: Sage.

Parrott, W. G. (1991). Mood induction and instructions to sustain moods: A test of the subject compliance hypothesis of mood congruent memory. *Cognition and Emotion, 5,* 41–52.

Parrott, W. G., & Sabini, J. (1990). Mood and memory under natural conditions: Evidence for mood incongruent recall. *Journal of Personality and Social Psychology, 59,* 321–336.

Peters, D. P. (1997). Stress, arousal, and children's eyewitness memory. In N. L. Stein, P. A. Ornstein, B. Tversky, & C. Brainerd (Eds.), *Memory for everyday and emotional events* (pp. 351–379). Mahwah, NJ: Erlbaum.

Petty, R. E., & Cacioppo, J. T. (1986). The Elaboration Likelihood Model of persuasion. In L. Berkowitz (Ed.), *Advances in experimental social psychology* (Vol. 19, pp. 123–205). New York: Academic Press.

Petty, R. E., Gleicher, F., & Baker, S. M. (1991). Multiple roles for affect in persuasion. In J. P. Forgas (Ed.), *Emotion and social judgments* (pp. 181–200). Oxford/New York: Pergamon Press.

Petty, R. E., Schumann, D. W., Richman, S. A., & Strathman, A. J. (1993). Positive mood and persuasion: Different roles for affect under high- and low-elaboration conditions. *Journal of Personality and Social Psychology, 64,* 5–20.

Petty, R. E., & Wegener, D. T. (1998). Attitude change: Multiple roles for persuasion variables. In D. T. Gilbert, S. T. Fiske, & G. Lindzey (Eds.), *Handbook of social psychology* (Vol. 1, pp. 323–390). New York: McGraw-Hill/Oxford University Press.

Pezdek, K., Finger, K., & Hodge, D. (1997). Planting false childhood memories: The role of event plausibility. *Psychologial Science, 8*, 437–441.

Philippot, P. (1993). Inducing and assessing differentiated emotion-feeling states in the laboratory. *Cognition and Emotion, 7*, 171–193.

Plutchik, R., & Ax, A. F. (1967). A critique of "Determinants of emotional state" (by Schachter and Singer, 1962). *Psychophysiology, 4*, 79–82.

Poole, D. A., Lindsay, D. S., Memon, A., & Bull, R. (1995). Psychotherapy and the recovered memories of childhood sexual abuse: U.S. and British practitioners' opinions, practices, and experiences. *Journal of Consulting and Clinical Psychology, 63*, 426–437.

Pope, H. G. J., & Hudson, J. I. (1992). Is childhood sexual abuse a risk factor for bulimia nervosa? *American Journal of Psychiatry, 149*, 455–463.

Priester, J. R., Cacioppo, J. T., & Petty, R. E. (1996). The influence of motor processes on attitudes toward novel versus familiar semantic stimuli. *Personality and Social Psychology Bulletin, 22*, 442–447.

Quigley, B. M., & Tedeschi, J. T. (1996). Mediating effects of blame attributions on feelings of anger. *Personality and Social Psychology Bulletin, 22*, 1280–1288.

Razran, G. (1940). Conditioned response changes in rating and appraising sociopolitical slogans. *Psychological Bulletin, 37*, 481.

Regan, D. T., Williams, M., & Sparling, S. (1972). Voluntary expiation of guilt: A field experiment. *Journal of Personality and Social Psychology, 24*, 42–45.

Reisenzein, R. (1983). The Schachter theory of emotion: Two decades later. *Psychological Bulletin, 94*, 239–264.

Reisenzein, R. (1994). Pleasure-arousal theory and the intensity of emotions. *Journal of Personality and Social Psychology, 67*, 525–539.

Rimé, B., Philippot, P., & Cisamolo, D. (1990). Social schemata of peripheral changes in emotion. *Journal of Personality and Social Psychology, 59*, 38–49.

Riordan, C. A., & Tedeschi, J. T. (1983). Attraction in aversive environments: Some evidence for classical conditioning and negative reinforcement. *Journal of Personality and Social Psychology, 44*, 683–692.

Riskind, J. H. (1983). Nonverbal expressions and the accessibility of life experience memories: A congruence hypothesis. *Social Cognition, 2*, 62–86.

Riskind, J. H., & Gotay, C. C. (1982). Physical posture: Could it have regulatory or feedback effects on motivation and emotion? *Motivation and Emotion, 6*, 273–298.

Rogers, R., & Wettstein, R. M. (1988). Drug-assisted interviews to detect malingering and deception. In R. Rogers (Ed.), *Clinical assessment of malingering and deception* (pp. 195–204). New York: Guilford Press.

Roseman, I. J. (1991). Appraisal determinants of discrete emotions. *Cognition and Emotion, 5*, 161–200.

Ross, L., Rodin, J., & Zimbardo, P. G. (1969). Toward an attribution therapy: The reduction of fear through induced cognitive-emotional misattribution. *Journal of Personality and Social Psychology, 12*, 279–288.

Rotton, J., Frey, J., Barry, T., Milligan, M., & Fitzpatrick, M. (1979). The air pollution experience and physical aggression. *Journal of Applied Social Psychology, 9,* 397–412.

Ruiz-Caballero, J. A., & Gonzalez, P. (1994). Implicit and explicit memory bias in depressed and nondepressed subjects. *Cognition and Emotion, 8,* 555–569.

Russell, J. A. (1980). A circumplex model of affect. *Journal of Personality and Social Psychology, 39,* 1161–1178.

Russell, J. A., & Carroll, J. M. (1999a). On the bipolarity of positive and negative affect. *Psychological Bulletin, 125,* 3–30.

Russell, J. A., & Carroll, J. M. (1999b). The phoenix of bipolarity: A reply to Watson and Tellegen (1999). *Psychological Bulletin, 125,* 611–617.

Russell, J. A., & Feldman Barrett, L. (1999). Core affect, prototypical emotional episodes, and other things called *emotion*: Dissecting the elephant, *Journal of Personality and Social Psychology, 76,* 805–819.

Schachter, S. (1964). The interaction of cognitive and physiological determinants of emotional state. In L. Berkowitz (Ed.), *Advances in experimental social psychology* (Vol. 1, pp. 49–80). New York: Academic Press.

Schachter, S., & Singer, J. (1962). Cognitive, social, and physiological determinants of emotional state. *Psychological Review, 65,* 379–399.

Schacter, D. L. (1996). *Searching for memory: The brain, the mind, and the past.* New York: Basic Books.

Scheier, M. F., & Carver, C. S. (1977). Self-focused attention and the experience of emotion: Attraction, repulsion, elation, and depression. *Journal of Personality and Social Psychology, 35,* 625–636.

Scheier, M. F., Carver, C. S., & Gibbons, F. X. (1981). Self-focused attention and reactions to fear. *Journal of Research in Personality, 15,* 1–15.

Scherer, K. R. (1993). Studying the emotion-antecedent appraisal process: An expert system approach. *Cognition and Emotion, 7,* 325–355.

Scherer, K. R. (1997). Profiles of emotion-antecedent appraisal: Testing theoretical predictions across cultures. *Cognition and Emotion, 11,* 113–150.

Scherer, K. R. (1999). Appraisal theory. In T. Dalgleish & M. Power (Eds.), *Handbook of cognition and emotion* (pp. 637–663). Chichester, UK: Wiley.

Scherer, K. R., & Tannenbaum, P. H. (1986). Emotional experiences in everyday life: A survey approach. *Motivation and Emotion, 10,* 295–314.

Scherer, K. R., & Wallbott, H. G. (1994). Evidence for universality and cultural variation of differential emotional patterning. *Journal of Personality and Social Psychology, 66,* 310–328.

Schimmack, U., & Diener, E. (1997). Affect intensity: Separating intensity and frequency in repeatedly measured affect. *Journal of Personality and Social Psychology, 73,* 1313–1329.

Schwarz, N., & Bless, H. (1991). Happy and mindless, but sad and smart? The impact of affective states on analytic reasoning. In J. P. Forgas (Ed.), *Emotion and social judgments* (pp. 55–72). Oxford/New York: Pergamon Press.

Schwarz, N., & Bless, H. (1992). Constructing reality and its alternatives: An inclusion/exclusion model of assimilation and contrast effects in social judgment. In L. L. Martin & A. Tesser (Eds.), *The construction of social judgments* (pp. 217–245) Hillsdale NJ: Erlbaum.

Schwarz, N., Bless, H., & Bohner, G. (1991). Mood and persuasion: Affective states influence the processing of persuasive communications. In M. Zanna (Ed.), *Advances in experimental social psychology* (Vol. 24, pp. 161–199). San Diego, CA: Academic Press.

Schwarz, N., & Clore, G. L. (1983). Mood, misattribution, and judgments of well-being: Informative and directive functions of affective states. *Journal of Personality and Social Psychology, 45,* 513–523.

Schwarz, N., Strack, F., Kommer, D., & Wagner, D. (1987). Soccer, rooms, and the quality of your life: Mood effects on judgments of satisfaction with life in general and with specific domains. *European Journal of Social Psychology, 17,* 69–79.

Sedikides, C. (1992). Mood as a determinant of attentional focus. *Cognition and Emotion, 6,* 129–148.

Sherrod, D. R., Armstrong, D., Hewitt, J., Madonia, B., Speno, S., & Teruya, D. (1977). Environmental attention, affect, and altruism. *Journal of Applied Social Psychology, 7,* 359–371.

Shobe, K. K., & Kihlstrom, J. F. (1997). Is traumatic memory special? *Current Directions in Psychological Science, 6,* 70–74.

Singer, J. A., & Salovey, P. (1988). Mood and memory: Evaluating the network theory of affect. *Clinical Psychology Review, 8,* 211–251.

Smith, C. A., & Ellsworth, P. C. (1985). Patterns of cognitive appraisal in emotion. *Journal of Personality and Social Psychology, 48,* 813–838.

Smith, C. A., & Lazarus, R. S. (1993). Appraisal components, core relational themes, and the emotions. *Cognition and Emotion, 7,* 233–269.

Smith, S. M., & Petty, R. E. (1995). Personality moderators of mood congruency effects on cognition: The role of self-esteem and negative mood regulation. *Journal of Personality and Social Psychology, 68,* 1092–1107.

Snyder, M., & White, P. (1982). Moods and memories: Elation, depression, and the remembering of the events of one's life. *Journal of Personality, 50,* 149–167.

Spanos, N. P. (1994). Multiple identity enactments and multiple personality disorder: A sociocognitive perspective. *Psychological Bulletin, 116,* 143–165.

Stapel, D. A., Martin, L. L., & Schwarz, N. (1998). The smell of bias: What instigates correction processes in social judgments? *Personality and Social Psychology Bulletin, 24,* 797–806.

Stein, N. L., & Levine, L. J. (1989). The causal organization of emotion knowledge: A developmental study. *Cognition and Emotion, 3,* 343–378.

Stein, N. L., & Levine, L. J. (1990). Making sense out of emotion: The representation and use of goal-structured knowledge. In N. L. Stein, B. Leventhal, & T. Trabasso (Eds.), *Psychological and biological approaches to emotion* (pp. 45–73). Hillsdale, NJ: Erlbaum.

Stein, N. L., Wade, E., & Liwag, M. D. (1996). A theoretical approach to understanding and remembering emotional events. In N. L. Stein, P. A. Ornstein, B. Tversky, & C. Brainerd (Eds.), *Memory for everyday and emotional events* (pp. 15–47). Mahwah, NJ: Erlbaum.

Stepper, S., & Strack, F. (1993). Proprioceptive determinants of emotional and nonemotional feelings. *Journal of Personality and Social Psychology, 64,* 211–220.

Strachey, J. (Ed.). (1953–1974). *Complete psychological works of Sigmund Freud* (Vol. XX, p. 29). London, Hogarth Press.

Strack, F. (1992). The different routes to social judgments: Experiential versus informational strategies. In L. L. Martin & A. Tesser (Eds.), *The construction of social judgment* (pp. 249–275). Hillsdale, NJ: Erlbaum.

Strack, F., Martin, L. L., & Stepper, S. (1988). Inhibiting and facilitating conditions of the human smile: A nonobtrusive test of the facial feedback hypothesis. *Journal of Personality and Social Psychology, 54*, 768–777.

Strack, F., Schwarz, N., Bless, H., Kubler, A., & Wanke, M. (1993). Awareness of the influence as a determinant of assimilation versus contrast. *European Journal of Social Psychology, 23*, 53–62.

Strack, F., Schwarz, N., & Gschneidinger, E. (1985). Happiness and reminiscing: The role of time perspective, affect, and mode of thinking. *Journal of Personality and Social Psychology, 49*, 1460–1469.

Taylor, S. E. (1991). Asymmetrical effects of positive and negative events: The mobilization-minimization hypothesis. *Psychological Bulletin, 110*, 67–85.

Termine, N. T., & Izard, C. E. (1988). Infants' responses to their mothers' expressions of joy and sadness. *Developmental Psychology, 24*, 223–229.

Tomkins, S. S. (1962). *Affect, imagery, and consciousness.* New York: Springer.

Tourangeau, R., & Ellsworth, P. C. (1979). The role of facial response in the experience of emotion. *Journal of Personality and Social Psychology, 37*, 1519–1531.

Ucros, C. G. (1989). Mood state-dependent memory: A meta-analysis. *Cognition and Emotion, 3*, 139–167.

Wallbott, H. G., & Scherer, K. R. (1988). Emotion and economic development: Data and speculations concerning the relationship between economic factors and emotional experience. *European Journal of Social Psychology, 18*, 267–273.

Watson, D., & Tellegen, A. (1985). Toward a consensual structure of mood. *Psychological Bulletin, 98*, 219–235.

Watson, D., Tellegen, H. (1999). Issues in the dimensional structure of affect – Effects of descriptors, measurement error, and response formats: Comment on Russell and Carroll (1999). *Psychological Bulletin, 125*, 601–610.

Watson, D., Wiese, D., Vaidya, J., & Tellegen, A. (1999). The two general activation systems of affect: Structural findings, evolutionary considerations, and psychobiological evidence. *Journal of Personality and Social Psychology, 76*, 820–838.

Weaver, C. A. (1993). Do you need a "flash" to form a flashbulb memory? *Journal of Experimental Psychology: General, 122*, 39–46.

Wegener, D. T., & Petty, R. E. (1994). Mood management across affective states: The hedonic contingency hypothesis. *Journal of Personality and Social Psychology, 66*, 1034–1048.

Wegener, D. T., & Petty, R. E. (1996). Effects of mood on persuasion processes: Enhancing, reducing, and biasing scrutiny of attitude-relevant information. In L. L. Martin & A. Tesser (Eds.), *Striving and feeling: Interactions among goals, affect, and self-regulation* (pp. 329–362). Mahwah, NJ: Erlbaum.

Wegener, D. T., & Petty, R. E. (1997). The flexible correction model: The role of naive theories of bias in bias correction. In M. Zanna (Ed.), *Advances in experimental social psychology* (Vol. 29, pp. 141–208). San Diego, CA: Academic Press.

Wegener, D. T., Petty, R. F., & Smith, S. M. (1995). Positive mood can increase or decrease message scrutiny: The hedonic contingency view of mood and message processing. *Journal of Personality and Social Psychology, 69*, 5–15.

Weiner, B., Graham, S., & Chandler, C. (1982). Pity, anger, and guilt: An attributional analysis. *Personality and Social Psychology Bulletin, 8*, 226–232.

Wessel, I., & Merckelbach, H. (1998). Memory for threat-relevant and threat-irrelevant cues in spider phobics. *Cognition and Emotion, 12*, 93–104.

Wilder, D. A., & Shapiro, P. (1989). Effects of anxiety on impression formation in a group context: An anxiety-assimilation hypothesis. *Journal of Experimental Social Psychology, 25*, 481–499.

Williams, L. M. (1994). Recall of childhood trauma: A prospective study of women's memories of child sexual abuse. *Journal of Consulting and Clinical Psychology, 62*, 1167–1176.

Wilson, T. D., & Brekke, N. (1994). Mental contamination and mental correction: Unwanted influences on judgments and evaluations. *Psychological Bulletin, 116*, 117–142.

Winkielman, P., Zajonc, R. B., & Schwarz, N. (1997). Subliminal affective priming resists attributional interventions. *Cognition and Emotion, 11*, 433–465.

Winton, W. (1986). The role of facial response in self-reports of emotion: A critique of Laird. *Journal of Personality and Social Psychology, 50*, 808–812.

Wood, J. V., Saltzberg, J. A., & Goldsamt, L. A. (1990). Does affect induce self-focused attention? *Journal of Personality and Social Psychology, 58*, 899–908.

Wood, W., Wong, F. Y., & Chachere, J. G. (1991). Effects of media violence on viewers' aggression in unconstrained social interaction. *Psychological Bulletin, 109*, 371–383.

Worth, L. T., & Mackie, D. M. (1987). Cognitive mediation of positive affect in persuasion. *Social Cognition, 5*, 76–94.

Yuille, J. C., & Cutshall, J. L. (1986). A case study of eyewitness testimony to a crime. *Journal of Applied Psychology, 71*, 291–301.

Yuille, J. C., Davies, G., Gibling, F., & Marxsen, D. (1994). Eyewitness memory of police trainees for realistic role plays. *Journal of Applied Psychology, 79*, 931–936.

Zajonc, R. B. (1968). Attitudinal effects of mere exposure. *Journal of Personality and Social Psychology (Monographs), 9*, 1–27.

Zajonc, R. B. (1980). Feeling and thinking: Preferences need no inferences. *American Psychologist, 35*, 151–175.

Zajonc, R. B. (1984). On the primacy of affect. *American Psychologist, 39*, 117–123.

Zajonc, R. B. (1998). Emotions. In D. T. Gilbert, S. T. Fiske, & G. Lindzey (Eds.), *Handbook of social psychology* (Vol. 1, pp. 591–632). New York: McGraw-Hill/Oxford University Press.

Zajonc, R. B., Murphy, S. T., & Inglehart, M. (1989). Feeling and facial efference: Implications of the vascular theory of emotion. *Psychological Review, 96*, 395–416.

Zevon, M. A., & Tellegen, A. (1982). The structure of mood change: An ideographic/nomothetic analysis. *Journal of Personality and Social Psychology, 43,* 111–122.

Zillmann, D., Baron, R., & Tamborini, R. (1981). Social costs of smoking: Effects of tobacco smoke on hostile behavior. *Journal of Applied Psychology, 11,* 548–561.

Zillmann, D., Bryant, J., Comisky, P. W., & Medoff, N. J. (1981). Excitation and hedonic valence in the effect of erotica on motivated intermale aggression. *European Journal of Social Psychology, 11,* 233–252.

Index

actions: and influence of feelings on helpfulness, 181–189; and influence of negative feelings on hostility and aggression, 167–181

activation, in memory network, 73–74

adaptation level, and influence of expectations on affect, 31, 196n40

Adelmann, P. K., 51, 52, 199n23–25, 200n27, 200n29, 201n33

aesthetics, of rooms, 26, 126, 134

affect and affective experience: bipolar and circumplex models of, 12–21; definition of, 11; psychological theories on origins of, 25–37. *See also* emotions; feelings; mood

affect infusion model (AIM), 127–130, 156–157, 216n19, 220n1

affective congruence: in decision making, 135–143, 204n14; in judgments, 122–130, 132–134; in memory, 74, 76–80, 82–85. *See also* mood congruence

affective-state dependency, and memory, 73–76

agency, and appraisal theory, 45–46

aggression, and influence of feelings on, 167–181, 221n12, 221n15

Ahn, Shin-Ho, 126, 134, 215n11

air pollution, and aggressive behavior, 171

Allman, A., 196n41

American Medical Association, Council on Scientific Affairs, 102

American Psychiatric Association, 110

American Psychological Association, 100, 116–117, 210n7, 213n43

amnesia, 109–110. *See also* repression

analytic processing, 128–141

Anderson, Craig A., 169, 170, 171, 176, 177, 220n6–7, 221n13

Anderson, J. A., 54, 59

Anderson, K. B., 220n7

anger: and appraisal theory, 48, 175–177, 179, 221–222n21–22; arousal and bodily sensations of, 23; and bodily feedback thesis, 57f, 58; differentiation of, 43, 189–190; and influence of negative affect, 167–181; and persuasion, 160–161. *See also* negative affect

anxiety, and attention, 79, 205n19

appetition, and positive versus negative affect systems, 18

appraisals and appraisal theory: anger and aggressive behavior, 175–177, 179; and attribution, 197n8; and bodily reaction-feedback concept, 52–53; development of concept of, 43–50, 197n9–12, 198n14

Arnold, Magda B., 43–44, 48, 197n7

arousal: and active-passive dimension, 14; and eyewitness accounts,

Studies in Emotion and Social Interaction

First Series
Editors: Paul Ekman and Klaus R. Scherer

DATE DUE

DEMCO, INC. 38-2931